# Introduction to
# Government

---

HARPERCOLLINS COLLEGE OUTLINE

# *Introduction to Government*

**Larry Elowitz, Ph.D.**
Georgia College

HarperPerennial
*A Division of HarperCollinsPublishers*

*An American BookWorks Corporation Production*

**Project Manager:** Jonathon E. Brodman

**Editor:** Thomas Quinn

Library of Congress Catalog Card Number: 91-58269
ISBN: 0-06-467156-9

99 00 01    ABW/RRD    20 19 18 17 16 15 14 13 12

# Contents

# Preface

*Introduction to Government*, part of the HarperCollins Outline series, is intended as a supplement to the main American government textbooks, both softcover and hardcover, currently used in senior high schools and at the freshman level in colleges and universities throughout the nation. *Introduction to Government* provides the "essentials" about American political institutions, leaders, and concepts so that the student can better comprehend related materials found in comprehensive textbooks. Real-life political examples are disseminated throughout in order to reinforce substantive material. This new title covers the three branches of government, federalism, public opinion, the media, parties, interest groups, the bureaucracy, voting, campaigns, and elections. There is also a chapter on public policy. The book contains a glossary of key terms important to the study of American government, as well as relevant appendices. This work can also serve as an effective review device to study for major course examinations.

I am grateful to Jonathon E. Brodman and Fred N. Grayson for their invaluable technical assistance and encouragement extended to me during this project's evolution. Finally, I would like to thank my wife, Sharon, whose support, patience, and computer skills were all essential to the book's completion.

Larry Elowitz
Georgia College

# 1

# *Government, Politics, and the Creation of the U.S. Constitution*

*It is virtually impossible for an American citizen to escape the personal impact of government and the political process. From the variety of taxes paid, to environmental and consumer regulations, voting and elections, or interest rates paid on a loan, the citizen confronts the diverse effects of political decision-making by an elected or appointed public official at the local, state, or federal governmental level. Conversely, a citizen can also influence his or her political world by exercising the constitutional freedoms incorporated and developed within the context of the Constitution.*

*That American constitutional system can be traced to the dramatic events of the 1787 convention in Philadelphia. The fifty-five delegates possessed certain political ideals and a desire to forge a stronger nation. The compromises they agreed to and the document they produced have clearly stood the test of time. This first chapter's coverage may explain why an eighteenth-century plan of government still can have considerable relevance for a nation that prepares to enter the twenty-first century.*

# GOVERNMENT, POLITICS, POWER— SOME BASIC DEFINITIONS

**What Do We Mean by Government?**

In the United States, government consists of those institutions (Congress, the Supreme Court, etc.), agencies (Federal Reserve Board, Environmental Protection Agency, etc.), and elected/appointed political officials whose purpose may be to write, enforce, or interpret laws and public policies in general. The main goals of local, state, and federal *governments* are to maintain public order, provide goods and services that help the lives of citizens, and protect basic freedoms and liberties.

**What Do We Mean by Politics?**

Politics refers to the activities of influencing or controlling government for the purpose of formulating or guiding public policy. Two commonly used definitions coined by political scientists David Easton and Harold Lasswell are, respectively, "the authoritative allocation of values," and "who gets what, when, and how." The two definitions suggest that there must be some authority (governmental personnel) who can decide on those preferences (values) which will be selected over other choices. In short, politics is rooted in the inevitability of social conflict.

**Why Are There Conflicts in American Society?**

First, individuals differ in terms of needs, values, abilities, and attitudes. Disagreements follow over moral issues of right or wrong, such as abortion or the death penalty. Second, individuals may quarrel over what problems are the most important to solve. For example, should the federal government spend more money on defense or social programs? Third, individuals compete for scarce goods and services. Senior citizens over the age of sixty-five want higher Social Security benefits, but workers in their mid-twenties would prefer that less money be taken from their paychecks. Will the elderly get "what" they desire this year ("when") by convincing Congress, a part of government, to pass a law benefiting them ("how")? Or will Congress be politically influenced by thousands of young workers writing letters of protest against higher Social Security deductions? Whatever the final decision, values will be "allocated" in an authoritative manner.

**What Is Power?**

Government has the power to enforce any law it passes. For example, a driver may feel that the fifty-five-mile-per-hour speed limit is a bad law, and refuse to obey it. But the driver does face the consequences of breaking the law if he speeds excessively, i.e., a fine, or even time in jail. Similarly, many American citizens do not like to pay federal income taxes. But the Internal Revenue Service, an agency of the federal government, can prosecute individuals who fail to pay. Power, then, is the ability of government to make a person do something he or she does not necessarily want to do. Still, the power of government is not unlimited. The people do have the right to question governmental power in a democracy.

**What Are Direct and Representative Democracies?**

The United States is a democracy, a term which means government by the people. Historically, there have been two types of democracies. One, termed direct democracy, originated in the ancient Greek city-state of Athens, where citizens were expected to participate in political life (women, slaves, and foreigners were ineligible for citizenship). All vital decisions were voted on by the entire citizenry. Contemporary America still practices direct democracy, most notably through the New England Town Meeting, in which nearly all of the town's voters play a role in deciding on tax rates, hiring city officials, adopting local laws, and so on, through a majority vote. But direct democracy in a nation of 250 million individuals is simply not practical.

The second type of democracy—*representative* or *republican democracy*—was selected by the framers of the U.S. Constitution. The exercise of political power ultimately rested with the people, but policy decisions and running the nation were delegated to the people's chosen representatives through the election process. (In the early days of the republic, only property owners were allowed to vote. While the electorate was gradually broadened, it would not be until the twentieth century that women's and black Americans' voting rights were guaranteed.)

# INDEPENDENCE AND THE ARTICLES OF CONFEDERATION

The only "national" political institution which evolved after the signing of the Declaration of Independence in 1776 was the Continental Congress. But the Congress had few resources with which to wage a war against the British. Small farmers and debtors preferred that power be held by state legislatures, rather than a national government, so that they could maximize their influence over local affairs. Wealthier farmers, merchants, land owners, and financial speculators preferred that property be protected by a strong central government. A compromise had to be reached between these two groups. The result was a government established under the Articles of Confederation.

**The Articles of Confederation**

The Articles of Confederation provided a plan of government which did have some successes. The American government negotiated a favorable peace treaty with the British, provided for payment of war debts, and successfully passed the Northwest Ordinance, which allowed settlements (and eventual statehood) in a large region north of the Ohio River. But the Articles suffered from some very serious defects. Under the Articles, Congress could not tax, regulate commerce, or control a national currency. Congress could only ask for voluntary tax contributions from the states. Furthermore, passage of controversial bills required a difficult-to-attain two-thirds vote of the states. Amendments to the Articles required a near-impossible unanimous agreement of the thirteen state legislatures. In short, government under the Articles was actually a "firm league of friendship" in which each state was a "sovereign" or independent political entity.

# EVENTS WHICH LED TO CALLS FOR A CONSTITUTIONAL CONVENTION

The Articles were unable to cope with a series of economic and social misfortunes in the 1780s. First, a serious economic depression followed the Revolutionary War. Contributing to the depression were economic "wars" between and among the states. For example, Rhode Island and Massachusetts placed protective tariffs on each other's manufactured goods. Second, there were troubles with European trade. Independence had led to American ships being barred from the British West Indies. The new government under the Articles was unsuccessful in obtaining important commercial treaties with Spain and France. Third, unstable monetary systems resulted from each state printing its own currency. Fourth, some states were controlled by the debtor class, which preferred inflationary monetary policies; others by the wealthy creditors who desired restrictions on credit.

**Shays' Rebellion**

In western Massachusetts, farmers who could not pay their mortgages or high taxes interfered with the conduct of foreclosures and tax delinquency proceedings. In the winter of 1786, a former captain in the Revolutionary War, Daniel Shays, led a group of some 2,500 angry, musket-bearing debt-ridden farmers in a march on the federal arsenal at Springfield. Although the state militia put down the insurrection, the fears of economic disintegration in the colonies and outright anarchy disturbed many of America's leaders. The Articles of Confederation were unable to provide a strong central government that could promote stable economic growth or even develop a strong national army. (Massachusetts had put down the rebellion by using a private army financed through individual contributions.) It was time for major political change.

# THE UNITED STATES CONSTITUTION

**The Constitutional Convention**

In 1786, a meeting was held in Annapolis, Maryland, to discuss problems associated with the Articles. Alexander Hamilton's resolution, approved by the Annapolis delegates, called for Congress to authorize a convention in Philadelphia which would consider the "trade and commerce of the United States." Congress so acted, setting a date of May 14, 1787, for the convention. The Continental Congress directed that the convention's purpose was to *revise* and possibly strengthen the Articles, not to create a *new* form of government. But amending the Articles would require the unanimous consent of the states.

## THE DELEGATES

Although seventy-four delegates were selected by twelve states (Rhode Island refused to send representatives), only fifty-five men attended. Some notable political figures of the day did not participate in the convention's proceedings. Thomas Jefferson was in France as U.S. ambassador, and John Adams was the British ambassador. Thomas Paine, Patrick Henry, Richard Henry Lee, Samuel Adams, and John Hancock all feared a tyrannical centralization of power. Generally, the delegates who did attend were well-to-do, college-educated, with ample political experience in colonial government. No blacks, women, Indians, or common workers attended. Most delegates did agree on a basic political philosophy—they believed in preserving property, had a pessimistic view of human nature (believing that people were selfish and base), and feared mass democracy. Therefore, government's role was to restrain humanity's love of power. As Madison phrased it, "Ambition must be made to counteract ambition!" When the framers referred to the "people," they really meant the educated men of property. Others, such as Benjamin Franklin, were more trusting, believing that government by the consent of the governed meant all the people or at least all white males, and not just the "better" classes.

The delegates convened on May 25, 1787, and quickly agreed that: (a) George Washington should be the presiding officer, and that (b) all proceedings be held in secret. Then, after a few days of procedural questions, Edmund Randolph, who headed the Virginia delegation, introduced fifteen resolutions which represented the large states' plan for a new government.

## THE VIRGINIA PLAN

Randolph's plan called for a strong national government with a legislative, executive, and judicial branch. There would be a bicameral or two-house Congress, with representation in both chambers being based on state population. Voters would elect members of the lower house. Upper-house members would be elected by the lower house from nominations proposed by the state legislatures. Congress would elect both the executive and Supreme Court judges. The national government would influence the people directly, in effect bypassing the states. One clear example of the central government's power was the concept of the executive and selected judges forming a Council of Revision which could veto both federal and state laws.

### THE NEW JERSEY PLAN

On June 15, William Paterson of New Jersey introduced the small-state plan. Congress would be a unicameral legislature, with each state being entitled to one vote. Its members would be elected by the state legislatures. Congress would elect a plural executive for a nonrenewable term. The Supreme Court would comprise the judiciary, its judges appointed to life terms by the executive. Congress was granted the authority to regulate interstate trade and collect additional taxes from the states. Finally, national laws and treaties would be considered supreme and binding upon all the states.

### THE CONNECTICUT COMPROMISE

In mid-July 1787, a compromise between the large- and small-state plans was devised by Roger Sherman and William Johnson of Connecticut. The House of Representatives would have representation based upon population. In the Senate, or upper chamber, the small states would have equality of state representation—two senators per state. The delegates accepted this compromise.

### THE COMPROMISE OVER SLAVERY

Roughly one-third of the South's population was slaves. Should these slaves count as citizens in apportioning representation to the southern states? After some heated debate, three-fifths of the slave population was counted. In addition, the South, in exchange for its approval of the national government controlling commerce, was allowed to continue the slave trade until 1808.

### THE RATIFICATION TEST

The signing of the Constitution meant only that the new document was a finished proposal. According to Article IV of the Constitution, nine states would have to ratify or approve the plan. Majorities in each state's ratifying convention were required. However, a bitter debate subsequently unfolded between constitutional supporters, the Federalists, and their opposition, the anti-Federalists.

**The Anti-Federalist Position.** Anti-Federalists objected to the Constitution on the grounds that: (a) the document benefited rich aristocrats who would use a strong national government to control public policies; (b) the political rights and independence of the states would be crushed; (c) there was no Bill of Rights guaranteeing individual freedoms.

*The Federalist Papers.* The Federalists counterargued through *The Federalist Papers*, a series of newspaper articles written by Alexander Hamilton, James Madison, and John Jay, that: (a) no one faction could gain political control in a large federation in which many groups contested for power (Madison's assertion that "ambition must check ambition"); (b) dividing the government into three branches—executive, legislative, and judicial—and allowing each branch to have partial control over the other two (example: the president could veto a bill, Congress could override that veto, the courts could interpret the meaning of a law) would ensure liberty; (c) the states would be granted "reserved powers" and have their existence protected; (d) a Bill of Rights would be added to the Constitution after ratification. Eventually, the Federalists would win the ratification struggle. But there were several close votes, as revealed in the following table.

| | State | Date | Against | For |
|---|---|---|---|---|
| 1. | Delaware | December 7, 1787 | 30 | 0 |
| 2. | Pennsylvania | December 12, 1787 | 46 | 23 |
| 3. | New Jersey | December 18, 1787 | 38 | 0 |
| 4. | Georgia | January 2, 1788 | 26 | 0 |
| 5. | Connecticut | January 9, 1788 | 128 | 40 |
| 6. | Massachusetts | February 6, 1788 | 187 | 168 |
| 7. | Maryland | April 28, 1788 | 63 | 11 |
| 8. | South Carolina | May 23, 1788 | 149 | 73 |
| 9. | New Hampshire | June 21, 1788 | 57 | 46 |
| 10. | Virginia | June 25, 1788 | 89 | 79 |
| 11. | New York | July 26, 1788 | 39 | 27 |
| 12. | North Carolina | November 21, 1789 | 195 | 77 |
| 13. | Rhode Island | May 29, 1790 | 34 | 32 |

*Fig. 1.1   State Ratification Votes*

**Amending the Constitution**

First, an amendment may be proposed by a two-thirds vote of both houses of Congress and then ratified by the legislatures of three-fourths of the states. Second, an amendment may be proposed by two-thirds of both houses of Congress and then ratified by conventions in three-fourths of the states (thirty-eight in all). Third, an amendment may be proposed by a national convention and ratified by the legislatures of three-fourths of the states. Fourth, an amendment may be proposed by a national convention and ratified by conventions in three-fourths of the states.

Of the twenty-six amendments added to the U.S. Constitution, all but one have been adopted by the first method. Only the twenty-first was adopted by the second method. There has not been a constitutional convention held since 1787.

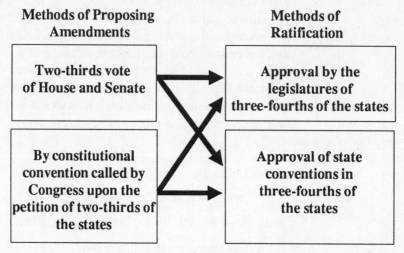

Fig. 1.2  *Amending the Constitution*

## POLITICAL IDEAS WHICH INFLUENCED THE FRAMERS OF THE CONSTITUTION

*John Locke and Natural Rights*

The framers of the Constitution were well versed in the political ideas of the English philosophers, particularly John Locke (1632–1704). In his *Two Treatises on Government,* Locke argued that human beings had the capacity to perceive and understand higher or natural law which posed standards for human conduct. Flowing from natural law are the natural rights of the individual—life, liberty, and property—which cannot be infringed upon by the state or government. It is the responsibility of those who rule to protect these natural rights. In turn, the people have the right to abolish those governments which violate such rights. Jefferson voiced these sentiments in the Declaration of Independence:

> To secure these rights, governments are instituted among Men, deriving their just Powers from the Consent of the Governed. That whenever any Form of Government becomes destructive of these ends, it is the right of the people to alter or abolish it . . .

Implied in such thinking was Locke's principle of self-government—that people were intelligent enough to rule themselves by creating government for protection and societal order. They could also change that government when it no longer performed justly those basic political and social functions.

## Other Views

Locke's theories were not universally accepted by the framers. Two other British philosophers, Thomas Hobbes (1588–1679) and David Hume (1711–1776), viewed humanity as far more irrational, passionate, selfish, and even evil. The role of the state was mainly to restrain the emotional and moral excesses of the ruled; otherwise, order would dissolve into chaos. As James Madison asserted in *The Federalist Papers, No. 17:* ". . . if men were angels, no government would be necessary." In short, the framers had to wrestle with an age-old political dilemma—how to guarantee individual freedom, protect it from governmental tyranny, and ensure that such freedom would not be abused by the individual himself.

## The Social Contract

Locke's theories seemed to offer a potential balance between individual freedom and societal anarchy. First, his social-contract theory postulated that there was a mutual obligation between the state and the individual. The members of society accepted laws as binding upon them—they gave their allegiance to the government in exchange for protection and, hopefully, justice. But the government also had to keep its contractual bargain by preserving and defending the natural rights of the people.

## Majority Rule and Minority Rights

Locke realized that individual freedom was not unlimited. The will of the majority was to be reflected in laws and policies, and these were to be obeyed by all, even the minority who might be opposed to those decisions. But how would the majority be prevented from tyrannizing the minority? Locke admitted that this was a possibility.

## Minority Rights and the Constitution

In the American system, the Constitution sets definite limits on the majority. Civil liberties are guaranteed in the Bill of Rights. This is why the absence of a Bill of Rights in the original Constitution troubled so many of the anti-Federalists. (The Bill of Rights was adopted in 1791, two years after ratification.) In addition, a Bill of Rights reaffirmed the doctrine of limited government, a doctrine popular in colonial America. Even a powerful centralized government had to respect such rights as a jury trial, freedom of speech, religion, and so forth.

## Equality

Jefferson's famous contention in the Declaration that "all men are created equal" referred to a moral and legal equality. The framers clearly accepted the reality of differences among people in terms of ambition, motivation, temperament, and intelligence.

# THE KEY CHARACTERISTICS OF CONSTITUTIONAL DEMOCRACY

## Separation of Powers and Checks and Balances

The constitutional framers wished to control government by a division of government into three branches—the legislative, executive, and judicial. This separation-of-powers principle was the work of the eighteenth-century French political philosopher Baron de Montesquieu. Montesquieu also insisted that a system of checks and balances, or overlapping of the powers of the branches of government, would prevent a potentially dangerous concentration of power. For example, the president would have the power to appoint Supreme Court justices. But the Senate would have to confirm these appointments.

As Madison phrased it, the objective was "to divide and arrange the several offices [of government] in such a manner as that each may be a check on each other. . . ."

## Free Elections

Free elections are indispensable to a democracy. In the United States today, regularly scheduled elections are open to registered voters who are eighteen years of age or older. Elections are frequent in America, constantly forcing candidates for public office to win the approval of the voters and respond to the challenge of the opposition.

Elections perform several important political functions: (a) they transfer power from one set of leaders to another in a peaceful fashion; (b) they promote stability and order in governing society over time; (c) they allow citizens a chance to express their preferences on public policy; (d) they promote accountability—i.e., elected officials must consider the wishes of the people.

## Freedom of Expression

Democratic dialogue is possible only if people are free and unafraid to express their opinions on issues and to listen to the views of others.

## Universal Education

Jefferson claimed that "a nation which expects to be ignorant and free expects what never was and what never will be." Jefferson contended that a democracy could be supported only by an informed citizenry instilled with democratic values and a willingness to defend those values from attack.

# A BRIEF REVIEW OF THE CONSTITUTIONAL AMENDMENTS

There are currently twenty-six amendments to the U.S. Constitution. The following represent brief summaries of each amendment:

## BILL OF RIGHTS

**Amendment #1** Guarantees the "free exercise" of religion, freedom of speech, the press, assembly, and petition.

**Amendment #2** Establishes the people's right "to keep and bear Arms" within the context of a "well-regulated Militia."

**Amendment #3** Prohibits quartering of soldiers in private homes.

**Amendment #4** Prohibits "unreasonable searches and seizures" and establishes the issuance of search warrants upon "probable cause."

**Amendment #5** Creates the device of the grand jury; prohibits double jeopardy (an individual can't be tried again for the same crime once found innocent); no one can be coerced into testifying against oneself; also guarantees "due process of law" and right of eminent domain (public acquisition of private property must be duly compensated).

**Amendment #6** Guarantees to the accused the right "to a speedy and public trial" by a jury. The rights of knowing the charges, being confronted with witnesses, and having the assistance of a lawyer for the defense are also included.

**Amendment #7** Preserves the right of a jury trial in common lawsuits exceeding twenty dollars.

**Amendment #8** Prohibits excessive bail (monetary guarantee that the defendant will appear in court at a particular time in the future) and "cruel and unusual punishments."

**Amendment #9** Enumerated or detailed rights in the Constitution do not eliminate other rights "retained by the people."

**Amendment #10** There are "reserved" powers granted to the states or the people.

NOTE: The first ten amendments constituted the original Bill of Rights added in 1791. The remaining sixteen amendments were added from 1789 to 1971.

## ADDITIONAL AMENDMENTS

**Amendment #11** The judicial power of the United States does not extend to any law or equity suit brought by a foreign state or citizen against any state.

**Amendment #12**  Details the role and operation of the electors in the electoral college; also describes the mechanics of the House of Representatives' selection of the president and the Senate selection of the vice-president.

**Amendment #13**  Abolishes the practice of slavery.

**Amendment #14**  Forbids any state from depriving a person of life, liberty, or property, without due process of law.

**Amendment #15**  Citizens cannot be denied the right to vote on the grounds of "race, color, or previous condition of servitude."

**Amendment #16**  Congress is granted the power to establish the federal income tax.

**Amendment #17**  Provides for direct popular election of U.S. senators, rather than the previous method of selection by state legislatures.

**Amendment #18**  Prohibits the "manufacture, sale, or transportation of intoxicating liquors" within the United States (the Prohibition Amendment).

**Amendment #19**  Grants women the right to vote in the United States.

**Amendment #20**  Presidential and vice-presidential terms are set to begin on January 20; congressional representatives' and senators' terms to begin on January 3.

**Amendment #21**  Repeals the Eighteenth Amendment.

**Amendment #22**  Limits the president to a maximum of two elected terms.

**Amendment #23**  Grants the District of Columbia electors in the electoral college.

**Amendment #24**  Abolishes the poll tax as a requirement for voting in the United States.

**Amendment #25**  When there is a vice-presidential vacancy, the president may appoint a new vice-president with the approval of a majority vote by Congress. Also, when the president is unable to perform his office duties, the vice-president becomes acting president. Finally, if a conflict ensues between the acting president and the original president over who should occupy the office, Congress decides by a two-thirds vote within twenty-one days.

**Amendment #26**  Grants eighteen-year-old American citizens the right to vote.

*T*he Constitution limits and fragments political power. Over 200 years, the Constitution's modifications through amendments and judicial interpretation have solidified the Lockean principles relating to governmental protection of life, liberty, and property. The American system of government, while certainly not perfect, has largely remained true to the social-contract ideal.

However, the American experiment in democratic self-government is still evolving. For example, the delicate balance of power between the national government and state governments must still be redefined for each *generation. Federalism, the subject of chapter 2, is an apt reminder that the revolution of 1787 is far from over.*

**Selected Readings**

Bernstein, Richard B. *Are We to Be a Nation? The Making of the Constitution* (1987)

Levy, Leonard W., ed. *Essays on the Making of the Constitution.* 2nd ed. (1987)

MacDonald, Forrest F. *Novus Ordo Seclorum: The Intellectual Origins of the Constitution* (1985)

Mead, Walter B. *The United States Constitution; Personalities, Principles, and Issues* (1987)

Rossiter, Clinton. *1787: The Great Convention* (1965)

# 2

## Federalism

*Federalism in America refers to the division and sharing of constitutionally assigned or implied powers between the national and state governments. America's federal system, a mixture of states' rights and national supremacy, permits the states and municipalities control over a number of important programs—highways, some welfare programs, education, the police, and land-use regulations (zoning). While the federal government possesses enormous power, it must persuade the states to govern in ways that will meet national political, economic, and social goals. The states may not always be so persuaded—witness the years of resistance to progressive civil rights legislation passed by Congress, or the desegregation rulings of the United States Supreme Court. Despite federalism's imperfections, American federalism has been an attractive political arrangement shared by other nations such as Canada, Australia, India, West Germany, and Switzerland.*

## UNITARY AND CONFEDERATION GOVERNMENTS

Unitary and confederation governments represent two other ways of distributing political power. In the unitary system, almost all of the political power is vested in the central government. Many democracies use this model, such as France, Israel, and the United Kingdom. By comparison, a confederation is an association of several sovereign units (states, provinces, and so on) in which the central government has little power. The national government depends upon cooperation from the states in order to function effectively. In 1786, that cooperation was far from satisfactory, hence the call for a constitutional convention. States may also secede from a confederation, but not from a federal system. (The American Civil War established this principle by force of arms.)

# FEDERALISM AND THE CONSTITUTION

## The Perspective of the Framers

The founders were basically divided over the meaning of federalism. One group subscribed to the views of Alexander Hamilton, who argued for a powerful federal government—i.e., the concept of national supremacy. The other view, espoused by Thomas Jefferson, assumed the federal government to be a creation of the states. The Jeffersonians believed that an "oppressive" national government could threaten individual liberties. It should therefore have limited powers. This basic struggle between national supremacy and states' rights would intensify over time.

## Contemporary Federalism

Today, the United States consists of more than 80,000 separate governmental units. Along with the national and state governments, there are cities, counties, and special districts (the latter typically handle schools, water supplies, or sewage disposal) constituting local polities. The Constitution, however, recognizes only federal and state authority. Each state can create, abolish, or modify its local governmental units. For example, the state of Virginia could take territory away from any of its own cities.

## Constitutional Provisions Relating to Federalism

The states are given responsibilities in drawing congressional districts for members of the House of Representatives, ratifying or proposing constitutional amendments, and tapping the "reserved powers" granted to them by the Tenth Amendment. The federal government is allocated a long list of delegated or specifically granted powers in Article I, Section 8 of the Constitution—borrowing money, raising armies, declaring war, and regulating commerce are examples. In addition, the Constitution tells the states what they may not do—no state can make a treaty with a foreign nation, grant titles of nobility, pass a bill of attainder (a law declaring an individual or group guilty of a crime and administering punishment without benefit of trial), approve ex post facto laws (laws which retroactively make an earlier noncriminal act a crime), levy taxes on imports or exports (without permission of Congress), impair the "obligation of contracts," or keep military forces in peacetime. Finally, five amendments to the Constitution place restrictions on the actions of the states—the Thirteenth (prohibits slavery), the Fourteenth (no denial of due process, equal protection of the laws), the Fifteenth (no denial of vote due to race, color, or previous condition of servitude), the Nineteenth (no denial of vote on the basis of sex), and the Twenty-sixth (no denial of the vote to eighteen-year-olds).

## THE STATES ARE PROTECTED FROM THE FEDERAL GOVERNMENT

The U.S. Constitution declares that state representation in the U.S. Senate may not be altered without agreement from the affected state. Also, a state may not be divided or merged with another state without its consent. Finally, constitutional amendments may not be added without the ratifying vote of three-fourths of the states.

## CONSTITUTIONAL RULES GOVERNING RELATIONS AMONG THE STATES

These rules as set forth by the Constitution include the "full faith and credit clause," the "privileges and immunities clause," the "interstate rendition clause," and the implied use of interstate compacts.

**The Full Faith and Credit Clause.** Found in Article IV, the clause mandates that a state must accept the official records, documents, and civil rulings (a property sales contract, as one example) of other states in the union. In addition, a marriage or divorce obtained under the laws of one state are normally (but not always) considered legally valid by all other states.

**The Privileges and Immunities Clause.** According to Article IV, "The citizens of each state shall be entitled to all privileges and immunities of citizens in the several states." Each state is expected to extend the same courteous treatment to citizens of other states as well as the same legal protections. (For example, a citizen has access to the courts in another state.) Thus, this clause protects fundamental rights across the nation.

**The Interstate Rendition Clause.** This clause, found in Article IV, Section 2, states the following:

> . . . a person charged in any state with Treason, Felony, or other Crime, who shall flee from Justice, and be found in another State, shall on Demand of the executive authority of the State from which he fled, be delivered up to be removed to the State having jurisdiction of the Crime.

Normally, a fugitive who flees to another state is willingly extradited or sent back to the state where the alleged crime was committed. However, the Supreme Court has ruled that the federal courts cannot compel a governor to extradite a fugitive.

**Interstate Compacts.** Article I, Section 10 asserts that "no State shall, without the Consent of Congress, enter into any Agreement or Compact with another State." However, assuming congressional permission, interstate compacts or agreements have been realized through negotiations by the governors of those involved states. Currently, there are more than 170 compacts which try to manage problems which cross state borders. In recent years, these compacts have dealt with interstate problems such as transportation, crime, and trade. For example, the Port Authority of New York–New Jersey, founded in 1921, supervises interstate bridges and tunnels, ports for ships, and bus and railroad routes. Future compacts may deal with such difficult problems as radioactive waste disposal.

## THE NATIONAL GOVERNMENT'S RELATIONSHIP WITH THE STATES

*Guarantee of a Republican Form of Government/ Protection Against Internal Violence*

According to the Constitution (Article IV, Section 4), the national government is required to guarantee a "republican" form of government within each state and to protect each state against foreign invasion or internal violence. (States have requested federal aid to suppress domestic violence sixteen times in American history.) The president may use federal troops or "federalize" the state militia. As an example, President Lyndon B. Johnson sent federal troops to Selma, Alabama, in 1965 in order to protect a voting rights march led by the Rev. Martin Luther King, Jr.

The "republican form of government" guarantee is not defined clearly in the Constitution, nor has the Supreme Court ruled conclusively on its meaning. The Court considers the issue a "political question" which should be treated by the president and Congress. However, the term is generally understood to mean a "representative democracy" whereby fundamental liberties are preserved.

After the Civil War, Congress charged that several southern states did not have a republican form due to continuing discriminatory practices against blacks. Congress refused to admit "elected" senators and representatives from these states.

*Respect for Territorial Integrity*

The federal government is constitutionally required to acknowledge the legal existence and boundaries of each state in the Union. Consequently, Congress cannot carve out a new state from the existing territory of another state without the approval of that state's legislature.

*The Principle of National Supremacy*

Article VI is clear on the issue of national supremacy—the states may not pass laws or enact policies which are in conflict with the Constitution, acts of Congress, or national treaties. If there is a conflict, state laws/policies are clearly inferior to federal statutes.

### McCULLOCH V. MARYLAND

The concept of national supremacy was established in the 1819 Supreme Court case of *McCulloch* v. *Maryland*. Chief Justice John Marshall declared that the state of Maryland did not have the power to tax the national bank of the United States, an act which clearly violated the Supremacy Clause. As Marshall phrased it:

> If any one proposition could command the universal assent of mankind we might expect it to be this—that the government of the Union, though limited in its powers, is supreme within its sphere of action. The States have no power to retard, impede, burden, or in any manner control the operation of the constitutional laws enacted by Congress.

**Marshall's Argument.** To Marshall, the government of the United States was established by the people, not the states. The federal government and its related institutions were accordingly immune to destructive policies passed by the states. In Marshall's words, "The power to tax was the power to destroy." Hence, the Maryland law was unconstitutional. The Marshall Court also expanded congressional controls over interstate commerce, through such historic cases as *Gibbons* v. *Ogden* in 1824. But the battle between states' rights and federal power was far from over.

**Nullification and War.** The doctrine of nullification, first proposed by Thomas Jefferson and James Madison and later revived by John C. Calhoun, argued that the states could declare a federal law invalid if interpreted by them as a violation of the Constitution. Jefferson and Madison had invoked the doctrine in 1798 over a federal law which punished newspaper editors for printing critical stories about the federal government. Calhoun, of South Carolina, used the doctrine to attack national tariffs and federal efforts to ban slavery. The Civil War resolved the nullification issue. The Union could not be dissolved and the states could not unilaterally obviate federal law.

## Dual Federalism

In the era after the Civil War, the states promulgated the theory of dual federalism, which held that the national government was supreme in its sphere of influence, but that the states were equally supreme in their areas of political jurisdiction. The Tenth Amendment was perceived by the Supreme Court as a barrier to national power. For example, Congress could regulate interstate commerce, but it was up to the states to handle intrastate (within each state) commerce. Industrial production was construed as a local activity under the jurisdiction of the states. The same philosophy was extended to child labor laws. However, the national scope of huge corporations and the growing complexity of the economy obliterated these artificial distinctions.

The election of Franklin D. Roosevelt as president in 1932 accelerated the decline of dual federalism. The Supreme Court eventually approved the federal government's power to regulate commerce and the economy. By the 1940s, farming and manufacturing were clearly defined as falling under the scope of federal supervision. Today, dual federalism has yielded fully to the contemporary model of cooperative federalism.

## Cooperative Federalism

Cooperative federalism has been compared to a "marble cake," as opposed to dual federalism's "layer cake" analogy. The states and federal government frequently share the administrative costs and responsibilities associated with public programs. A good example is the field of public education. The national government provides considerable monetary aid to elementary and secondary schools, but state and local officials handle such areas as curriculum standards and teacher certification requirements. For hundreds of other cooperative programs, Washington may pay for part of the bill, but states and cities must also bear some of the costs of the project, be it airport construction or sewage treatment plants.

# WHY THE STATES/LOCALITIES REMAIN IMPORTANT IN THE FEDERAL SYSTEM

The states and localities continue to play a significant role in American politics. There are three governmental services in which they have major control—law enforcement, education, and land controls (zoning and housing patterns). There are two reasons explaining these areas of influence—the traditional belief held by the American people that the police and schools should come under local jurisdiction, and the support of locally elected legislators for such views. House and Senate members would oppose strong federal supervision over the curriculum of the schools or a "national" police force.

# FEDERAL GRANTS-IN-AID

## The Early Era of Fiscal Federalism

The earliest federal grants given to the states were land grants for colleges and universities. Grants also assisted the construction of railroads, wagon roads, flood-control zones, and canals. In subsequent decades, grants increased in popularity as states willingly accepted plentiful amounts of federal tax dollars. The federal government, in keeping with the concept of dual federalism, allowed state control over the administration of grant programs.

Politically, conservative state governors could attack wasteful federal spending while still accepting federal money for "important projects" in their respective states. This remains a standard political ploy even today.

## The Modern Era of Federal Grants

The modern concept of a federal grant-in-aid derives from the presidency of Franklin D. Roosevelt. FDR established categorical grants for specific problems such as children's health and vocational education. Categorical grants were expanded even more under the Great Society programs of Lyndon Johnson in the 1960s. Five new federal programs accounted for this growth: (1) aid to low-income families; (2) Medicaid (health insurance for the poor); (3) building of highways; (4) assistance to the unemployed; (5) welfare payments to low-income mothers who had disabled children or no spousal support. State and local governments now were required to put up matching funds, a share of the total cost of the particular program being promoted. Also, these grants had "strings" attached, such as not using federal funds to discriminate against minorities or approving construction projects which paid workers a below-union wage. Finally, some grants bypassed the states entirely, allocating funds directly to local governments or even community civic groups.

### PROJECT AND FORMULA CATEGORICAL GRANTS

There are two basic types of categorical grants—project and formula:

**Project Grants.** The most common type of categorical grant, these are awarded on the basis of competitive applications. An example would be university professors applying for funds to be used for scientific research.

**Formula Grants.** These grants are distributed according to a complex formula incorporating population, income, rural population, or other variables. The total amount of money allocated for a school lunch program to a particular state or locality would be formula-based.

### BLOCK GRANTS

These grants, begun in 1966, involve federal funding to the state and local governments in general; they encompass broad areas such as mental health or criminal justice. Block grants were more consistent with the conservative political philosophy of allowing greater discretion to the states/localities in determining how and where the funds should actually be spent. Still, federal "strings" gradually multiplied even with these ostensibly "no-strings" grants.

## A NOTE ON FEDERAL CONTROLS: MANDATES AND "CONDITIONS OF AID"

Mandates are federal laws or court rulings which compel cities and states to implement certain policies even if no aid is received. Examples would include protection of the environment and federal pure-drinking-water standards. "Conditions of aid" do not have to be accepted by the states or localities; however, rejection of these conditions will usually prevent the receipt of federal dollars. For example, in the past, western states lost highway construction funds when they did not comply with the federal fifty-five-mile-per-hour speed-limit standard.

## *Federalism Under Nixon and Carter*

Lyndon Johnson's Great Society was based on the premise that the states could not be trusted to use federal grant money wisely—i.e., to help the poor and disadvantaged. But starting with the Nixon administration, this assumption was challenged with new programs intended to give fiscal decision-making powers back to the states. General revenue-sharing allocated federal tax dollars back to state and local officials who in turn were given wide discretion as to how those funds would be spent. Categorical grants were also combined into general funding areas such as the Model Cities or Urban Renewal programs. These block grants proliferated with the Comprehensive Employment and Training Act (CETA) in 1973. CETA was modified by President Jimmy Carter in 1978 in order to send funds directly to the needy, rather than relying on state and locally elected politicians to make the allocation decisions.

## *Reagan's "New Federalism"*

The Reagan administration tried to reverse even further the centralization trend begun by FDR in the 1930s. Reagan conservatives opposed big government, federal programs to help the poor, and federal expenditures on costly social programs which they argued contributed to economic inflation and stagnation. They stressed the theme of devolution, which basically meant shifting federal responsibilities to the states, localities, and the private sector. President Reagan promptly consolidated seventy-seven categorical grants to nine new block grants to be administered by the states. He also proposed the "Great Swap," whereby the federal government would assume full responsibility for Medicaid (health care for the indigent elderly), while the states would handle the food-stamp and other welfare programs. But Congress rejected this plan.

Another Reagan argument was that state and local officials should not depend as much on federal "hand-outs." These officials should tap other revenue sources at their respective governmental levels. But state officials resented these federal cuts. They also objected to revenue-sharing being canceled by the Reagan administration as a way of further reducing federal spending. The states reacted by developing new revenue sources, such as lotteries, which raised billions of dollars. States also cut expenses through such devices as "privatizing" formerly public services (trash collection) and encouraging more welfare recipients to find employment.

# ADVANTAGES AND DISADVANTAGES OF FEDERALISM

## Introduction

The founders created a federal structure to prevent a tyrannical concentration of political power which might silence the voice of the states. The ultimate goal of the federal system would be to strengthen the foundations of democracy through power-sharing. Has the federal vision of the framers been fulfilled?

## Advantages

Federalism is seen as having a number of advantages: (a) it promotes a measure of local control over political life and multiplies the opportunities for political participation through the elections of thousands of state and local officials; a citizen or interest group denied access at one level of government can seek redress at another; in short, the opportunity to gain political power is widely disseminated among the fifty states, 3,000 counties, and thousands of municipal governing units; (b) it encourages experimentation and diversity vis-à-vis the nation's social and political needs; Georgia was the first state to allow eighteen-year-olds the right to vote, and California was a pioneer in devising air-pollution policies long before the federal government passed a comprehensive clean-air act for the entire nation.

## Disadvantages

Some notable negative aspects of federalism are: (a) its local orientation encourages provincialism and obstruction of progress; (b) local autonomy can create wasteful duplication, such as the plethora of agricultural agencies at all three levels of government. The bureaucracies become bloated and administrative costs increase proportionately; (c) federal systems may have difficulty coordinating problems that "spill over" state lines, such as air and water pollution. Acid rain that falls upon states in New England originates in the industrial centers of the Midwest, but those polluting states can refuse to pay for damages.

*The sharing of political power is the trademark of contemporary federalism. While national supremacy is now accepted, the states are clearly partners with the federal government on both policy coordination and implementation. Even after the Reagan era, billions of federal grant dollars continue to reinforce the "marble cake" relationship.*

*In the past, some experts have predicted that an all-powerful federal government would eventually render the states politically meaningless. However, state governments have markedly improved their performance during the last twenty-five years in such policy areas as education, urban renewal, and the environment. Political leadership in the states has also improved. In short, the federal tradition seems to be in no danger of extinction.*

**Selected Readings**

Anton, Thomas. *American Federalism and Public Policy* (1989)

Dye, Thomas R. *American Federalism: Competition Among Governments* (1990)

Elazar, Daniel J. *American Federalism: A View from the States.* 3rd ed. (1984)

Kettl, Donald F. *Government by Proxy: (Mis?) Managing Federal Programs* (1988)

Reagan, Michael, and John G. Sanzone. *The New Federalism* (1981)

Wright, Deil S. *Understanding Intergovernmental Relations.* 3rd ed. (1988)

# 3

## Public Opinion and the Mass Media

*P*ublic opinion may be defined as the collection of views and attitudes held by different groups and individuals in America toward the political system in general, and important public issues specifically. There is no one "public," but many "publics," separate groups with different views. Leaders must try to consider these diverse publics when creating new policies.

The mass media—books, films, radio, newspapers, television, magazines—transmit information to the American people and their political leaders. The media play an important role in supporting democracy and influencing public opinion. As Thomas Jefferson wrote in 1787: "Were it left to me to decide whether we should have a government without newspapers, or newspapers without a government, I should not hesitate a moment to prefer the latter." The media report on the government's actions (or inaction), the political behavior of public officials, the many events which impact upon the lives of citizens, the views of candidates running for office, and unresolved social problems. The public's degree of respect for, and belief in, the political system can also be shaped by the tone that the media set in their news coverage. In short, the media play a large role in providing the "information base" from which citizens develop their opinions; conversely, elected officials can learn from media reports and polls what the chief policy concerns of the public may be.

# PUBLIC OPINION IN A DEMOCRACY

**The Importance of Public Opinion**

People do have different opinions on issues. But in order for a democracy to function effectively, the many individuals and groups within society must accept democracy's fundamental ideas and values. These ideas and values include an acceptance of majority rule, individual rights, minority protection, peaceful resolution of social problems, and tolerance for dissent. Also, the people must believe that their opinions count and that leaders can be trusted to act responsibly.

**The Qualities of Public Opinion**

Political scientists have specified five qualities of public opinion which can vary over time. These are: intensity, fluidity, stability, quiescence, and relevance.

### INTENSITY

This quality measures how strongly people feel about a given issue and their determination to express their private opinions publicly. For example, most Americans have strong opinions about the right of a woman to have an abortion, both pro and con. Truly intense opinions can frequently help a minority win on a public policy issue over a less concerned, politically inactive majority. Thus, the National Rifle Association, the largest anti-gun-control group in America, with 2.6 million members, has been successful in thwarting the passage of comprehensive gun-control laws by Con- gress, despite polls which reveal that a majority of the public favor such legislation.

### FLUIDITY

Public opinion can change very quickly, sometimes overnight. A classic example of opinion fluidity was America's strong isolationism (avoiding a war against Germany or Japan) prior to December 7, 1941. After the Japanese attack on Pearl Harbor, national opinion changed to a full support of the war effort.

### STABILITY

Some individuals maintain their opinions for a very long time. The vast majority of Americans believe that democracy is a good, if not the best, form of government. This fundamental acceptance seems constant from generation to generation.

### QUIESCENCE

Quiescent, or latent, public opinion refers to potential opinion which can become activated through events or the communication of more information, especially by the media. Thus, the American people were ready for a president who was an "outsider"—i.e., not a Washington politician—after the presidential scandals of the 1970s. Hence, the appeal of Jimmy Carter, an ex-governor of Georgia, who won the presidency in 1976. As another example, the media's emphasis on the dangers of the fatal disease AIDS in the late 1980s and early 1990s forced millions of citizens to think about the problem and form appropriate opinions.

### RELEVANCE

Relevant public opinion deals with how important or unimportant an issue may be to individuals. An elderly citizen facing serious medical expenses will be concerned over increased costs of Medicare or Medicaid health coverage. An eighteen-year-old must think about the possibility of future military service (or even the reinstitution of the draft) when he registers with his local selective service board. Home owners will be upset over a projected increase in property taxes, but apartment renters will be indifferent since these taxes will not directly affect them.

# HOW PUBLIC OPINION IS FORMED

## The Agents of Political Socialization

Americans learn about their leaders and develop their opinions about government through the process known as political socialization. Important to this process are the family, schools, peer groups, the media, and generational events.

### FAMILY

A child's parents, brothers and sisters, grandparents, or other relatives can all influence his or her early political attitudes. A family which discusses politics around the dinner table can bequeath to the child a lifelong interest in public affairs. Conversely, a family of nonvoters, whose members describe politicians as "crooks," may transmit to children negative feelings toward government.

### THE FAMILY AND PARTY IDENTIFICATION

One clear legacy of the family is the transfer of party or partisan identification to children. Research reveals that nearly one-third of school-children can identify with a party by the second grade. If both parents are strong supporters of the Republican (or Democratic) party, then their children will tend to adopt that party as their own as they begin political life. However, recent studies suggest that young people are becoming more "independent," so that the family's partisan influence is somewhat weaker today than it was two decades ago.

## FAMILY INFLUENCE AND ATTITUDES TOWARD POLITICAL AUTHORITY

Most children identify with the president as a benevolent figure by the time they are age six or seven. However, low-income, poorly educated families tend to produce children whose attitudes are more hostile to the presidential "figure," and political authority in general.

## SCHOOLS

The educational system tries to reinforce the legitimacy of the political system through civics courses, student participation in school government, and treatments of American history and governmental institutions in textbooks. Students who go to a college where most professors are political liberals are likely to be influenced in that ideological direction. By "liberal," we mean that students will be more tolerant of rapid social change and likely to favor an active American role in world affairs.

## PEER GROUPS

Groups consisting of friends and associates who share similar social or workplace characteristics can influence opinions as well. Thus, members of a labor union may have fairly uniform views toward the government's protection of their right to collective bargaining. Corporate executives may agree on the desirability of minimum governmental interference in the marketplace.

## MEDIA

The media's role in opinion formation will be elaborated on later. The media bombard the citizen with all kinds of political information. However, studies show that people have "selective perception"—i.e., they will ignore media reports which run counter to their existing beliefs or are of little interest to them.

## GENERATIONAL EVENTS

Major, traumatic events can permanently shape attitudes of each political generation. During the 1960s and 1970s, the Vietnam War and the Watergate scandal led millions of Americans to question the integrity of the presidency, and politicians in general (many schoolchildren acquired a less favorable view of the president as well).

Similarly, the Great Depression of the 1930s convinced a majority of the electorate that the Democratic party could best handle the issue of economic prosperity. The stability of this opinion persisted until the era of Ronald Reagan in the 1980s.

## Personal Characteristics and Opinion Differences

Personal characteristics can have a definitive impact upon opinion as well; included are such factors as race, religion, region and place of residence, and gender.

### RACE

White and black Americans often have different opinions regarding such issues as school busing (more blacks than whites may see the practice as promoting integration), the death penalty (more whites favor it), higher spending for defense (whites are more supportive), or national health insurance (blacks are more supportive). Furthermore, blacks have consistently voted Democratic, while many blue-collar whites have turned their support to the Republican party.

### RELIGION

Religious backgrounds also affect opinion. For example, Catholics tend to be more liberal than white Protestants on economic issues; Jewish-Americans are even more liberal than either Catholics or Protestants on both economic and noneconomic concerns. Born-again Christians favor school prayer and oppose abortions with a greater intensity than many other religious groups. In short, different religious teachings will affect the individual's conceptions of morality, social justice, human nature, and obedience to authority.

### REGION AND PLACE OF RESIDENCE

A person's geographic region and residence can influence political attitudes. The South, for example, remains more conservative than the Northeast, especially on racial issues and "law and order" policies. Southerners also tend to be more supportive of defense spending than other regions (the presence of many military bases in the South may account for this opinion). Midwesterners may have a special interest in farm policy. Regarding place of residence, most of the nation's largest cities have voted Democratic; the suburbs have traditionally supported Republican candidates.

### GENDER

Until the mid-1970s, few major differences existed between the political views of men and women. One difference was in regard to the use of military force; more women than men were opposed to the Vietnam War. But by the mid-1980s, women became convinced that Republicans, led by President Reagan, were likely to send troops into combat. Hence, they identified with the Democratic party. Still, on other issues, the so-called "gender gap" was virtually nonexistent. For example, majorities of both men and women approved of abortion.

# PUBLIC OPINION POLLS

**The History
of Polling**

Prior to the era of modern scientific polling, magazines and newspapers would solicit opinions from their readers by face-to-face straw polls or mail surveys. However, despite a large number of responses, these techniques were unreliable. The straw vote emphasized quantity of responses over the quality of the sample. In other words, an accurate cross-section of the voting population was by no means assured.

### THE LITERARY DIGEST MISTAKE OF 1936

A famous case of faulty surveys was *The Literary Digest* poll that predicted the outcome of the presidential election of 1936 between the Republican candidate, Alfred Landon, and the Democratic incumbent, President Franklin D. Roosevelt. The *Digest*, a popular magazine of its day, mailed postcard ballots to more than 10 million individuals whose names had been taken from automobile registration lists and telephone directories. After more than 2 million ballots were returned, the magazine stated that Landon would easily win the election. The opposite occurred, as Roosevelt won in a landslide, capturing 60 percent of the vote and winning every state except Maine and Vermont.

What had been the *Digest*'s mistake? The magazine had contacted wealthier Americans who could afford cars and telephones during a depression year. Poorer classes of American had been omitted—the unemployed, blue-collar workers, and ethnic minorities. These groups were the heart of FDR's voting strength. Shortly thereafter, the *Digest* went out of business.

### THE 1948 GALLUP POLL'S ERROR

After the *Digest* debacle, more-sophisticated scientific pollsters developed far better techniques, using personal interviews with small samples of selected voters. George Gallup's organization became famous, but it, too, unwittingly created a "biased" (inaccurate) sample in the 1948 election between Republican challenger Thomas Dewey and the incumbent Democratic candidate, President Harry S. Truman. Roughly two weeks before election day in November, Gallup confidently predicted Dewey to be the winner. Thinking Dewey to be far ahead, it stopped interviewing voters. Subsequently, many voters changed their minds, switching from Dewey to Truman. The result was a Truman victory.

**The Sample Must Mirror the Voting Population.** Clear lessons of 1936 and 1948 are that the sample of individuals polled must be a microcosm of the much larger population and that interviewing must be continued up to election day since opinion can be very fluid. A poll only represents a "snapshot of opinion" at a particular time.

## *Proper Polling Procedures*

Accurate polling procedures must: (a) construct a representative sample; (b) use valid or reliable questions; (c) carefully communicate with respondents.

### CONSTRUCTING A REPRESENTATIVE SAMPLE

A sample must be representative in that every major characteristic of the population from which the sample has been drawn must exist in the sample in approximately the same frequency as in the much larger population. For example, if 4 percent of the U.S. population was Hispanic, a similar proportion of the sample should also be Hispanic. Most national polls interview between 1,200 and 1,500 people who collectively represent the national U.S. adult population of 190 million. The sample size must be large enough to reflect the major social, economic, and political characteristics of the American electorate.

A representative sample is chosen through the process of random sampling, which is basically a lottery system whereby every individual in the population and each geographic region has an equal mathematical chance of being included in the sample, just as in a lottery every number has the same probability of being selected. If the sample is large enough and is truly randomly selected, then the law of probability states that final results will be satisfactory, usually within a small margin of error—typically no more than plus or minus 3 percent in national polls. If a poll projects that candidate A will receive 52 percent of the vote on election day, his/her actual percentage could vary within a range of 49 to 55 percent. (Over the years, the Gallup Poll, with few exceptions, has accurately predicted the winner of each presidential election.)

### THE USE OF VALID QUESTIONS

The manner in which questions are phrased is quite important to a poll's final results. Questions which are emotionally loaded can predetermine responses from those being interviewed. For example, the question "Do you agree with a woman's freedom of choice to have an abortion?" will elicit different responses than will the question "Do you agree with a woman's right to murder her unborn child by means of an abortion?"

### COMMUNICATION WITH RESPONDENTS

Questioners conducting polls through face-to-face interviews or over the phone must avoid contaminating truthful responses through their voice inflections, preexisting attitudes toward the questions asked, or unintentional coaching of interviewees. To avoid these problems, organizations exercise great care in hiring and training their field personnel.

## Problems with the Polls

In addition to *The Literary Digest* and 1948 classic mistakes, polls in recent years have encountered greater volatility in public opinion, with the consequent need of polling more often, especially during a presidential campaign. In 1984, several polls seriously underestimated the final margin between Reagan and Mondale (eighteen percentage points); and in 1988 the polls were in error by as much as seventeen percentage points in the various presidential primaries.

Two other problems related to polling are the bandwagon effect and exit surveys.

### THE BANDWAGON EFFECT

Critics charge that publishing poll results will influence voters to vote for the candidate who appears to be far ahead of his opponent. People want to select the obvious winner. While there is little empirical evidence to support this claim on the national level, some studies suggest it has influenced election outcomes in state and local races.

### USE OF EXIT POLLS

Exit pollsters interview voters regarding their ballot choices as they leave the voting booth on election day. By taking a random sample and collating voter responses, predictions as to whom the eventual winner will be can be made relatively early. One problem with exit polls is that some voters will not be truthful with interviewers about how they have voted, thus distorting the process.

Exit polls have been utilized by the networks to predict both congressional and presidential victors, thus discouraging citizens who planned to vote later in the day from even going to their respective precincts. Apparently, exit polls in previous elections have reduced voter turnout in the western states based on poll projections made earlier from the Northeast and South. To resolve this problem, the networks have agreed not to broadcast election predictions until the polls have closed in the Pacific time zone.

## Polls and the Media

The media publish national and regional poll results on a regular basis. In fact, major newspapers such as *The New York Times* and *The Washington Post* frequently conduct their own polls on important policy questions. Media poll coverage can influence the opinions of those undecided or even uninformed Americans. The reciprocal relationship between the media and American public opinion is not new. Indeed, the media's role in both reacting to and creating opinion has been historically significant.

# A BRIEF HISTORY OF THE MEDIA

**Early Partisanship and the Press**

Partisan newspapers were published during the early years of the American republic. The *Gazette of the United States*, a pro-Federalist newspaper, was sponsored by Alexander Hamilton, while Jefferson countered with the *National Gazette*, a pro-Republican party publication. Both papers were too expensive for the average citizen to afford (most citizens were illiterate, anyway), and their small circulation was almost exclusively directed at the party faithful. They usually appeared only once or twice a week. Clearly, early newspapers did not seek the goal of impartial reporting. It was not until the 1830s that newspapers moved toward independent ownership and mass circulation.

**Press Partisanship Declines, Mass-Circulation Newspapers Become Prominent**

In 1845, the invention of the high-speed rotary press ushered in low-cost, mass-produced newspapers. The telegraph permitted a rudimentary wire service, relaying stories between cities at a faster pace. Improved literacy rates caused circulation and sales to increase. This new financial status liberated newspapers from their previously strong ties to party patronage. While newspapers became more issue-oriented, many editors practiced more flamboyant methods of boosting sales.

### RISE OF "YELLOW JOURNALISM"

A new style of reporting evolved by the late 1800s, stressing coverage of scandals, violence, disasters, and sports in an effort to expand circulation. This so-called "yellow journalism" (the name came from the inexpensive yellow paper used by these newspapers) contributed to the outbreak of the Spanish-American War after William Randolph Hearst's paper, *The New York Journal*, printed inflammatory stories about Cuba, Spain, and the sinking of the American battleship *Maine*.

### "MUCKRAKERS"

Opinion magazines such as *McClure's* and *Collier's* promoted the art of investigative reporting, or muckraking, a term coined by Theodore Roosevelt to refer to the "dirt" being uncovered. Typical muckrakers were Ida M. Tarbell, who analyzed John D. Rockefeller's Standard Oil monopoly in a series of magazine articles; and Lincoln Steffens, whose book, *Shame of the Cities*, recognized the pervasiveness of urban corruption in America.

**The Era of Objective Journalism**

American journalism reacted against Hearst's excesses by embracing the concept of objective journalism. Led by Adolph Ochs, owner of *The New York Times*, objective journalism avoided partisanship and exaggerated opinions in favor of the "facts" of a story and the presentation of all sides.

(One other factor promoting objectivity was the profit motive—i.e., sales depended on reaching as many groups in society as possible.) In addition, newspapers began to separate advertisements from the news, eliminating a source of bias. Finally, newly formed journalism schools at Columbia University and the University of Missouri reinforced the merits of objective journalism. Today, most newspaper publishers follow the principles of objectivity (as they see it), trying to achieve a liberal-conservative "balance" even in their opinion columns.

## The Development of Radio and TV Broadcast Journalism

Technology in the twentieth century extended the media's reach dramatically. The "electronic media"—radio and TV—now reached millions of citizens.

### RISE OF RADIO

National political leaders, especially President Franklin D. Roosevelt in the 1930s, grasped the idea of the potential power of radio. Roosevelt used his radio "fireside chats" to talk directly to the American people. Later presidents did not have to rely upon newspaper editors and reporters to reinterpret their political messages. Radio became the first national media form, reaching millions of Americans instantaneously and simultaneously. Today, 99 percent of American homes have radios.

### RISE OF TELEVISION

The widespread use of television in the 1950s brought political life into the homes of millions of Americans. TV's full political potential was first realized with the broadcast of the national party conventions in 1952. Republican candidate Eisenhower then pioneered TV political commercials in the following campaign. Presidential candidate John F. Kennedy and Vice-President Richard M. Nixon held the first nationally televised debate in 1960. The importance of "looking good" on TV and projecting competence became apparent when Kennedy, appearing youthful, handsome, and knowledgeable, won the debate handily over Nixon, who looked tired, ill, and unshaven. (Ironically, radio listeners thought Nixon had won the debate, but the TV audience was far larger.) Subsequently, President Kennedy became the first chief executive to utilize TV fully in speeches and live press conferences during the early 1960s.

TV presidential debates in 1960, 1964, 1976, 1980, 1984, and 1988 added to the medium's impact. Televised congressional hearings, dealing with an issue like the Watergate scandal in the 1970s, brought viewers closer to another vital political institution. Also, TV network news expanded dramatically in terms of amount of time on the air and range of topics covered. By the early 1990s, 98 percent of all homes in America had at least one TV set, and the medium had become the major source of political news for the public. Polls revealed that two out of every three Americans considered TV news stories to be more accurate than newspaper accounts. Thus, it was not surprising that the importance of the electronic media had required governmental regulation.

**Broadcasters Are Licensed by the Government.** The Federal Communications Commission (FCC) was established in 1934 to regulate the performance standards first of radio and then eventually of television stations. The FCC develops regulations covering station ownership, signal strength and frequency location, advertising rates, and general access to the airwaves by citizens and public officials. The FCC requires that a license to each station be renewed after seven years for radio and five years for TV.

**Federal Regulations Regarding Political Content.** Federal law dictates that stations give "equal time" to all candidates running for the same office. Until 1987, they also operated under the provisions of the fairness doctrine.

**The "Equal Time Provision."** If radio or TV broadcasters make air time available to one candidate running for public office, they must allow equal time to all other candidates who seek that same office. All air costs must be the same for each candidate. Rates must also be comparable to those charged to commercial advertisers.

**The "Fairness Doctrine."** Until 1987, broadcasters adhered to the "fairness doctrine," which mandated the airing of opposing opinions on significant public issues. But frequently issues have more than two sides, so strict adherence to the doctrine consumed inordinate amounts of broadcast time. Owners of stations frequently avoided controversy altogether. They also objected to the fact that the FCC imposed the doctrine upon their operations, but not upon newspapers or magazines.

Subsequently, the FCC abolished the doctrine in 1987 on the basis that it: (a) violated freedom of the press—i.e., broadcasters should be free to cover issues as they wish; (b) the great diversity of media outlets already allowed different opinions to be aired. Congress, fearing that broadcasters would shun in-depth examination of controversial material even more than previously, subsequently passed a bill in 1987 reinstating the fairness doctrine, but President Reagan vetoed it.

Although the media had evolved to a prominent and influential position in American political life, critics warned that their concentrated structure was harmful to democratic dissent and discussion. An exploration of that issue now follows.

# THE SCOPE AND STRUCTURE OF THE MEDIA

**Media Scope**

Collectively, adult Americans purchase more than 60 million newspapers each day. An average citizen will also watch three to four hours of TV daily. Americans can choose from some 10,000 weekly or monthly periodicals and make their listening or viewing choices from nearly 9,000 radio and 1,600 television stations nationwide. There are more than 10,000 movie theaters and 1,300 book publishers across the country.

**Media Structure**

Experts on the media suggest that their structure can be divided among three circles of importance—the inner, middle, and outer.

### INNER CIRCLE

This circle includes the three major news networks, NBC, CBS, ABC; the news organization CNN; the three major national news magazines (*Time, Newsweek, U.S. News and World Report*); four key or nationally popular newspapers (*The New York Times, The Washington Post, The Wall Street Journal, USA Today*); and the national wire service (Associated Press). The power of this media circle is immense, since its units decide what stories, domestic and foreign, will reach over 80 percent of the nation's households. Also, these twelve organizations have significant influence over journalists within the other two circles.

### MIDDLE CIRCLE

The *Los Angeles Times*, the *Chicago Tribune*, the *Christian Science Monitor*, the Scripps-Howard news service, and the Knight-Ridder newspaper chain are included here. While both national and local reporting are covered, the importance of the middle-circle media is primarily regional. Magazines included in this circle typically include *The New Republic* and *The National Review*.

### OUTER CIRCLE

This circle is composed mainly of local newspapers and TV stations. Most newspaper articles and TV stories will have originally appeared in the inner-circle media, and are subsequently reproduced by the various outer-circle media outlets.

**Media Concentration**

In the early 1900s, there were more than 2,500 daily newspapers in the United States. By 1990, the number had dropped below 1,700. Furthermore, large corporate newspaper chains, such as Gannett and Newhouse, control three out of every four newspapers sold today. Gannett owns *USA Today* and more than 90 other newspapers. Ten corporations own eight of the inner-ring media and a large number of TV stations, cable TV systems, radio stations, and newspapers found within the second and third circles. Furthermore, as a result of mergers, only about 2 percent of American cities have the benefit of competing newspapers.

### IS CONCENTRATION A DANGER?

Freedom to present diverse points of view is essential to the preservation of democracy. Will concentration of ownership blunt diversity? Do the media represent only the values and priorities of corporate America?

### SUPPORTERS OF THE CURRENT SYSTEM

One side argues that new forms of communication, such as cable television, satellite TV, and electronic mail, ensure diversity. Second, although much of the media are owned by corporations, usually reporters and editors are left alone to present the news in their own way (profits are the concern of corporate directors, not slanted news). Third, the FCC prohibits the same person or company from owning both a television station and a daily newspaper within the same urban area. Fourth, the American tradition of free speech is typically hostile to censorship.

### CRITICS OF CENTRALIZATION

Critics charge that media corporations are so powerful that their owners can suppress dissent and the views of the minority. A democracy is based on power checking power: How can media monopolies be consistent with that principle? In addition, society depends upon the media to check and balance other political and economic institutions. But if the media belong to corporate America and profits are the main goal, do anti-business views have a fair hearing? In short, can the media report events and issues fairly, openly, and objectively? Can the media's vital political roles be jeopardized?

## THE MEDIA'S POLITICAL ROLES

The media play a number of important political roles. Included among them are: (a) alerting the public to new developments; (b) shaping the public agenda; (c) molding public opinion; (d) linking the public and its leaders; (e) evaluating, positively or negatively, public leaders' reputations; (f) serving as a watchdog for the public.

**Alerting the Public to Fast-Breaking Stories**

Media journalists alert the public to each and every fast-breaking story, be it an unexpected disaster at a nuclear power plant, the president falling ill, a jump in inflation, a major scandal in Congress, or the explosion of a space shuttle. Media representatives can be at the scene of a particular news story in minutes due to modern communication technology.

**Shaping the Public Agenda**

The media focus attention on particular issues in contrast to others, and suggest solutions to society's problems as well. In effect, the media inform the public as to which problems are the most urgent. The media may not be able to tell people how to think, but they can tell the populace what issues they should be thinking about. Problems and issues not mentioned will usually be ignored. Thus, the issue of protecting the environment was not on the public agenda thirty years ago. The media generally ignored pollution, destruction of endangered wildlife, recycling of metals or paper, or holes in the earth's ozone layer. But the media began stressing ecological issues in the early 1970s and over the following decades. Currently, environmental issues are uppermost in the public's consciousness. A similar example was the media's coverage of drug abuse in America, which made millions of citizens even more aware of how extensive the problem was.

**Molding Public Opinion**

The media transmit information to the electorate. The "two-step flow" of opinion formation is important for this role. In the first step, a person receives information from a TV news broadcast or other media form. Then, this information, in theory, is compared by the alert citizen to other data sources so as to confirm or deny the first source's validity.

**A Link Between the Public and Leaders**

The media are natural links between the public and leaders. As an illustration, reporters explain the policy positions of a president to the voters and periodically survey the electorate's reaction to those positions. Accordingly, presidents pay close attention to these media stories. For example, President Lyndon Johnson often watched three television news shows simultaneously. Other public officials will frequently use the media to propose new programs or justify their decisions to the citizenry.

**Making or Breaking Public Reputations**

The media can tarnish or improve a public figure's reputation. For example, Gary Hart's bid for the presidential nomination in 1988 ran afoul of two reporters from *The Miami Herald* who staked out his home and learned of his affair with a young woman, Donna Rice. The resultant story of Hart's sexual infidelity forced him to resign his candidacy. Similarly, in the same year, Democratic Senator Joe Biden was forced to end his presidential campaign when the media learned of his plagiarized campaign speeches (taken from a British politician). In 1992, Democratic presidential hopeful Bill Clinton, governor of Arkansas, was plagued by media charges that he was an adulterer. Even Ronald Reagan's public image was tarnished when the media revealed a number of scandals in his administration. Conversely, the media can catapult an unknown candidate to prominence. Jimmy Carter received such media treatment in 1976 after doing well in the Iowa caucus. Eventually, he garnered the presidential nomination.

## Watchdog for the Public

Media representatives increasingly see themselves as a collective watchdog for the American people. They point to their role in criticizing the conduct of the Vietnam War and hastening its end, exposing the Watergate scandal during the Nixon administration, and uncovering governmental corruption at the federal, state, and local levels. But critics argue that the media only occasionally play the watchdog role, preferring to concentrate on safe or dramatic stories which will least offend advertisers. The media are also highly selective in their coverage of events and issues. These biases in news reporting are delineated in the next section.

# NEWS PRESENTATION

How is the news presented? Is the presentation biased? The American people depend almost entirely on the media for the information they receive about politics and government. But are the media truthful and unbiased? Whose interests do reporters serve? Following is a discussion of items that represent recurring problems associated with news reporting.

## News Reporting—a Business Seeking Profit

There must be a presentation of stories which will hold the attention of the audience. The chances of a sponsor's products selling are severely minimized if an audience is very small. TV must be entertaining to the average American, if high ratings are to be attained. Which news stories, over others, will attract the greatest number of viewers?

## Objectivity in News Reporting

Ideally, news reporters are supposed to report events truthfully and objectively. However, it is impossible to report every important story in the papers or on TV. Journalists must be selective. Also, reporters are human beings with their own emotions and sensitivities. Invariably, stories will be slanted in one direction or the other. Unfortunately, news and truth rarely go hand in hand. The news can appear to be fair, but it seldom conveys all of the facts necessary whereby viewers can make an independent, informed, responsible, and intelligent judgment.

## PERSONAL BACKGROUNDS OF JOURNALISTS

Surveys of journalists, both in print and electronic media, reveal similar backgrounds. White males still dominate, despite impressive gains by women and minorities in recent years. Both groups are overwhelmingly college-educated and come from upper-middle-class homes with parents who were professionals or in business.

## ARE REPORTERS BIASED?

Social science studies suggest that media representatives are not biased toward one party or ideology. For example, while many journalists may be liberals in their support for governmental services, many others support the free enterprise system. Journalists' stories may criticize the political leadership, but rarely the legitimacy of political institutions or values which comprise the American credo. As another example of a mixed-partisan picture, editors of newspapers usually endorse Republican candidates, but reporters identify more often with the Democratic party.

*Need for Brevity in Reporting*

Newspaper articles dealing with important political events must be relatively brief so that other pages can be reserved for advertising, sports, or local issues. The electronic media have an even greater need for brevity. For example, the evening news on TV may have only twenty to twenty-two minutes for actual stories, with the remaining time allotted to commercials. Many stories will be reported in a minute or two (or less). But how can complex issues like inflation, toxic wastes, crime, or the arms race be covered in such a short period of time? Furthermore, TV will cover campaigns through sound bites. Instead of a candidate's full speech being reported, a sound bite of fifteen seconds or less, highlighting a key phrase or slogan, will be the prime type of media coverage. Fortunately, television documentaries do exist, breaking a general pattern of superficiality through an in-depth look at problems in society. Shows like "60 Minutes" are also helpful in altering TV's penchant for being mainly a headline service.

*Dependence upon Government Officials*

Broadcasters and journalists acquire most of their information from elected or appointed officials in government. There are two reasons: (1) officials are available for questioning; (2) many reporters develop friendships with these officials. Studies reveal that domestic and foreign officials are the source of 75 percent of all reports in two of America's leading newspapers, *The New York Times* and *The Washington Post*. Still, there are examples of investigative reporting at its finest: for example, reporters Carl Bernstein and Bob Woodward of *The Washington Post* uncovered important evidence in the Watergate scandal which eventually led to President Nixon's resignation in 1974.

**Personal Side of the News Dominates Reporting**

News stories stress the "human-interest factor"—i.e., individuals' personal tragedies and triumphs. For example, when American hostages were seized by terrorists in the Middle East, network reporters interviewed the families of the hostages at length, but devoted far less time to the underlying reasons for the hostages' being seized or the specific demands of the terrorists. Similarly, the media devoted considerable TV air time and newspaper coverage to the sexual-harassment allegations made by Anita Hill against Supreme Court Justice nominee Clarence Thomas. Far less coverage was given to the weeks of hearings prior to the Hill-Thomas confrontation.

**News Stresses Drama, Violence, Action**

Lead stories of TV news shows or the newspaper's front page will stress murders, earthquakes, airplane crashes, tornado damage, wars, and so forth. Rioting by protesters attracts media coverage, but reporters will often neglect the underlying causal factors which led to the riot in the first place.

# HOW THE MEDIA COVER ELECTIONS AND GOVERNMENTAL INSTITUTIONS

**Coverage of Presidential Elections**

Media reports in presidential election years will indicate who is ahead or behind in securing each party's nomination. Frequently, the media will cite poll results to show the potential winner or loser in the November election. The same media mentality will apply to televised debates. For example, Michael Dukakis was labeled as the "loser" by *The New York Times* after his second TV debate against George Bush in 1988.

**Coverage of the Presidency**

The president is the focal point of news coverage. His activities are of major interest to the viewing public. The media, always mindful of the ratings, naturally give the president more air time and print space than any other political official. Presidential press conferences, major speeches, policy proposals, overseas trips, health status, or even personal family matters—all will attract considerable media attention.

**Coverage of Congress**

Floor proceedings of Congress are covered by the C-SPAN network. The House permitted TV coverage beginning in 1979, the Senate in 1986. Originally, there was fear that legislative debate would be disrupted by television and that legislators would posture before the cameras. However, C-SPAN has been successful in allowing the public to at least view and partially understand the workings of Congress. The major networks rarely cover committee hearings in depth. (Notable exceptions have included the

Watergate hearings and Iran-Contra hearings.) They seem to prefer reporting final floor votes or the actions of congressional leaders in both houses.

*Coverage of the Courts*

Of the three branches, the legislative, executive, and judicial, it is the judiciary that probably receives the least amount of media coverage. Judges are usually reluctant to grant interviews to reporters; cameras and microphones are normally prohibited in federal courts (state trials can be televised). Ironically, the media tend to be more favorable in their treatment of the courts and judges. Still, many lawyers and judges alike have complained that the media may report inaccurate details about legal procedures and problems.

## THE MEDIA AND DEMOCRACY

Many observers have remarked that information is the essence of democracy. Responsible citizens cannot practice self-rule if the factual bases and diverse values underlying controversial issues are not presented to them by a conscientious, efficient media. Critics contend that the media have failed in this mission. They have provided a vast amount of information, but the end result has not been an informed society.

Media representatives argue that the superficial treatment of the news fits the needs and desires of the American public. Americans want to be entertained by the media. They are indifferent to media presentations involving complex issues. Media representatives suggest that if citizens began demanding more TV shows like "60 Minutes" or the "MacNeil-Lehrer Newshour," the networks would be glad to oblige them.

*The precise configuration and content of the public's opinions can be measured by modern scientific polling procedures within a reasonable margin of error. The "roots" of those opinions can be found in the political socialization process and its agents—the family, schools, and peer groups, among others. Personal characteristics, such as race or religion, also play a key role in opinion formation.*

*Historically, the media have played a number of important roles, from promoting partisan views to defining the public agenda to guarding the public interest. Some critics fear that the contemporary media's concentration of ownership will threaten freedom of thought and dissent; others see the proliferation of media outlets and constitutional guarantees of free speech as firm barriers to this threat. Additional criticisms of the media include an emphasis on their profits over the public interest, the super-*

*ficiality of the news coverage, the penchant for stressing violence and drama over the "why" behind news events, and possible biases among reporters and TV journalists.*

**Selected Readings**

Asher, Herbert. *Polling and the Public: What Every Citizen Should Know* (1988)

Crespi, Irving. *Public Opinion, Polls, and Democracy* (1989)

Graber, Doris A. *Media Power in Politics.* 3rd ed. (1990)

Jennings, M. Kent, and Richard G. Niemi. *Generations and Politics: A Panel Study of Young Adults and Their Parents* (1981)

Niemi, Richard G., John Mueller, and Tom W. Smith. *Trends in Public Opinion: A Compendium of Survey Data* (1989)

Parenti, Michael. *Inventing Reality: The Politics of the Mass Media* (1986)

# 4

# *Political Parties and Interest Groups*

*I*t is hard to imagine American democracy without political parties or interest groups. Both parties and interest groups are representative devices which allow the people to interact with government and which employ political power to implement or influence the policy process. Parties try to elect their members through maximization of support within the electorate. Interest groups, while not placing candidates on the ballot, do play the important roles of supporting/opposing office-seekers, molding public opinion, and gaining access to government decision-makers. Parties have been weakened in recent years, but interest-group activities have increased.

## POLITICAL PARTIES—FUNDAMENTALS AND COMPONENTS

Political parties provide an important link between the people and their governments. Through parties, voters can make their political will known and hold representatives accountable.

Parties recruit individuals to run for political office under the party label. If a political party is successful in getting enough of its candidates elected, the party can control the government and develop appropriate public policies.

Parties are important to a democracy in yet another way. They can develop political compromises among contending groups in society so that the legitimacy of the political system is maintained.

## Party Components

A political party has three components:

### THE PARTY IN THE ELECTORATE

This component consists of citizens who identify with a political party (a majority of Americans consider themselves Democrats or Republicans) and who vote for or against their party's candidates.

### THE PARTY IN GOVERNMENT

This component refers to those appointed or elected officeholders in the legislative and executive branches of government who are considered representatives of a specific political party.

### THE FORMAL PARTY ORGANIZATION

This component comprises active party "professionals" who actually control and direct the party at the local, state, and federal levels. These individuals are involved in important campaign and fund-raising activities. They also wish to attract citizens to their party banner, so that a stronger base of volunteers and supporters can be established. Professionals usually enjoy the "game" of politics and seek positions of power in the party or government. Their major goal is winning elections.

# THE FUNCTIONS OF POLITICAL PARTIES

## Mobilization of Voters

Party workers will urge or help voters to go to the polls on election day. Workers may use telephone calls; visit homes, apartments, or offices; and even provide transportation for voters.

## Personnel Agencies

As indicated earlier, parties seek out individuals who might make attractive candidates for public office. Parties present these individuals to the voters. If a party's candidates win, then the party achieves political power.

## Providing Campaign Resources

Parties help in fund-raising so that their candidates will have the financial means to run increasingly expensive campaigns.

**Simplifying
Elections/
Educating the
Public**

Many citizens do not have the time or motivation to become informed about every candidate's stand on the issues of the day or even to know the background qualifications of each candidate. These voters simply rely on party affiliation and select all of their party's nominees (a "straight" party ticket) listed on the ballot. The parties also try to educate the public about contemporary public issues through campaign speeches, debates, TV newscasts, and so on. Therefore, parties do influence public opinion by identifying society's problems and suggesting political solutions. As President John F. Kennedy once observed, the responsibility of parties was to place the unfinished policy agenda before the American people for their consideration.

**Aggregating
Interests**

Parties help to coordinate the combined (aggregate) interests and demands of the electorate. When there is conflict among diverse interests, parties facilitate compromise. It bears repeating that parties encourage peaceful change and allegiance to the political system through the aggregation function.

**Organizing the
Decision-
Making Process**

Both state legislatures and Congress are organized by party affiliations. Party leaders are influential in selecting the legislature's members to serve on specific committees and subcommittees.

**The Watchdog
Role, or "The
Loyal
Opposition"**

The party which is out of power will be sure to criticize the policies and decisions taken by the ruling party. The minority party may hope to influence the majority party's thinking, while also laying the groundwork for an electoral victory in the near future.

# HISTORY OF AMERICA'S PARTY SYSTEMS

**Founders'
Views**

The framers of the Constitution envisioned political parties as being both dangerous and disruptive. (Parties are not even mentioned in the Constitution.) To them, party members promoted societal divisions, pursued selfish interests, and stifled dissent. James Madison considered parties "factions" which threatened the common good in society. In George Washington's famous 1796 Farewell Address, the first president warned that the young nation could be destroyed by the "baneful effects of the spirit of party."

However, parties became a political reality early in the nation's history, and five distinct party systems would follow.

## First Party System, 1796–1828

Despite the founders' fears, the early division between Federalists and anti-Federalists, as symbolized by the philosophical clash between Hamilton and Jefferson during Washington's administration, intensified partisan divisions. Hamilton's Federalists represented the northern commercial and manufacturing interests, believed in a strong central government, and supported a ruling national aristocracy. (Hamilton once told Jefferson that the people were a "great Beast.") By contrast, the Jeffersonians spoke for agricultural concerns in the South, a limited role for the federal government, and a faith in the common man.

Jefferson's victory over John Adams in 1800 meant the eventual demise of the Federalist party (it disappeared completely around 1816). Thereafter, Jefferson's Republicans dominated presidential and congressional politics. This period of one-party rule led to the "Era of Good Feeling," symbolized by James Monroe's near-unanimous election in 1820. However, after 1820, rival factions within the Republicans led by John Quincy Adams (the National Republicans) and Andrew Jackson (the Democratic Republicans) developed into the Whig and Democratic parties, respectively.

## Second Party System— Jacksonian Democrats and the Whigs, 1828–1860

Andrew Jackson's election in 1828 ushered in the Democratic party, a party which stressed the common man's participation in the political system. Jackson's party introduced suffrage to all white adult males, the popular election of presidential electors (formerly implemented by the state legislatures), and national nominating conventions (instead of congressmen choosing their party's nominee). The Democrats had the support of small farmers, Catholics, the new immigrants, and those Americans residing in frontier towns.

The Whigs, or the anti-Jacksonians, favored both a strong national government and business interests. Northeastern manufacturers, southern planters, and Protestants constituted the party's core. The Whigs were successful in electing William H. Harrison to the presidency in 1840.

## Third Party System—the Republican Party Is Born, 1860–1896

The slavery debate divided the Whig party and led to its dissolution by the time of the Civil War. Northern Whigs and some disgruntled Democrats, plus members of a third party, the Know-Nothings, created the anti-slavery Republican party, or the GOP (Grand Old Party). The party elected its first president, Abraham Lincoln, in 1860.

After the Civil War, the Republicans dominated both Congress and the presidency. The Republicans drew their support from ex-Union soldiers, blacks, English immigrants, and northern Protestants. The GOP was very much pro-business. By comparison, the Democrats drew support from southerners, Irish Catholics, farmers, labor unions, and anti-Prohibitionists. The Democrats continued to support the doctrines of states' rights and limited government. But during this period the Democrats were able to win only with one presidential candidate—Grover Cleveland, in 1884 and 1892.

## Fourth Party System, 1896–1932

The election of 1896 was a turning point in American politics. The Democrat, William Jennings Bryan, represented the agrarian faction of the party. Although he carried the rural South and West, the industrialized and urban areas of the nation went for the GOP. In effect, the 1896 realigning election (a long-term change in the underlying party loyalties of voters) meant that the GOP would be the dominant party for more than three decades (except for the election of the Democratic president Woodrow Wilson in 1912 and 1916).

The GOP appealed to a wide base of voters by opposing social-welfare assistance to the individual but supporting government efforts to assist business. The Democrats' only real base of support was in the rural South and among ethnic Americans, such as the Irish.

### THE RISE OF THE PROGRESSIVES

During this era, the Progressives became an important third-party movement, emphasizing political reform of corrupt big-city machines found in the Northeast and Midwest. (Many of these party machines and their party bosses would stuff the ballot boxes on election day.) Several Progressive ideas eventually became law—voter registration, the secret ballot, direct primary, and civil service laws. The reforms' ultimate impact was to weaken the hold of party bosses by giving voters greater influence over the nomination and election processes.

## Fifth Party System— Democratic Dominance, 1932–1980

President Herbert Hoover's aloof reaction to the stock market crash of 1929 and the resultant Great Depression (Hoover had stated that "economic depression could not be cured by legislative action") convinced millions of disillusioned and unemployed voters to select the Democratic nominee, Franklin D. Roosevelt, in 1932. Under FDR's leadership, many economic recovery laws were passed. The 1932 election represented another realigning election, whereby the Democrats became the dominant political party. Roosevelt's "New Deal Coalition"—an alliance of urban dwellers, blue-collar workers, Catholics, Jews, southern conservatives, and northern liberals—held together long enough to elect FDR to four consecutive terms. After World War II, Republicans did elect to the presidency Dwight D. Eisenhower (1952 and 1956), Richard Nixon (1968 and 1972), Ronald Reagan in 1980 and 1984, and George Bush in 1988. The Democrats have not won the presidency since 1976, leading some analysts to pose the possibility of a new party system. However, the Democrats have, with a few exceptions, maintained control of both houses of Congress as well as a majority of state legislatures.

## Sixth Party System—1980 to the Present

The 1980s witnessed "divided government"—GOP presidential domination, but continued Democratic control of the House (the GOP was the majority party in the Senate during most of Reagan's two terms, but the Democrats regained control in 1987).

Was there a sixth party system? Was the Republican party the new majority party in America? The evidence remains inconclusive. But there are indicators of change in party loyalties and philosophies. The reader may wish to consider the cumulative impact of these trends, as listed below, and whether a new party system will emerge in the not-too-distant future.

## Decline of Party Loyalty/Rise of Independent Voters

Many voters now see no significant policy differences between the two parties but are increasingly aware of candidate styles and personalities. Increasingly, voters do not identify strongly with their parties. (By 1990, nearly 35 percent of the electorate considered themselves independents; in 1950, only a little more than 20 percent had claimed that label.)

### INCREASED TICKET-SPLITTING

Two to three times more voters divided their candidate selections between the two major parties during the 1980s, as compared to the 1950s. For example, southern white voters continued to support Democrats for congressional offices, but preferred the more conservative Republican candidates for president in recent elections. Republicans have carried the South in every presidential election since 1968, except for Jimmy Carter's victory in 1976 (Carter was a former governor of Georgia).

## The Two Parties Today: Summary of Differences

While both parties have similar functions, they do have differences. The Republican party attracts large numbers of wealthy, college-educated, and conservative supporters. Democrats still appeal to a greater number of minorities, the poor, lesser-educated voters, and liberals. The GOP typically stresses rugged individualism, a strong national defense, minimal governmental intervention into the economy, and limited regulation of big business. Democrats see government as a social "referee" promoting social justice and fair employment policies. Finally, it should be stressed that each party's membership represents a mixture of diverse viewpoints and policy preferences.

# WHY DOES AMERICA HAVE A TWO-PARTY SYSTEM?

Despite a plethora of minor political parties in American history, the nation has essentially maintained a two-party system. The two-party system is not common to most nations. (Democracies in Europe have multiparty systems, with three or more parties competing for power.) Only five other nations have two-party systems: Australia, Austria, Canada, Great Britain, and New Zealand. While minor parties in America—Progressives, American Independents, Libertarians, Socialist Workers, among others—have periodically challenged the two major parties, they have not supplanted either one of them at any governmental level. What are the reasons for the strength of the two-party system in America?

**History and Tradition**

As already discussed, the Federalist–anti-Federalist division constituted partisan politics early in America's political history. Since then, Americans have been conditioned through the political socialization process to the permanence of two parties. In general, most citizens see little value in voting for a minor party, considering such action to be wasteful and nonsensical.

**The Electoral System**

The single-member district system in America means that there can be only one winner per office. The victor is the candidate who receives the greatest number of votes, a plurality, even if the plurality is not a majority. The United States does not have proportional representation, a system common in Europe whereby legislative seats are awarded to each party on the basis of popular vote totals. Under proportional representation, a minor party which receives 15 percent of the national vote would receive 15 percent of the seats in the national legislature. In America, this party would probably win nothing.

**Election Laws**

In many states, it is difficult for a minor party to get on the ballot. For example, in 1968, George Wallace's American Independent party found that more than 400,000 signatures would be needed to get on the presidential ballot in Ohio (Wallace appealed to the Supreme Court, and this requirement was ruled unconstitutional). In 1988, Bush and Dukakis were on all fifty state ballots, but virtually all of the minor parties were unable to get on even half of the ballots.

Another factor is that election laws are primarily the responsibility of the states. The 7,500 state legislators across the nation are virtually all Republicans or Democrats. These legislators have little incentive to pass election procedures which will facilitate minor party challenges against the two major parties.

*Flexibility and Adaptability of the Two Parties*

The Democratic and Republican parties are broad-based, or "umbrella parties." They both accept members from nearly all groups and social classes in America. By clinging to the political center, they maximize their voting appeal. Minor parties with new ideas find that their ideas are frequently co-opted by either or both of the major parties.

*Voter Beliefs*

Americans have historically agreed on the rules of the political and economic game. They have accepted democracy, capitalism, and diversity of religious belief. Rich–poor class hatreds, monarchist or socialist parties, and religious control of political life have fortunately not been part of American history. Furthermore, America's abundant resources have furnished a decent standard of living to the vast majority of the population. In short, there is an "ideological consensus" among Americans. The two major parties' philosophies reflect this consensus. A purely religious party, or parties composed solely of black Americans, farmers, or environmentalists, would not have broad enough appeal for the voters.

Presidential candidates whose views are perceived as being extremist or too distant from the political center will not be supported by a majority of the moderate electorate. When Republican Senator Barry Goldwater ran for the presidency in 1964, his brand of conservatism was seen as being too far to the political right; Senator George McGovern, the Democratic presidential candidate in 1972, was seen as being an extreme liberal or too far to the political left. Both men were badly defeated at the polls by Lyndon Johnson and Richard Nixon, respectively.

# MINOR PARTIES—TYPES AND FUNCTIONS

Minor parties in American politics cannot be dismissed as being unimportant. While many disappear with time, they can have a major impact upon elections and issues during specific historical eras.

*Categories of Minor Parties*

The four main types of minor parties are ideological, one-issue, economic protest, and factional or splinter.

### IDEOLOGICAL

Ideological minor parties espouse radical ideas or values from the perspective of most Americans. But these parties do attract some votes. A specific example was the Socialist party of Eugene V. Debs, who won nearly 6 percent of the vote in the 1912 presidential election.

## ONE-ISSUE

The Prohibition party would exemplify the one-issue minor party (abolition of alcoholic beverages). Another example is the Free Soil party, which opposed slavery. Because they are so narrowly based, one-issue parties have difficulty attracting a broad spectrum of the electorate. In addition, their issues may be addressed and resolved by a major party.

## ECONOMIC PROTEST

An example of the economic-protest party was the Populist party of the 1890s, which demanded government ownership of rail and phone companies. The Greenback party (1876–1884) called for the free coinage of silver and an income tax.

## SPLINTER

Teddy Roosevelt's Bull Moose party of 1912 was a "splinter" or faction from the regular Republican party (T.R. opposed William Howard Taft, the GOP candidate, and the Democrat Woodrow Wilson). In 1968, George Wallace's American Independent party followers claimed that their political views opposing desegregation and strong law-and-order policies had been ignored by the mainstream Democratic party.

## Importance of Third Parties

Minor parties have attracted new groups of voters, served as forums for different opinions, and brought new issues to the national political agenda. The Socialist party first raised the issue of a Social Security program, a policy subsequently adopted by FDR's Democratic party in the 1930s. Teddy Roosevelt's Bull Moose party encouraged leaders within the two major parties to consider new laws regulating corporations. It also urged adoption of "direct democracy" devices, such as the initiative (citizens propose laws), referendum (voters approve legislation), and the recall (citizens can remove officeholders for unsatisfactory job performance between elections).

Minor parties have also begun important political innovations, such as the anti-Masons, who, in 1831, employed a national nominating convention for the first time. Finally, minor parties can play the role of election "spoiler," siphoning off enough votes from a major party candidate to change the electoral outcome. Theodore Roosevelt's 1912 candidacy divided the Republican vote to ensure Wilson's election. In 1968, George Wallace garnered over 13 percent of the popular vote and 46 electoral votes, achievements which probably hurt most the Democratic candidate Hubert Humphrey in his losing race against Republican Richard Nixon.

# POLITICAL PARTY ORGANIZATION

American political parties exist at all three levels of government—national, state, and local. While an American political party appears hierarchical and integrated, the reality is that parties are decentralized and fragmented. The national party can rarely dictate policy or "discipline" state or local party officials. Furthermore, power seems concentrated more at state and local levels.

## State and Local Party Organizations

At the bottom of a state party is the precinct, a small voting district which selects party committee members. The party committee member may be chosen by a local party caucus, state party convention delegates, or in a primary election. Larger cities use a ward system instead of the precinct unit. In New England, the "town" is the local unit.

Above the local levels, parties are organized at the city and/or county levels. Intermediate levels can include city, legislative, and judicial committees, then county committees, and congressional district committees. The state committee, headed by the state's party chairman, represents the top level. In some states the party chairman may be very powerful. However, the more typical case is that the county committee remains the center of party power, since this committee often selects important local officials.

State party organizations try to recruit candidates, raise money for campaigns, devise campaign strategies, mobilize voters on election day, and distribute campaign literature.

## National Party Organization

The national party organization is headed by the national committee and its chairman. The national committee, composed of representatives from the states and territories, has limited authority. It decides where and when the next national nominating convention will be held and engages in fundraising duties. The national party chairperson is usually selected by the presidential nominee of the party. His or her responsibilities include hiring personnel and handling the party's administration. The national nominating convention meets every four years, writes the party's platform, and then the assembled delegates select the party's ticket—i.e., its presidential and vice-presidential nominees.

# AMERICAN POLITICAL PARTIES— A FUTURE DEALIGNMENT?

To some observers, political parties are losing much of their importance. Voters identify less with parties today and more with candidate image, style, and personality. Candidates prefer to use their own campaign organizations rather than rely on traditional party machinery. Once elected, officeholders cannot be controlled by party leaders or be held accountable for any campaign promises. In short, dealignment, a decline in loyalty or identification with the two major parties, rather than realignment, a switching of voter allegiance from one party to the other, may be the future pattern. Periodic calls by political reformers for parties which are more centralized, disciplined, and issue-oriented have been largely ignored. Conversely, the power of interest groups has increased substantially.

# INTEREST GROUPS

**Definition and Comparison with Parties**

Unlike political parties, interest groups do not nominate candidates for public office. Interest groups are mainly concerned with influencing the policies of government by applying pressure upon public officials. A good example is MADD—Mothers Against Drunk Driving—an interest group which pressured Congress into passing a 1984 law withholding federal highway funds from those states which did not raise the legal drinking age to twenty-one. In addition, interest groups are normally concerned with a narrower range of issues; parties must be involved with the entire range of public affairs and issues. Thus, interest groups are usually accountable only to their members, not to society as a whole.

Interest groups will also try to influence public opinion through advertisements, letters, radio/TV spots, and so forth. Finally, interest groups will oppose or support candidates for public office, depending on how those candidates stand on key issues. For example, the National Rifle Association would be unlikely to make campaign contributions to a candidate who favored strong gun-control legislation. Conversely, right-to-life groups back anti-abortion candidates on a regular basis.

In short, an interest group is composed of individuals who have similar or shared attitudes on specific issues and who collectively try to influence government decisions. The thousands of interest groups in America may try to prevent a particular action or purposely seek change in existing policies.

# *INTEREST GROUPS—TECHNIQUES AND STRATEGIES OF INFLUENCE*

Interest groups approach their task of trying to influence public policy by two fundamental methods. The first is by meeting legislators and other public officials. The second is to pressure policy-makers through a more circuitous route involving the media. These two approaches can be classified as direct and indirect.

## *Direct Techniques*

Direct techniques include lobbying, compiling ratings of legislative behavior, and providing campaign assistance.

### LOBBYING AND LOBBYISTS

A lobbyist is a paid representative of an interest group. The term "lobbying" comes from the historic practice of citizens waiting for and contacting representatives in the lobbies outside legislative chambers. Today, lobbyists, many of whom are ex-legislators themselves, try to persuade legislators to vote for or against a bill or convince members of executive agencies that a program is desirable or undesirable. Their techniques may involve any of the following:

  a. private meetings with public officials whereby needed information is disseminated;
  b. testifying before congressional committees and executive agencies;
  c. assisting legislators in drafting laws or regulations, or furnishing legal advice;
  d. socializing with legislators in order to win their confidence—this is also called "wining and dining";
  e. filing lawsuits or *amicus curiae* briefs in the courts; *amicus curiae* ("friend of the court") briefs are third-party statements which try to influence the judges' decisions in the particular case under consideration;
  f. discussing campaign contributions with the legislator.

### RATINGS OF LEGISLATORS

Legislators are given a score based on how many times they have voted in accordance with the views of the interest groups involved. For example, a high ADA rating—Americans for Democratic Action—would mean a very liberal voting record. A high ACA rating—Americans for Constitutional Action—would signify a conservative voting pattern. One group, Environmental Action, lists legislators with good or bad records on ecological issues.

### CAMPAIGN ASSISTANCE

Legislators wish to be reelected, so a group's endorsement and financial backing are both important. Many interest groups establish their own fund-raising committees, or PAC's. PAC's are Political Action Committees which represent corporations, labor unions, and other special-interest groups. There are more than 4,000 known PAC's today. PAC's are limited by law to $5,000 contributions for each candidate per election (although PAC's frequently find ways to get around this limit).

## Indirect Techniques

Interest groups using indirect techniques of influence try to convince the public that their causes are worthy or just. Ads in magazines or newspapers, television sponsorship, and radio messages are some of the devices that can be used. A good example of this technique occurred during the late 1970s, when American oil companies spent millions of dollars on ads explaining that oil shortages were due to the restrictive policies of Middle Eastern nations. The ads explained that American oil firms were trying to end those shortages through heavy investments (costing the firms billions of dollars) in drilling hundreds of new wells.

Interest groups can also use their membership to send thousands of letters or telegrams to legislators. In 1988, the National Rifle Association spent close to $2 million urging its membership to contact key legislators. More than 10 million pieces of mail flooded congressional offices. A bill proposing a seven-day waiting period before a gun could be purchased was defeated, perhaps reflecting this mail "pressure."

# THE GROWTH OF INTEREST GROUPS

## Historic Diversity and Tradition

How and why do interest groups form? In the United States, traditional racial, religious, and ethnic diversity has multiplied the number of group interests. Culturally, Americans have always seemed to constitute a nation of "joiners." The French observer Alexis de Tocqueville noted this characteristic in the 1830s, when he observed that the "principle of association" had deep roots in the American psyche. Finally, groups are also free to organize under the constitutional protections of free speech, assembly, and petition.

## Structure of American Government

Federalism and the separation of powers promote interest-group activity. An interest group which fails to accomplish its goals at the state level can work for change in Washington. A group which is unsuccessful with Congress can try to influence the courts through a test case. Civil rights groups, such as the NAACP (National Association for the Advancement of

Colored People), were successful in having the Supreme Court eventually rule segregation unconstitutional in 1954 after decades of congressional resistance. (See chapter 10.)

**Socioeconomic Changes/New Technology**

A good example of the former is the large numbers of women since 1960 who have entered the workplace, hence the formation of new women's groups. New technology, such as word processors, computerized mailing lists, and WATS lines, has enabled group leaders to raise money more easily and to stay in touch with rank-and-file members.

**Growth of Government**

The expansion of government has meant additional programs and new groups organized to protect those programs. For example, the AARP, the Association for the Advancement of Retired People, was created to resist any changes in Social Security laws and to persuade Congress to pass new legislation helping the elderly, especially in the area of health care.

## MEMBERSHIP IN INTEREST GROUPS

Among many different reasons people have for becoming members of interest groups are the following incentives: material, solidarity, and purposive.

**Material Benefits**

Groups can offer members all kinds of benefits, from low-cost insurance to reduced prices for goods and services to special travel packages. Direct monetary benefits can include higher wages, as when a labor union pressures big business. Nonmonetary benefits might include better safety conditions for workers.

**Solidarity Benefits**

The benefits of making friends and participating in social events can be a major incentive for group membership. There is also the satisfaction of belonging to a group which has a unique cause—be it protecting the environment or reducing taxes.

**Purposive Benefits**

These are benefits which are extended to individuals outside the interest group's own members. A member of an environmental group working for cleaner air and water knows that success will benefit everyone.

**Who Joins?**

Those citizens who have more education plus higher incomes are more likely to join interest groups. This stratum of the population generally has more time and political motivation than lesser-educated, low-income citizens.

# TYPES OF INTEREST GROUPS

In the past, most interest groups have pursued economic goals for their membership—i.e., farmers, businessmen, workers in labor unions, and professionals. However, noneconomic interest groups have proliferated in recent years, dealing with such issues as the environment, race, or even the "public interest." Other noneconomic groups have fought for the rights of women, Hispanics, and gays. A third category includes governmental interest groups.

*Economic Interest Groups*

These groups have traditionally involved agriculture, business, labor, and professionals. They are primarily concerned with attaining material benefits, such as profits, better pay, or improved job security.

## AGRICULTURE

The largest agricultural interest group is the American Farm Bureau Federation (AFBF). The AFBF has more than 2.5 million members. The National Farmers' Union (NFU), National Grange, and the National Farmers Organization are smaller in size and represent narrower constituencies. There are clear differences in regional appeal, specific farm groups represented, and political philosophy among these groups. The AFBF is strongest in the South and Midwest, and represents large farmers. It opposes restrictive federal regulations on agriculture, and generally is supportive of conservative Republicans. Conversely, the NFU has its greatest support among Midwestern grain farmers and supports government subsidies. It leans toward the Democratic party. In short, there is no one group which can represent all of the nation's farmers.

## BUSINESS

More than half of all groups registered to lobby Congress are business firms. The three most powerful business interest groups are the United States Chamber of Commerce (USCC), the National Association of Manufacturers (NAM), and the Business Roundtable (BR). The USCC represents well over 200,000 medium and small businesses and has been an opponent of consumer-protection laws and stricter antitrust policies. The NAM is a group which mirrors the wishes of about 14,000 fairly large corporations. In the past, the NAM has worked for legislation restraining labor unions and creating protective tariffs. The BR is composed of the leaders of the 200 biggest corporations in America. Like other business groups, it is firmly against government regulation of corporations, anti-monopoly legislation, and higher corporate taxes.

## SMALL BUSINESS

Groups even more representative of small businesses include the National Federation of Independent Business (NFIB) and the National Small Business Association (NSBA). The NFIB represents more than 600,000 small-business proprietors. The NSBA has some 45,000 small-business members.

## TRADE ASSOCIATIONS

Trade associations are concerned with benefiting a particular industry. A good example is the American Petroleum Institute, which has an annual budget of $10 million.

## ORGANIZED LABOR

The largest labor interest group is the AFL-CIO, which represents more than 15 million workers and over 100 affiliated unions. The AFL-CIO (created in 1955 by a merger of the American Federation of Labor and the Congress of Industrial Organizations) supports pro-labor policies such as national health insurance and higher minimum-wage standards. In addition to the AFL-CIO, there are other independent unions which are politically influential, such as the United Auto Workers.

Organized labor has suffered a decline of members in recent years, with only one-sixth of the work force now unionized (compared to one-third twenty years ago). However, labor interest groups can still be effective. In 1988, labor groups were successful in having a law passed requiring business firms to give workers a sixty-day notice before layoffs or plant closings were to begin.

## PROFESSIONAL GROUPS

Typically included in this category would be the American Medical Association (doctors), the American Bar Association (lawyers), the National Education Association (teachers), and the National Association of Realtors (real estate brokers). Most of the important professional groups have lobbyists in Washington, D.C.

## Noneconomic Groups

These groups form in reaction to a specific public issue or controversy, such as the Right to Life Association, which evolved after the 1973 Supreme Court decision allowing abortion (*Roe* v. *Wade*). Under this category are included public interest, ideological, consumer, women's, religious, political action, environmental, and single-issue interest groups.

## PUBLIC INTEREST

These groups seek political rewards that extend beyond the actual group membership so that much of society benefits from their lobbying efforts. Where economic groups seek direct private, material gain, a public interest group such as the League of Women Voters works for simpler procedures to register voters, a goal which could theoretically strengthen democracy throughout the nation.

## IDEOLOGICAL

As indicated earlier, these groups espouse a particular political and/or moral philosophy which they wish to see incorporated into public policies. The ADA or the once-active Moral Majority (fundamentalist Christian values) are good examples of the genre.

## CONSUMER

A famous consumer advocate is Ralph Nader. Nader first publicized the issue of automobile safety, then proceeded to establish Public Citizen, Inc., with fifteen suborganizations covering such problems as nuclear power, health care, ethical congressional procedures, pollution control, pure food and drugs, and so forth. While Nader's organization is very prominent, there are countless other consumer groups whose interests can range from producing safe infant toys to lowering interest rates on credit cards.

## WOMEN

Groups backing greater equality for women in the workplace have become important. NOW, the National Organization for Women, although failing to pass an Equal Rights Amendment, remains a strong political force. NOW has 150,000 members.

## RELIGIOUS

Religious groups have frequently taken positions on social issues, raging from abortion to nuclear power to the rights of minorities. Foreign policy has also been an area of interest. For example, Jewish groups have strongly backed Israel. The Catholic Church has supported the nuclear-freeze movement.

## POLITICAL ACTION

A good example is Common Cause, which was established in 1970 by John Gardner and now has 225,000 members. Common Cause is concerned with accountability of government officials to the citizenry, campaign reforms, stricter laws governing campaign contributions, and public financing for presidential elections.

## ENVIRONMENTAL

Environmental groups have multiplied as the public has become more conscious of environmental problems such as oil spills, pollution, and conservation. The Sierra Club, founded in 1892, lobbies for clean air and water and unspoiled wilderness areas. It has a membership of more than

250,000. The National Wildlife Federation, National Audubon Society, Friends of the Earth, Inc., and the Wilderness Society are other prominent examples. Currently, there are more than 500 environmental interest groups in the United States.

### SINGLE-ISSUE

These groups are primarily concerned with influencing policy in one substantive area. Examples would include the National Rifle Association, which opposes gun control; the National Taxpayers Union, which desires a constitutional amendment to balance the federal budget; and Planned Parenthood, which is concerned with reproductive freedom for women.

## *Governmental Interest Groups*

Because the federal government can influence other nations through arms sales, foreign aid, or trade policy, foreign governments will send their own lobbyists to Washington. In 1990, there were about 1,000 lobbyists representing overseas interests.

State and city governments in America have their own interest groups. Groups such as the Council of State Governments or the National League of Cities will try to pressure Washington for grant money, defense contracts, federal construction projects, urban renewal, or low-cost housing subsidies. The states and cities continually inform Washington policy-makers about current problems and future needs.

## *Why These Groups Fail or Succeed*

The effectiveness of both economic and noneconomic interest groups depends upon a number of variables—membership size, money, quality of the lobbying effort, the dedication and intensity of the leadership, general organizational cohesion, and political timing. Interest groups also differ on their alliance-building capabilities, or their willingness to work with other like-minded groups to achieve a specific political goal. While it is true that large, well-financed groups have distinct advantages over smaller groups with fewer resources, "David" can sometimes best "Goliath," as has been the case with victories of environmental groups over the representatives of big business.

# *SHOULD INTEREST GROUPS BE REGULATED?*

## *Criticisms of Interest Groups*

Critics of the American interest-group system argue that it is biased toward the upper social classes and ignores the needs of the poor and minorities. Furthermore, they assert that big business dominates the system.

Finally, critics point to the unsavory techniques used by lobbyists to influence legislators, from influence-peddling (paying for gifts and expensive junkets) to threatening the loss of campaign contributions if acquiescence is not forthcoming. In short, interest groups eventually "buy" political influence and thus need governmental regulation (see following section, on the 1946 Lobbying Act).

Proponents of interest groups argue that no group can dominate the political system for long. Influence will vary over time as different coalitions of groups clash over public policy alternatives. These group struggles promote stability, fairness, and democratic participation. Furthermore, most lobbyists are men and women of integrity—blackmail, under-the-table payments, and outright corruption are rare, especially at the federal level. Finally, every group has the constitutional freedom to organize and play a role in the political arena. In recent years, the underprivileged strata of American society have become more vocal in articulating their group needs through the media or protest demonstrations. Finally, the growing weakness of political parties requires that interest groups fill the void as representatives of the people.

## The Federal Regulation of Lobbying Act

In 1946, Congress tried to regulate lobbying activities through the Federal Regulation of Lobbying Act. The act required lobbyists to register their names, give background information on their salaries and expenses, and provide quarterly reports on their activities to Congress. The penalty for noncompliance was a possible fine of $10,000 and/or five years in prison.

However, in a Supreme Court ruling testing the act's constitutionality, the Court found that the act pertained mainly to lobbyists who "directly" influenced federal legislation. In short, the act was applicable only to lobbyists who communicated with legislators on proposed or pending legislation or those individuals who solicited, collected, or received money for lobbying. Indirect lobbying (trying to influence public opinion) or social gatherings of lobbyists and legislators would not be covered by the act.

Consequently, 6,500 lobbyists of the estimated 80,000 lobbyists in Washington, D.C., are registered under the act. Most of the act's provisions have been ignored. Some argue that stricter regulation of lobbying could violate First Amendment rights—i.e., the guarantee of the right to petition for redress of grievances.

*P**olitical parties are indispensable tools of democracy, encouraging citizen participation, informing the electorate, linking government to the people, and recruiting those individuals who will serve in official public positions at all three levels of government. In addition, America's two-party system has been congruent with the nation's history and ideological moderation. Despite the prevalence of America's two parties, minor parties have periodically forced* the major parties to adopt new programs and ideas. Finally, the organization of American parties mirrors the decentralized and loose chain of command common to our federal structure.

Unlike parties, interest groups do not propose candidates for public office. Interest groups, both economic and noneconomic, are mainly concerned with influencing public officials to accept or reject specific programs and policies. Their methods of influence are both indirect and direct, the former involving grass-roots pressure, the latter skilled lobbyists who personally contact important decision-makers in the executive and legislative branches of government. Members of interest groups are usually drawn from the better-educated, wealthier strata of the population.

Critics of the interest-group system argue that it is undemocratic and unethical. Proponents see the system as necessary to democracy and possessing the capability to represent both the poorer and wealthier classes.

**Selected Readings**

Berry, Jeffrey M. *The Interest Group Society* (1989)

Cigler, Alan J., and Burdette A. Loomis, eds. *Interest Group Politics.* 2nd ed. (1986)

Frantzich, Stephen E. *Political Parties in the Technological Age* (1989)

Goldman, Ralph M. *The National Party Chairman and Committees: Factionalism at the Top* (1990)

Sabato, Larry J. *The Party's Just Begun: Shaping Political Parties for America's Future* (1988)

Schlozman, Kay Lehman, and John T. Tierney. *Organized Interests and American Democracy* (1986)

# 5

## Voting, Campaigns, and Elections

*The real meaning of democracy occurs on election day when a citizen steps into the voting booth and secretly chooses his or her representative for a local, state, or federal office. (There are more than 500,000 elective offices in America.) The voter's decision is a result of both psychological variables—party loyalty, candidate style, issues, and sociological factors—socioeconomic background, and group affiliations. The candidates' campaigns which preceded election day may have confused, enlightened, or even had a negligible impact upon the voter. Meanwhile, millions of other "voter-eligible" Americans pay little attention to election day. It is truly ironic that as universal suffrage has been finally realized, voter participation in elections has actually declined. The reasons for voting or nonvoting and the interaction among campaign, election, and voter dynamics will be explored in this chapter.*

## THE HISTORICAL EXPANSION OF THE SUFFRAGE

In 1789, only a small number of Americans could vote in elections, perhaps one out of every fifteen citizens. The suffrage, the right to vote, was open only to white, adult males who owned property. The next 200 years would witness the elimination of voter restrictions for nonpropertied white adult males, blacks, women, and eighteen-year-olds.

### Elimination of Religious/ Property-Ownership Tests

During the twenty-five years after the Declaration of Independence (1776), many of the states believed that only citizens who belonged to a majority church (the dominant church in terms of total membership) and who owned property deserved the right to vote. Why should propertyless individuals have any interest in voting? Fortunately, nearly all of the states had abolished religious voting tests by the early 1800s. Property requirements persisted much longer. However, they were legally abrogated by the middle of the nineteenth century.

### The Passage of the Fifteenth and Nineteenth Amendments

Ratified in 1870, the Fifteenth Amendment barred the states from using race as a voting requirement. (However, most southern blacks were prevented from voting for close to a century through such unfair devices as the white primaries, grandfather clauses, or literacy tests.) In 1920, the Nineteenth Amendment gave women the right to vote for the first time. Congress had finally responded to decades of political pressure from the women's suffrage movement.

### Voting Rights Act of 1965; Twenty-third, Twenty-fourth, and Twenty-sixth Amendments

The Voting Rights Act suspended literacy tests and allowed federal voting examiners to register voters. The result was a dramatic increase in black voter registration, especially in the South. The Twenty-third Amendment, ratified in 1961, extended the suffrage to voters in Washington, D.C. The Twenty-fourth Amendment (1964) eliminated the poll tax as a requirement for voting in any federal election. The Twenty-sixth Amendment (1971) stipulated that eighteen-year-olds were now eligible to vote in both state and national elections. Prior to this amendment, twenty-one had been the minimum age for voting. But the argument that if "young Americans were old enough to be drafted into the military, they were then old enough to vote" prevailed.

## CURRENT REQUIREMENTS FOR VOTING

The achievement of universal suffrage extends to any American eighteen years of age or older the political right to vote, provided he or she complies with the legal requirements of citizenship, residence, and registration.

### Citizenship

An alien, or noncitizen, may not vote in any election throughout the nation. Approximately 6 million resident aliens are disenfranchised.

*Residence*

The residence requirement stipulates that a citizen must have lived in a state's election district for a prescribed period of time, typically thirty days, before becoming eligible to vote. The residence requirement is based upon the assumption that a voter must have enough time to learn about local and state candidates and issues.

*Registration*

Registration is a process of identifying voters so that electoral fraud is avoided. Except for North Dakota, all states mandate voter registration. A voter must register his or her name, place of residence, date of birth, and other appropriate information with a county clerk or local election registrar. A voter remains registered until he or she moves to another locality or state, where the registration procedure must occur again. Voters are removed from the registration rolls if they fail to vote in a number of consecutive elections, are convicted of felonies, or are confined to mental institutions. In all, 52 million eligible voters were not registered prior to the 1988 presidential election.

| Year | Percent voting of those eligible |
|------|------|
| 1932 | 56.9% |
| 1936 | 61.0% |
| 1940 | 62.5% |
| 1944 | 55.9% |
| 1948 | 53.0% |
| 1952 | 63.6% |
| 1956 | 60.6% |
| 1960 | 64.0% |
| 1964 | 61.7% |
| 1968 | 60.6% |
| 1972 | 55.9% |
| 1976 | 54.4% |
| 1980 | 53.9% |
| 1984 | 54.0% |
| 1988 | 50.1% |

*Fig. 5.1   Voting Turnout in Presidential Elections, 1932–1988*

### REGISTRATION AND VOTER TURNOUT

Obviously, registration requirements reduce voter turnout. America is a mobile society, and many Americans who change their residence each year forget to reregister. In some states, the cutoff date for registration is relatively early, some fifty to sixty days before the election. Also, until quite recently, many registration centers were open only during working hours, not on weekends or evenings. Note that voters are registered by the government in many of the nations of Western Europe and Scandinavia—in effect, citizens have lifetime registration.

### REGISTRATION BY MAIL OR ON ELECTION DAY

More than half of the states now permit voting registration to be done through the mail. Two states, Maine and Wisconsin, permit election-day registration. It has been estimated that national turnout could increase by 5 to 10 percent if election-day registration were available in more states. However, on the debit side, the voting process might be delayed considerably if significant numbers of citizens decided to register on election day.

# WHY CITIZENS DO NOT VOTE

**How Many People Don't Vote?**

In the 1988 presidential election, there were 182 million individuals of eligible voting age nationally. However, only slightly more than 50 percent of those eligible actually voted for the presidential candidates, and only 44 percent for congressional races. Turnout is even lower for state and local political races, typically 20 to 25 percent of the electorate.

Since 1960, voter turnout has been declining in national elections, from 63.1 percent in 1960 to the 50 percent figure just mentioned. (Compare these figures to the 1876 presidential election, when 85 percent of eligible voters cast ballots.) America has among the lowest turnout percentages when contrasted with other democracies like Austria or Sweden (over 90 percent). Note also that other democracies provide automatic registration for citizens, or even fine people who do not vote, such as in Uruguay or Australia.

**Reasons for Nonvoting**

### HANDICAPPED OR INELIGIBLE VOTERS

Millions of American voters, perhaps 6 or 7 million, cannot vote because they are physically or mentally handicapped. Another million or so are in prison or will not vote due to their religious convictions. Finally, perhaps 2 or 3 million are traveling on election day and are unable to get back to their home voting precincts in time. (Absentee ballots are available, but they are used by a relatively small percentage of the electorate due to the paperwork and time involved.) In short, when aliens are included in this category, the "real" nonvoters numbered more than 70 million in the 1988 presidential election, an amount that is definitely not inconsequential. These citizens might have cited one of the following explanations for not going to the polls.

### "IT MAKES NO DIFFERENCE WHO WINS"

Many citizens feel that regardless of which party's candidate is elected, the political system will continue to operate effectively. Both parties (and their candidates) are seen by these individuals as virtually identical in philosophy and policy preferences. Others within this category distrust politicians in general, so to them elections have little value or meaning.

### "I CAN'T INFLUENCE THE POLITICAL SYSTEM BY VOTING"

These citizens lack "political efficacy," or the feeling that their votes will make a difference in public policies. To them, politics is a mysterious, immovable force that is well beyond their control. In addition, many citizens with this view are voter "dropouts" who no longer find any of the candidates worthy of their time or attention. Contributing to this attitude is the absence of real competition in many elections.

### "I KNOW NOTHING OR CARE NOT ABOUT POLITICS"

These citizens are largely apathetic, disinterested, and uninformed about political life, campaigns, candidates, issues, or elections. To some observers, it is better that these individuals do not vote, since democracy should depend upon that segment of the population which is really concerned about public life.

### "I WASN'T REGISTERED," OR "THE POLLING LINES WERE TOO LONG"

This type of voter is stymied by the registration requirement previously discussed or by the inconvenience of going to the polls after a long work day. Some observers have suggested that election day be made a national holiday, with the polls open from 7:00 A.M. to midnight so as to accommodate working voters. Of course, the longer hours might facilitate election-day registration procedures as well.

## WHAT KIND OF PEOPLE VOTE?

***Factors Associated with High Voter Turnout***

It is clear that voters have different perceptions of their political world than do nonvoters. These perceptions are a reflection of socioeconomic backgrounds, loyalty to a political party, occupation, race, and age. Specifically, the following factors are crucial in determining whether a particular citizen will enter the voting booth on election day.

## EDUCATION AND INCOME

In general, voters have higher levels of education and income than nonvoters. For example, college graduates vote more regularly than high-school graduates; high-school graduates vote in greater numbers than those with only a grade-school education. The reason is that individuals with more schooling tend to be better informed about politics, follow the news more closely, possess a greater sense of political efficacy, and believe that voting is an important civic duty. (Low-income voters have less of a sense of involvement with, or control over, the political environment.) Similarly, high-income citizens are more likely to be property owners who perceive political choices as important to their standard of living and personal futures.

## PARTY IDENTIFICATION

Voters identify more strongly with political parties than do nonvoters. Party identification intensifies a voter's interest in supporting his or her partisan candidates on election day.

## OCCUPATION

Businessmen, white-collar professionals, and union members vote more frequently than unskilled workers, blue-collar laborers, or nonunion members. The reasons again relate to questions of education, income, efficacy, and group affiliation. For example, union members will be pressured by their fellow workers and union leaders to back pro-labor candidates who are running for office. Their self-interest dictates the voting decision.

## RACE

Whites vote more often than members of minority groups. The fact that African-Americans, Hispanics, and Puerto Ricans are underrepresented in the voting population can be explained by their generally lower levels of income and schooling. But whites and those minority voters who have comparable educational and income levels do vote in approximately the same proportions.

## AGE

Voters in their thirties, forties, or fifties are more likely to vote than very young voters, especially the eighteen-to-twenty-one age category. The latter, many of whom are still in school or preoccupied with starting a career, are simply less interested in politics. Conversely, persons over seventy vote less due to their physical infirmities.

# VOTING BEHAVIOR: PSYCHOLOGICAL AND SOCIOLOGICAL FACTORS

**The Three Basic Psychological Variables**

What are the crucial factors which influence the actual voting decision? The three underlying psychological variables are: (a) the individual voter's perceptions of party identification; (b) campaign issues; (c) the candidate's style, image, or personality.

### PARTY IDENTIFICATION

Party identification is the long-term variable. While chapter 4 revealed that voters can switch party loyalties and that party identification is weakening (ticket splitting and the increase of independent voters have reduced the level of partisan support), "PI" still explains roughly 70 percent of all voting in presidential elections. In short, PI remains the best predictor of a person's vote.

### CAMPAIGN ISSUES

Voters can be swayed by the particular issues of a campaign. Issues represent a short-term influence on the voting decision. For example, in 1988, many Democrats did not like their nominee's (Michael Dukakis) opposition to the death penalty. Accordingly, the Dukakis stand on this issue forced Democrats to "switch" to the pro–death penalty Republican candidate, George Bush. One out of six Democratic voters cast his or her ballot for George Bush. The significance of particular issues will vary from election to election and may involve both domestic (example: the economy) or international (the Vietnam War during the 1960s and 1970s) affairs.

### CANDIDATE STYLE, PERSONALITY, IMAGE

Voters whose party loyalty is weak and who are uninformed about the issues may vote on the basis of how the candidate looks on TV or whether he or she seems sincere, honest, or trustworthy. Ronald Reagan's likable personality on TV attracted millions of Democrats. Similarly, in 1964, GOP candidate Barry Goldwater's image of a nuclear risk-taker compelled droves of Republican voters to vote for Democrat Lyndon Johnson.

**Sociological Voting Factors**

Sociological factors refer to a voter's socioeconomic background and his or her group affiliations. These factors include the following:

### INCOME AND OCCUPATION

Republicans attract higher-income voters, Democrats lower-income voters. For example, in both 1984 and 1988, Ronald Reagan, the Republican candidate, attracted those with incomes above $35,000 by a margin of two to one over the Democratic nominee, Dukakis. Conversely, majorities of voters with incomes of $15,000 or less chose Carter in 1980, Mondale in 1984, and Dukakis in 1988.

Regarding the occupation variable, professionals and business people have overwhelmingly voted for the GOP from 1952 to 1988 (except for the 1964 presidential election). Conversely, Democratic nominees can usually attract a majority of blue-collar or manual workers' votes.

## EDUCATION

College graduates are likely to back GOP candidates, while high-school- and grade-school-educated citizens tend to vote Democratic.

## SEX, AGE

Men and women appear to support both parties in roughly equal proportions, although women voters have given an edge to the Democrats during the last decade (in 1988, 50 percent of female voters selected Bush, 57 percent Dukakis). Regarding the age factor, younger voters (under thirty) have traditionally supported the Democratic party, older voters (over fifty) the GOP. This was the pattern until 1984 and 1988, when Reagan and Bush, the Republicans, received majority support from voters under thirty.

## RELIGION AND RACE

Northern Protestants typically vote Republican, while Jewish and Catholic voters prefer the Democrats. The parties' stands on various issues can affect support from various religious groups—for example, abortion among Catholic voters. Concerning race, black Americans have supported the Democratic party by a clear majority in all presidential elections since 1952, largely due to the party's pro–civil rights record. The Democratic party has won a majority of white votes in only one national election—1964— during the last four decades. This racial division is even more salient in the South. For example, in 1988, 57 percent of the national white vote went for Republican George Bush, but he was selected by 74 percent of southern white voters.

## GEOGRAPHY

The Democratic party once dominated the "Solid South." However, southern voters have chosen Republican presidential candidates in recent years, while continuing to select Democrats in congressional or local races. The Republican influence remains strong in New England, the Midwest, and the far West, including California. While the Democrats still carry the big cities of the North and East, GOP voters dominate the suburbs.

### FAMILY, GROUP MEMBERSHIPS

It is generally true that family members tend to vote alike, since they are influenced by similar religious, economic, and social experiences. (There are, of course, exceptions, for many families are composed of strong-willed, independent individuals.) Consequently, the overwhelming majority of husbands and wives vote the same. Two out of three children, once grown, also identify with their parents' political party. In the workplace, groups who associate with one another in the office or on the assembly line tend to vote alike, perhaps due to peer pressure or similar socialization patterns. However, some voters are "cross-pressured" since they may work among associates who are Democrats but belong to a social club which consists mainly of Republican voters.

# CAMPAIGNS

**Timing and Circumstances**

Before a prospective candidate decides to run for office, he or she must consider the "timing" of the race—is it a good year for the party? Also, if applicable, how strong or weak is the incumbent? Does the candidate have wide contacts—i.e., do enough people know the candidate and will they be supportive?

**Modern Campaigns**

The goal of a campaign is to win public office on election day by a voting plurality. To accomplish this fundamental goal, modern presidential and congressional campaigns require building an organization through qualified personnel, formulating effective campaign strategies, and acquiring adequate funding.

### CAMPAIGN PERSONNEL

A well-organized campaign will rely upon the professional political consultant. A political consultant, for a fee, will be responsible for devising campaign strategies, formulating campaign themes and ideas, handling advertising, interpreting poll results, and even budgeting resources. Other important personnel may include speechwriters, clerical workers, direct-mail fund-raisers, computer programmers, professional pollsters, public-relations experts, lawyers, accountants, and skilled media producers.

### CAMPAIGN STRATEGIES

Campaign strategies can involve the achievement of name recognition for challengers, acquiring newspaper endorsements, maintaining the loyalty of party supporters while attracting "switchers" from the other party, and utilizing negative campaigning, poll "tracking," televised debates, especially in presidential races, and effective political commercials.

## ACHIEVING NAME RECOGNITION

Challengers have a major problem in unseating incumbents, especially in congressional races. Incumbents have the advantages of greater access to campaign funds, free mailings to constituents (the franking privilege), job experience, media recognition, and large campaign staffs. In 1990, 96 percent of House and Senate incumbents were reelected. During the last three decades, the "incumbency reelection" averages in Congress have been 95 percent (House) and 85 percent (Senate), respectively. An unknown challenger will have to get the attention of the voters through innumerable speeches, a simple, memorable campaign theme, countless personal contacts, door-to-door canvassing, or by placing ads in newspapers, or on TV and radio. Unfortunately for the challenger, these efforts will take time and money. Contributors may be reluctant to give funds to a long-shot challenger against an entrenched incumbent. In 1990, no more than 15 percent of House challengers were able to raise enough money to run a credible campaign. By contrast, incumbents outspent challengers by as much as three to one.

## ATTAINING NEWSPAPER ENDORSEMENTS

Newspaper endorsements can benefit a candidate, especially if the particular newspaper has a wide circulation. GOP candidates normally receive a larger number of newspaper endorsements than do Democrats. However, Democratic endorsements typically come from large metropolitan dailies, GOP endorsements from smaller-circulation papers.

## AVOIDING PARTY DEFECTIONS WHILE ENCOURAGING "SWITCHERS"

Candidates, in particular those in competitive races, must endeavor to retain loyal party supporters while attracting independent voters and "switchers" (crossover voters from the opposition party). The latter voters can determine the outcome of a close election. A candidate must understand what issue positions or personal messages will appeal to this potentially fluid sector of the electorate.

## NEGATIVE CAMPAIGNING

To some observers, an unfortunate development in modern campaigns has been to "sling the mud" at every opportunity (although this is really not new in American political history), especially in televised political commercials. Rather than running on "what I stand for and what I will do if elected," a campaigner will pillory or besmirch the integrity of the opponent, in effect saying to the voter that "better you elect me than my inferior, incompetent, unethical opponent." Negative campaigning was especially noticeable in the 1988 presidential race between Michael Dukakis and George Bush. However distasteful this may be to many, scholarly studies suggest that negative campaigns do influence voters. So, it is probable that this campaign tactic will remain a fixture of American politics.

## POLL "TRACKING"

Candidates increasingly rely on public-opinion polls during the campaign to see if their issue stands and personal style are effective with voters. Sophisticated "tracking" polls go beyond traditional surveys. Instead of taking a poll covering the entire sample every few days or once a week, interviews of voters are conducted continuously, revealing how important groups within the electorate are reacting to campaign themes and candidate appeals. For example, a congressional challenger who is a Democrat might find from tracking poll surveys that labor-union members increasingly believe he is not sympathetic to the average "working man." The challenger may quickly produce a TV ad which conveys support for union workers or deliver a pro-worker speech before the local chapter of the AFL-CIO.

## TV DEBATES

Because television plays such an important role in running an effective campaign, televised debates between presidential, congressional, or state/local candidates have become more common than ever. The first nationally televised debate occurred in 1960 between Kennedy and Nixon. Other presidential debates followed in 1976 (Carter–Ford), 1980 (Reagan–Carter), 1984 (Reagan–Mondale), and 1988 (Bush–Dukakis). It appears that Kennedy's and Carter's performances may have helped them to achieve a narrow victory in 1960 and 1976, respectively. But Reagan clearly bested Carter in 1980 ("Are you better off now than you were four years ago?"), and Bush did well against Dukakis in 1988. While TV debates are not always conclusive on the presidential level, TV is still a campaign weapon which politicians must master. Since voters increasingly rely on TV for most of their political information and perceptions, a poor performance or physical appearance by a candidate on TV can prove politically harmful. In the first 1960 nationally televised debate, Republican presidential candidate Richard Nixon, suffering from an illness, improper makeup, poor on-camera lighting, and the wrong-color suit (gray against a gray background), appeared unimpressive in contrast to a rested, tanned, and properly attired John F. Kennedy. Media experts for future presidential debates would be sure their candidates did not repeat Nixon's on-air mistakes.

One criticism of televised debates is that they become "side by side" press conferences rather than real debates in which the candidates challenge each other directly. Candidate answers to reporters' questions are well rehearsed, and frequently evasive. Nevertheless, viewers do have the benefit of gauging each candidate's level of knowledge and his ability to handle the pressures of the debate.

## TV POLITICAL COMMERCIALS

Political commercials on TV can help attract votes for a candidate, since evidence suggests that they may influence up to one-third of the electorate during a presidential campaign. Most commercials try to convey a simple image or theme which will be remembered by the viewer. For example, the famous 1964 "daisy girl" political commercial run by the Lyndon Johnson campaign committee depicted a small girl plucking petals from daisies and then being enveloped in a nuclear explosion. The implied message was that the Republican candidate, Barry Goldwater, could start a nuclear holocaust that would destroy America's children, and ostensibly all of humanity (the Republicans protested so strongly that the commercial was aired only one time). In 1988, the Bush campaign ran the infamous Willie Horton ad, claiming that Dukakis had furloughed Horton from prison on weekends, allowing Horton to commit the additional crimes of rape and robbery. The ad, and several others like it, convinced many voters that Dukakis was weak on the crime issue.

Many TV ads are almost wholly devoid of substantive policy, instead depending upon patriotic symbols or pleasing images. It was not accidental that George Bush was filmed giving a speech in a flag factory with hundreds of American flags placed in the background, or that Michael Dukakis spoke to the voters with his wife beside him in front of a cozy fireplace. These images can be very influential for many voters.

## CAMPAIGN EXPENSES, SPENDING, AND FUNDING

Modern campaigns are incredibly expensive. A presidential campaign requires extensive travel arrangements; TV time; newspaper ads; written materials including posters, brochures, pamphlets, and bumper stickers; polling costs; data processing; and staff salaries. Television time rapidly consumes campaign funds. A thirty-second ad on national TV during prime time will cost $150,000 or more. In 1988, more than $2 billion was expended on all federal political campaigns.

## Campaign Legislation

While the presidential race is federally funded (Dukakis and Bush were each limited to spending $23.05 million on their 1988 campaigns), congressional campaigns require private fund-raising efforts. Thus, escalating campaign costs have resulted. In 1974, a victorious House campaign cost about $90,000; in 1990, the cost was more than $400,000. For winning Senate races, the 1974 figure was about $500,000; in 1990, the cost had ballooned to more than $4 million. Critics are alarmed by these stupendous expenses, arguing that "money buys political office." In the past, Congress has tried to correct potential fund-raising abuses by passing various forms of legislation.

### THE 1971 FEDERAL ELECTION CAMPAIGN ACT (FECA)

The Federal Election Campaign Act of 1971 restricted the amount of campaign money that could be spent on mass-media advertising, mandated disclosure of all campaign contributions and expenditures over $100, and limited amounts that candidates and their families could donate to their own campaigns.

### THE REVENUE ACT OF 1971

This 1971 act encouraged private contributions through a system of tax deductions and credits. Also created was a $1 check-off feature on all federal income-tax returns which would subsidize the campaign costs of major party presidential candidates. Both of the 1971 statutes did not become operative until the 1976 presidential election.

### 1974 FECA AMENDMENTS

Congress decided to change the campaign finance laws once again after the Watergate scandal, when it was learned that illegal and improper amounts of campaign funds had been given to Richard Nixon's reelection campaign committee. (One example: Dairy producers had donated $680,000 to Nixon's campaign in exchange for favorable treatment from his administration.) This act established a six-person Federal Election Commission (FEC) to enforce the law, created public financing for presidential candidates in primaries and general elections (there was no public financing of congressional campaigns), and restricted contributions so that:

> a. each citizen was limited to contributing $1,000 per candidate in each federal election or primary, $20,000 to a national party committee, and $5,000 to other PAC's;
>
> b. the total amount of all contributions annually per individual was limited to $25,000;
>
> c. groups, such as PAC's—Political Action Committees—were limited to a maximum contribution of $5,000 per candidate in any election. No individual could give more than $5,000 per year to any one PAC;
>
> d. personal contributions from candidates or their families could not exceed $50,000 in the pre-nomination stage, or $50,000 for the general election, provided the candidate voluntarily accepted federal funds. Candidates not accepting federal funds at all could spend unlimited amounts of their own money. A provision of the act limiting these personal ex-

penditures was eventually ruled unconstitutional by the Supreme Court (*Buckley* v. *Valeo*) in 1976.

## PAC's

The 1974 act, and amendments passed in 1976, permitted special interests, unions, and corporations to form Political Action Committees as a way of raising funds for candidates' campaigns. A PAC had to raise money from at least fifty contributors and in turn disseminate these funds to a minimum of five candidates in a federal election. Individual corporations and labor unions were restricted to having only one PAC each.

PAC contributions account for a growing share of campaign funds. In 1974, PAC's accounted for about 15 percent of all congressional campaign funds. By 1990, the figure was over 35 percent.

## 1979 AMENDMENTS TO FECA

These amendments strengthened reporting requirements to the FEC (all contributions and expenditures of $200 or more had to be reported), allowed state and local party committees to spend unlimited and unregulated "soft money" funds (see page 77) on voter-turnout activities, and increased funding support for the national nominating conventions.

**The Impact of Campaign Finance Laws.** First, due to these laws, presidential campaigns now rely far more on public subsidization, rather than depending on the potentially corrupting influence of wealthy private donors. Second, the law has not reduced the total costs of other national campaigns, especially since congressional campaigns are not entitled to public funding. Private money, especially from the PAC's, has benefited congressional incumbents. Third, candidates who are independently wealthy are not restricted from contributing as much as they want to their own campaigns, prompting critics to charge that qualified, but moderate-income, candidates are at a clear disadvantage. Fourth, subsidies go to presidential candidates and not to strengthen the national parties. However, the parties have exploited a loophole in the campaign finance laws, accumulating "soft money" funds which are spent on "voter turnout" activities—operating telephone banks, printing and mailing out campaign literature, and recruiting field organizers. This money is distributed to state and local parties as a way of helping the national campaign. Both parties have turned to wealthy contributors to build up these soft-money accounts, which totaled $130 million in 1988. Soft-money amounts and individual contributors do not have to be reported to the FEC.

# PRESIDENTIAL ELECTIONS—DEMOCRACY'S ULTIMATE TEST

Every presidential election has two stages: (1) the nomination stage, in which hopeful candidates from each major party seek the presidential nomination, which is formally awarded at the national nominating convention every four years; (2) the general election stage, in which the two presidential contenders (and perhaps other, third-party presidential candidates) seek to win the presidency by receiving a majority of electoral votes in the electoral college.

## The Nomination Stage

The important steps in the nomination stage are the "presidential announcement," the winning of convention delegates through primaries and caucuses, and the selection of the party ticket at the national nominating convention.

### "PRESIDENTIAL ANNOUNCEMENT"

Presidential hopefuls will usually announce their intention to seek their party's nomination a year or more before the convention meets. Candidates who are not well known nationally may start even earlier, as was the case with Jimmy Carter's candidacy. Carter, a former governor of Georgia, was known to only about 2 percent of the American people in 1975.

### WINNING DELEGATES

Candidates may win delegates through two major avenues—caucuses and primaries.

### CAUCUSES

A caucus is basically a meeting of party members. While used in some twenty states, the Iowa caucuses are particularly important since they represent the start of the presidential campaign, usually in February of the election year. In a complicated process, Iowa party voters have local meetings (at the precinct or town level) at which they select delegates to a county or district convention. (Candidates must have large numbers of their supporters organized effectively and participating at these grass-roots levels.) From this level, delegates to the full Iowa state convention are selected. Then, delegates to the national convention are chosen. In 1988, fewer than 25 percent of all delegates to both parties' conventions were chosen by the caucus method. But Iowa remains psychologically important, since the media will focus on which candidates do well, labeling them the "front-runners." However, in 1980, George Bush did well in Iowa, but lost to Ronald Reagan in the New Hampshire primary. Reagan's poor showing in

Iowa was soon forgotten as he proceeded to secure the nomination. Ironically, in 1988, Bush lost in Iowa to Senator Bob Dole, but in February he recovered by getting the most votes in the New Hampshire primary. Iowa's significance was dimished in 1992, since its own Democratic senator, Tom Harkin, was victorious (he had little opposition from other Democrats).

### PRESIDENTIAL PRIMARIES

Presidential primaries are the main method of selecting delegates. In 1988, presidential primaries existed in thirty-six states, plus the District of Columbia and Puerto Rico. These primaries allowed voters to select national convention delegates and/or to express their preference among presidential contenders on the ballot. Because state laws differ, the precise nature of each primary must be examined state by state. Nevertheless, the central importance of primaries is clear—a presidential contender who does well in as many states as possible will win his or her share of delegates. To achieve the nomination, a candidate must win a majority of all delegates at the national convention. George Bush would win every primary election except South Dakota's in 1988, but other GOP candidates were far less successful.

**The Problem of Matching Funds.** Once again, a candidate who fares poorly in the early primaries, as in New Hampshire, may be forced to withdraw from the nomination race. One reason is budgetary—candidates who appear to be "losers" will find private campaign contributions "drying up" and public funding cut off. Under the federal campaign laws, major party contenders who raise $5,000 in twenty states in contributions of $250 or less, a total sum of $100,000, can expect matching federal grants during the pre-nomination period. Candidates who start their nomination quests early can usually comply with these requirements. But maintaining their eligibility for matching funds is far more difficult. A presidential hopeful who receives less than 10 percent of the popular vote in two consecutive primaries loses federal matching dollars until he or she is able to win 20 percent of the vote in another primary. Thus, Jesse Jackson twice lost his eligibility in the 1984 nomination campaign. So without federal money, the campaign is doomed.

**The Lack of Media Attention.** A sharp decrease in campaign funds due to failures in the early primaries is compounded by the problem of media inattention. Having no money translates into a lack of TV time, a minimal campaign at best, and newspaper/TV reporters "writing off" an individual's candidacy. These problems engulfed numerous candidates early in the 1988 primaries, including Democrats Pat Schroeder and Paul Simon, and Republicans Pat Robertson and Jack Kemp. (In 1992, both Democratic senators Bob Kerrey and Tom Harkin were forced to withdraw from the presidential race in March after doing poorly in the early primaries.) But note that in 1988, some candidates ignored Iowa and New Hampshire.

Tennessee Senator Al Gore decided upon a "southern strategy," hoping to win big on "Super Tuesday" (March 8, 1988), when sixteen primaries and five caucuses were held. However, Jesse Jackson compiled the most votes for the Democrats.

**Judging the Presidential Primary System.** Presidential primaries have helped to democratize the selection of each party's nominee, while compelling would-be nominees to test their candidacies throughout most of the nation. However, critics argue that the primaries actually test a candidate's media appeal more than those qualities needed for presidential leadership. Also, the large number of primaries fatigues both the candidates and the public. Reformers suggest an elimination of the current primary system in favor of a single, nationwide primary in which each party's nominee would be selected. The national conventions, if retained, could help select the vice-presidential nominees. But a national primary would hurt candidates who had less money to spend on TV time. Another proposal is Colorado's "national pre-primary convention" plan, whereby caucuses/state conventions would send delegates to the national nominating conventions to select two or three possible nominees. A national primary would then be held to select the party's final ticket. However, it is apparent that the major parties do not wish to change or abolish the national convention, which is held every four years in a major city such as New York, Atlanta, New Orleans, or Los Angeles. In 1992, the Republican convention would be in Houston, the Democratic meeting in New York City.

## THE NATIONAL NOMINATING CONVENTIONS

In the last twenty years, thanks to the primary system, each party has known who its presidential nominee would be. Thus, in 1988, Republican George Bush and Democrat Michael Dukakis had both attained a majority of the delegates pledged to them through numerous primary victories.

## THE DEMOCRATIC PARTY'S "SUPERDELEGATES"

In 1982, the Democrats had added the "superdelegates"—governors, big-city mayors, congressional representatives, state party chairpersons—delegates who were largely unpledged to any one nominee prior to the convention. In 1984, the superdelegates had supported Walter Mondale, in 1988 Dukakis. In future conventions, the superdelegates, if retained by the party, could help a candidate who may have a smaller total of pledged delegates from the primaries and caucuses, but generates considerable support from these party leaders.

Recent conventions have performed the important functions of writing and adopting a party platform, unifying the party faithful, and formally approving the party's "ticket."

## THE PARTY PLATFORM

The platform represents how the party "stands" on the important issues in an election year. Frequently written by party leaders and/or presidential staffers (if an incumbent president is running for reelection), the platform can represent a mixture of both specific and general "answers" to policy problems. Individual issues or "planks" within the platform statement—such as abortion or civil rights—can sometimes prove divisive among convention delegates, requiring compromise. Contrary to popular belief, most presidential nominees take platforms seriously, and they try to implement many of the document's policy proposals once in office.

| Issue | Democratic Plank | Republican Plank |
|---|---|---|
| Abortion | Supported freedom of reproductive choice | Favored amendment to outlaw abortion |
| AIDS | Promised additional research and education for prevention | Supported research and education for prevention |
| Crime | Supported increased federal assistance for local law enforcement | Supported death penalty |
| Drugs | Opposed legalizing illicit drugs | Supported use of military to fight drugs |
| Housing | Supported increase in public and subsidized housing | Supported cutting red tape for housing rehabilitation |
| National Defense | Questioned expenditures on certain weapons systems | Supported military buildup |
| Taxes | Supported a fairer share to be paid by the wealthy and corporations | Opposed any tax increases |

*Fig. 5.2    1988 Democratic and Republican Planks*

## UNIFYING THE PARTY

During the four or five days of a national convention, numerous speeches are delivered by party leaders. The "keynote address," typically delivered by one of the party's better orators, is the first major speech of the convention. The opposition party is lambasted and a call for party harmony echoes throughout the convention hall. Later in the convention, each candidate's name will be placed in nomination by a supporter, along with several seconding speeches. Normally, delegates backing each nominee will start floor demonstrations, which can last for some time. After all of the nominating speeches are over, balloting begins with each state's delegation called in alphabetical order. To reiterate, a majority of delegate votes is required. Unlike the 1924 Democratic convention in New York City, which went through 123 ballots, recent conventions have selected a presidential nominee on the first ballot. The most recent convention at which more than one presidential ballot was needed was in 1952, when Democrat Adlai Stevenson was nominated on the third roll call.

## APPROVING THE PARTY'S "TICKET"

The new presidential nominee must now choose his vice-presidential running mate. An important principle guiding his selection is "balancing the ticket," which means that the vice-presidential nominee's background should contain political and personal traits helpful to the ticket's national appeal. For example, in 1960, Massachusetts Senator John F. Kennedy, a Catholic, chose Lyndon Johnson, a U.S. senator from Texas and a Protestant, as his V.P. running mate. In 1988, George Bush chose Senator Dan Quayle, from Indiana, who was younger and more conservative than he. The ultimate balance occurred in 1984, when Walter Mondale chose Geraldine A. Ferraro, the first woman vice-presidential nominee, as his running mate. Mondale wanted to strengthen his appeal to women voters across the nation.

A presidential nominee may also choose a running mate who can help carry a pivotal state with a large number of electoral votes. Thus, in 1988, Michael Dukakis selected Senator Lloyd Bentsen of Texas (the state has twenty-nine electoral votes). But Texas and its important twenty-nine electoral votes were won by George Bush on election day.

## ACCEPTANCE SPEECHES AND THE CONVENTION'S END

Both nominees deliver their acceptance speeches on the final evening of the convention, typically in prime-viewing time so that the television networks can carry them live to the nation. The speeches are again designed to forge party unity by inspiring convention delegates and the party faithful to support the ticket during the upcoming campaign. For the candidates themselves, the aftermath of the convention is a time to plot campaign strategy so as to secure at least 270 electoral votes—a bare majority for victory—on election day in November.

# THE GENERAL ELECTION STAGE AND THE ELECTORAL COLLEGE

The presidential campaigns usually begin shortly after Labor Day in September and end on election day, the Tuesday after the first Monday in November. The campaign's decisions involving use of time and allocation of resources will largely be determined by the constraints posed by the electoral college system.

## What Is the Electoral College?

On election day, the voters technically do not directly select a presidential candidate, but rather choose a slate of presidential electors within each state of the Union, and the District of Columbia. The number of electors within each state equals its total representation in Congress. For example, in 1988, Georgia possessed 12 electoral votes since it had 10 representatives in the House, and, like all states, two senators (10 + 2 = 12). By contrast, California had 47 electoral votes (45 in the House, 2 in the Senate) due to California's being the most populous state in the nation. The entire electoral college had 538 votes, based on 435 in the House, 100 in the Senate, and 3 electoral votes awarded to the District of Columbia through the Twenty-third Amendment (435 + 100 + 3 = 538).

On election day of 1988, a voter in Georgia choosing George Bush was actually selecting 12 men and women, the electors, who had pledged to support the Bush–Quayle ticket. A voter choosing Dukakis was really selecting a different 12 electors, similarly pledged to support the Democratic ticket. Since Bush obtained a plurality of all popular votes cast in Georgia, he received all of Georgia's 12 electoral votes. Bush also won the most popular votes in California, thereby gaining that state's 47 electoral votes.

After election day, the electors meet in their respective state capitals on the Monday after the second Wednesday in December. They cast their electoral votes. The votes are then sent to the president of the Senate, where they will again be counted by the vice-president in early January when Congress reconvenes. If no presidential candidate has received at least 270 electoral votes (a bare majority of 538), the House of Representatives would choose the president, the Senate the vice-president.

### THE ELECTORAL COLLEGE—PROBLEMS AND SUGGESTED REFORMS

To critics, the electoral college has outlived its usefulness. The framers originally created the college to prevent direct popular election of the president and allow the electors to exercise their own judgment. Neither idea is reasonable today. A quick review of the college's defects and reforms may be helpful.

**A Popular Vote Winner, but a Presidential "Loser."** Under the prevailing system, it is possible for a ticket to accumulate the most popular votes nationally, but lose due to the electoral college's "winner take all" philosophy. A candidate could win the 11 biggest electoral-vote states by the smallest of popular vote margins, then lose by sizable popular vote totals in the other 39 states and the District of Columbia. The candidate picked by a national voting majority would be denied the presidency, because he did not win such states as California, New York, Texas, Pennsylvania, or Illinois.

This could have happened in the 1976 Ford–Carter race, with a switch of a few thousand popular votes in Ohio (25 electoral votes) and Hawaii (4 electoral votes) from Carter to Ford, giving the latter the necessary 270 electoral votes.

**The "Faithless Elector."** Note that electors are "pledged" to vote for their party's ticket, but they are not legally required to do so. Nine times in American history an elector has changed his or her vote. While the outcome of a presidential election has not been affected, the possibility still remains that this could occur. Imagine a close presidential race in which the final electoral vote total is 270 for candidate A, 268 for candidate B. If one "candidate A" elector switches to B, there is an electoral tie, 269 to 269, and the House must then select a president. If one more elector switches to B, then B is the winner.

**A Third-Party Bid Leads to Congressional Deadlock or Chaos.** A final problem is the specter of a third party siphoning off enough electoral votes to deny either of the two major parties an electoral college majority. This almost happened with George Wallace's American Independent party's candidacy in 1968, which claimed 46 electoral votes. Having the House choose the president could lead to a number of complications, since 26 of the 50 state delegations must approve a candidate, each delegation having one vote (a state whose delegation was evenly divided could not cast a vote). If the House was incapable of deciding, then the Senate's choice of a vice-president might become acting president.

**Reform #1: Direct Popular Election.** The reform with the greatest support is the one whereby the electoral college would be eliminated entirely, and direct popular election would be substituted through a constitutional amendment. Hence, the ticket which received a national voting plurality would always be the winner (provided it received at least 40 percent of the popular vote; if not, there would be a runoff election). But opposition from smaller states, the political difficulty of passing another constitutional amendment, and the added pressures on candidates of having to campaign arduously in virtually every state work against this reform. Unless there is an electoral crisis, a direct-election amendment is unlikely to be passed by Congress and ratified by the states.

**Reform #2: The National Bonus Plan.** This plan would give a bonus of 102 electoral votes to the candidate who received the most popular votes. If the bonus plus the electoral votes already won by the candidate equaled 321, a majority (538 + 102 = 640; 321 is a majority of 640), the candidate would be declared the winner. Otherwise, a runoff election between the two frontrunners would then be scheduled. The plan has received little support.

**Reform #3: The Proportional Plan.** This plan tackles the "winner take all" feature by awarding electoral votes according to percentages of a state's popular vote realized by each candidate. If candidate A received 40 percent of the total popular vote in a state with 20 electoral votes, A would be entitled to 8 electoral votes (20 x .40 = 8) instead of 0. The problem with this plan is that minor parties could gain enough electoral votes to prevent a 270-vote majority from being attained.

**Reform #4: The District Plan.** This plan would keep the electoral college but change the way electoral votes within the state are allocated. Only two electoral votes would be decided by the total statewide vote, not the entire slate of electors. The state's remaining electoral votes would be based on the popular vote within each congressional district (Maine and Nebraska already choose their electors in this manner). An electoral vote majority would still be required. If no majority existed, then a joint session of Congress would make the presidential selection. Small states would benefit from this plan, but large states would lose political power. However, the plan would not eliminate the danger of a candidate's receiving a minority of the popular vote but an electoral college majority. If the plan had been in effect in 1960, Richard Nixon, who won fewer popular votes than did John F. Kennedy, would have received 278 electoral votes, not 219, and thus would have become president.

## THE ELECTORAL COLLEGE—IMPACT ON CAMPAIGN STRATEGY

Obviously, a presidential candidate must do well in the large states if he is to win the presidency. In 1988 both Bush and Dukakis concentrated their time, efforts, and funds in the electoral-rich states of California (47); New York (36); Texas (29); Pennsylvania (25); Illinois (24); Ohio (23); Florida (21); New Jersey (16); Massachusetts (13); Georgia and Virginia (12 each); Missouri, Wisconsin, and Tennessee (11 each). It made little sense to spend days campaigning in a state like South Dakota, with only 3 electoral votes.

## THE 1988 ELECTORAL COLLEGE TOTALS AND ELECTION RESULTS

In the 1988 election, George Bush collected 426 electoral votes to 111 for Michael Dukakis (1 electoral vote went for Lloyd Bentsen). Bush won 40 states, Dukakis 10. The popular-vote totals were 48,886,097 (54 percent) for the Bush–Quayle ticket, 41,809,074 (46 percent) for the Dukakis–Bentsen ticket.

In Congress, the Democrats picked up one more seat in the Senate, eight more in the House. Voters continued their "split ticket" pattern, electing a Republican president, but consolidating the Democratic majorities in both houses of Congress.

## WHY BUSH WON

Bush was victorious for a number of reasons, including the following: (a) good economic conditions in the nation, with low unemployment and inflation; (b) peace abroad; (c) the link between Bush and Reagan's popularity; (d) the negative campaign of Bush, portraying Dukakis as an extreme liberal (in 1988, twice as many voters viewed themselves as conservatives rather than liberals); (e) the experience of Bush in government (former congressman, CIA director, vice-president) appealed to voters; (f) the stilted campaign style of Dukakis and his ineffective campaign strategy, which did not counter Bush's accusations quickly enough.

## VOTER PATTERNS

While liberals, blacks, and loyal Democrats supported Dukakis, southerners, white males, and white Protestants continued to support Bush. A good number of Democratic "switchers" and a majority of independent voters (55 percent) also selected the GOP candidate. In short, the 1988 election symbolized the electorate's preference for divided government. The GOP maintained its grip on the electoral college, with the Democrats showing few signs of losing control over Congress. Whether this pattern would continue in the 1992 election remained an open question. A faltering economy posed possible problems for President Bush, and a number of Democratic hopefuls scrambled for the nomination in 1992. President Bush had to cope with his own Republican challenger, conservative Pat Buchanan.

*In the American political system, voting, campaigns, and elections represent the very essence of democracy. Yet, despite the near achievement of universal suffrage, millions of eligible citizens in America do not vote due to apathy, residence and/or registration requirements, or a low sense of political efficacy. Studies show that high levels of education and income, group membership, white-collar occupations, a strong sense of party identification, and middle age are correlated with high voting turnout.*

*Modern campaigns have become expensive enterprises, requiring large amounts of funding, skilled staffers, political consultants, and polling and media experts. The stress on TV advertising has also emphasized candidate imagery over substance. The costs of campaigning have led to abuses, and a number of campaign finance laws are directed at controlling the "money can buy elections" mentality. However, while public subsidization of presidential campaigns has limited the role of private money, nonsubsidized congressional campaigns increasingly rely on PAC's.*

*Finally, presidential campaigns have two stages—the pre-nomination and general-election periods. The pre-nomination period requires presidential candidates to do well in caucuses and primaries in order to gain the support of convention delegates. Defeats in the early caucuses and primaries can doom a campaign. At the national nominating convention, a party ticket is chosen, a platform written, and party unity (hopefully) forged. In the presidential campaign which follows, both presidential candidates seek to win a majority from the electoral college. Although critics see flaws*

in the electoral college system and propose reforms, there is little likelihood
of changing the system in the near future.

**Selected
Readings**

Bartels, Larry. *Presidential Primaries and the Dynamics of Public Choice* (1987)

Cloward, Richard, and Frances Fox Piven. *Why Americans Don't Vote* (1988)

Diamond, Edwin, and Stephen Bates. *The Spot: The Rise of Political Advertising
on Television* (1988)

Salmore, Barbara G., and Stephen A. Salmore. *Candidates, Parties, and Campaigns: Electoral Politics in America.* 2nd ed. (1989)

Sorauf, Frank J. *Money in American Elections* (1988)

Watson, Richard A. *The Presidential Contest.* 3rd ed. (1988)

# 6

## *Congress*

*A*mericans seem to approve of their own congressional representatives as
responsible and effective legislators. But, according to public opinion polls,
they have a relatively low opinion of Congress as an institution. Recent
House incumbents have successful reelection rates of well over 90 percent.
Senate incumbents are typically reelected at a rate of over 75 percent. Yet,
less than half of the public thinks Congress does a capable job overall. A
good indication was the public's outcry when the issue of congressional pay
raises was brought up in 1989. The overriding public attitude was that
representatives and senators were undeserving of higher salaries. But were
these public perceptions fair or accurate? Many members of Congress were
hard-working public servants whose difficult political missions of both
representation and policy-making were unappreciated. Furthermore, Congress was typically viewed as a doddering, painfully slow, undisciplined
assembly unable to cope with the many problems of American society. Was
it any wonder that many incumbents ran "against Congress" in order to win
reelection? Incumbents emphasized the favors they performed for their
constituents or economic benefits they had won for their district or state.
They rarely defended Congress, the institution.

But Congress remains a vital component of the American political
system. The 535 men and women of Congress mirror the American people's
diversity, needs, hopes, and aspirations for the future. The purpose of this
chapter is to provide essential information regarding the composition of
Congress, its constitutional powers, leadership, membership qualifications
and backgrounds, and the legislative process.

# CONGRESSIONAL POWERS

**Constitutional Delegated or Expressed Powers**

In Article I, Section 8 of the Constitution, twenty-seven different powers are specifically granted to Congress. In addition, Article IV gives Congress the power to admit new states into the Union. The Sixteenth Amendment gives Congress the power to collect the federal income tax. Congress also has the "power of enforcement" in relation to the Thirteenth, Fourteenth, Fifteenth, Nineteenth, Twenty-fourth, and Twenty-sixth amendments.

### POWER TO TAX

Congress has the power to "lay and collect taxes, duties, imposts, and excises, to pay the debts, and provide for the common defense and welfare of the United States. . . ." In fiscal year 1991, the federal government collected more than $1.2 trillion in taxes. Taxes finance government operations and programs. The Constitution specifies limitations on the congressional taxing power: (a) taxes imposed by Congress must benefit public, not private, interests; (b) Congress cannot tax exports; (c) taxes must be apportioned by population among the states (all federal taxes must be levied at the same rates across the nation, but the more populous states—New York, for example—will pay more in total tax dollars than a state with fewer people, such as Wyoming).

### COMMERCE POWER

Congress has the power "to regulate commerce with foreign nations, and among the several states, and with the Indian tribes." Historically, the commerce clause has led to the expansion of federal power. Supreme Court interpretations in such landmark cases as *Gibbons* v. *Ogden* (1824) and congressional applications as in the Civil Rights Act of 1964 (prohibiting discrimination in public accommodations) have contributed to this broadening of the commerce clause.

### CURRENCY POWER

Congress has the power "to coin money," and the states are forbidden to have their own currencies. The thirteen different state currencies of the Revolutionary era created financial havoc. The framers of the Constitution strongly desired a single, national currency system; they gave the power to Congress to create such a system.

## BORROWING POWER

Congress can "borrow money on the credit of the United States." A common practice has been to issue government bonds in order to finance wars or help the government pay for new social programs. In the early 1990s, the federal government's total debt was more than $2 trillion.

## BANKRUPTCIES

Congress has the power to establish uniform bankruptcy laws across the nation. Thus, individuals who are hopelessly in debt have a method of paying off their creditors with whatever assets they may still possess.

## OTHER EXPRESSED POWERS

Congress has control over naturalization proceedings (becoming a citizen of the U.S.), the post office (creating new post offices and legislating against mail fraud or other misuses of the mails), patents and copyrights, uniform weights and measures, and the federal judiciary. In regard to the latter, Congress can create new federal courts below the U.S. Supreme Court and alter the jurisdiction or kinds of cases heard by the lower federal courts.

## WAR POWER

Congress is given the sole power to declare war by the Constitution. While the president is commander in chief of the armed forces, Congress can limit a president's use of troops overseas under the 1973 War Powers Act. Since the Vietnam War, Congress has been sensitive to presidential usurpation of the war power, demanding greater input into decisions to go to war. The congressional debate in 1991 over whether to authorize President Bush to use force in the Persian Gulf exemplified this type of demand.

## IMPLIED POWERS

These powers flow from Article I, Section 8, Clause 18 of the Constitution. Implied powers are not stated specifically, but have been considered reasonable offshoots of delegated powers. Clause 18 has come to be known as the "elastic clause"—"To make all laws which shall be necessary and proper for carrying into execution the foregoing powers . . ." The doctrine was first stated clearly in *McCulloch* v. *Maryland* (1819), when the Supreme Court ruled that the federal government had the right to establish a national bank, even though the Constitution made no mention of this power. Chief Justice John Marshall ruled that in order to implement the delegated powers of borrowing money, raising an army, or regulating commerce, it was necessary for the national government to charter a national bank.

## The Constitution's Nonlegislative Powers

### ELECTION OF A PRESIDENT AND VICE-PRESIDENT

If no candidate receives a majority of votes from the electoral college (currently 270 electoral votes), the House selects a president (by a majority of the state delegations, or 26 of 50) and the Senate chooses a vice-president.

### THE TWENTY-FIFTH AMENDMENT

Congress approves the presidential selection of a new vice-president due to a vacancy in that office.

### IMPEACHMENT

The House brings the charges against the accused official, the Senate acts as the jury and can convict by a two-thirds vote. (Historically, seven officials, all of whom were federal judges, have been impeached and convicted.)

### PRESIDENTIAL APPOINTMENTS AND TREATY RATIFICATION

The Senate has the responsibility in both areas. Usually the Senate will approve the president's choice for the cabinet or the Supreme Court, although rejections do occur (Reagan's inability to secure Robert Bork's nomination to the Court is one example). The Senate can accept or reject treaties by a two-thirds vote, the "advise and consent" function.

# THE OVERSIGHT FUNCTION OF CONGRESS

The oversight, or investigatory, function of Congress remains a major responsibility of Congress. Through committee hearings, Congress has sensitized the public to important problems in American society—the environment, crime, drug testing, foreign trade, and so forth. Congress also investigates executive departments and agencies to see if they are implementing existing laws fairly, effectively, and efficiently. For example, during the Reagan administration, Congress investigated scandals in the Environmental Protection Agency, finding out that EPA administrators had misused their funds in combating toxic wastes and pollution problems.

A key oversight function deals with the budgetary power. The "power of the purse" gives Congress a chance to balance presidential power. The 1974 Congressional Budget and Impoundment Control Act mandated Congress to enact its own budget-spending ceilings and timetable. The act established: (a) budget committees in each chamber; (b) the Congressional Budget Office. The act also allowed the Government Accounting Office greater power in assessing how the executive branch was spending congressional appropriations.

# BACKGROUND CHARACTERISTICS OF MEMBERS OF CONGRESS

**Constitutional Qualifications**

According to the Constitution, House members must be at least twenty-five years of age and a citizen of the U.S. for a minimum of seven years. A senator is required to be at least thirty years old, and a U.S. citizen for at least nine years. Representatives must reside in the state from which they are elected, but House members need not live in their congressional district. Still, it is rare for a legislator to be an outsider, since tradition dictates that the representative should thoroughly know the people and the problems of the locality.

**Age and Race**

The members of Congress do not represent a cross-section of the American population. White, middle-aged males dominate Congress. Congressional leaders tended to be even older than rank-and-file members, generally being in their late fifties and early sixties. Women and blacks have been underrepresented as well. For example, there were only two women in the Senate in 1991—Nancy Kassebaum of Kansas and Barbara Mikulski of Maryland. Whereas women make up more than 50 percent of the U.S. population, they constitute only about 5 percent of congressional membership. (This may change over time, since more women are gaining their party's nominations for both House and Senate candidacies.) Black Americans account for 12 percent of the overall population. However, in 1991, there were no black senators. In the House, roughly 5 percent of the total membership was black. Similarly, Hispanics had no senatorial representatives, and averaged only 3 percent of the House membership.

**Wealth, Occupation, Education**

Members of Congress are also much wealthier than the general American population, with about one-fifth of the total membership being millionaires. Occupationally, lawyers, bankers, and businessmen dominate Capitol Hill. Lawyers have the requisite skills for political life—they know how to bargain and they understand legal-contractual relationships. Educationally, nearly all members of Congress have bachelor's degrees from a college or university. A good many have master's or Ph.D. degrees as well.

# THE ORGANIZATION OF CONGRESS

## Basics

Congress is a bicameral (two-house) legislature, consisting of a 435-member House of Representatives and a 100-member Senate. House members are elected from congressional districts in their states, one representative per district. The greater the population a state has, the more representatives it has in the House. Thus, California, the most populous state in the nation, had forty-five members in 1990. Georgia, with a smaller population base, had only ten House members. (After the 1990 census, it appeared that both states would gain representatives, since their respective populations had increased. States that had declined in population would lose House representatives.) Every state must have at least one representative. Given the fact that 435 members is a maximum size fixed by a 1922 law, currently each House member represents an average of 570,000 constituents.

Every state is entitled to have two senators. Each senator is elected by his or her entire state. Since there are fifty states, there are one hundred senators. The term of office for a House member is two years. A senator's term is six years. However, only one-third of the Senate is up for reelection every two years (the terms have been staggered historically). The entire body of the House of Representatives is up for reelection every two years.

## The Representative/ Senator and His/Her District or State

The typical representative or senator must devote a considerable amount of his or her time to political fence-mending—i.e., helping constituents with their problems. New members of Congress try to visit their districts/states as much as possible. Political speeches, town meetings with voters, media interviews, and one-on-one conversations all play a part in making the voters aware of who their representative or senator is and the fact that he or she cares about them and their political views. Typically, a representative can adopt four ideal types of legislator–constituent relationships: the trustee, delegate or agent, the partisan, or politico.

### TRUSTEE

Trustees mainly follow their own judgment when it comes to voting. Their belief is that their vote should not merely reflect what the voters back home desire. Trustees feel that they are better able to make the right choice due to their professional expertise and access to information.

### DELEGATE

Delegates see their vote as an expression of the majority view among their constituents. These legislators ignore what their party leaders desire or what special-interest groups want if those wishes run counter to popular will.

## PARTISAN

These legislators follow the advice and direction of the House and Senate party leadership on a majority of voting decisions.

## POLITICO

This is a mixture of all three roles, depending on the issue being voted upon. Only a few bills may really be heavily publicized or important to a representative's voters, so the delegate function may prevail. However, in cases where there is voter apathy or ignorance, the trustee function can be adopted. Finally, party voting is important in Congress—studies show that on important votes a majority of Democrats will oppose a majority of Republicans, especially in the House. The partisan orientation will also depend upon the effectiveness of the House and Senate leadership, as described in the next section.

## House and Senate Leadership

There are only three congressional officers mentioned in the Constitution: the Speaker of the House, the vice-president (as president of the Senate), and the president pro tempore of the Senate, who chairs the chamber when the vice-president is absent. The president pro tempore is normally a senator of the majority party who has considerable seniority. (The president pro tempore also succeeds to the presidency after the vice-president and Speaker.) The vice-president has little influence in the Senate, except to break a tie vote. By contrast, the Speaker of the House is very influential.

## THE SPEAKER OF THE HOUSE

The Speaker is the most influential member of the House. He is the presiding officer of the chamber and the recognized leader of his majority party (he is chosen by the members of the party). He is not a member of any standing committee but can still vote on bills and enter into floor debate. The Speaker interprets House rules, refers bills to appropriate committees, rules on procedural questions, puts questions to a vote, and announces the outcome of floor voting. The most effective Speakers work closely with their staff, the House majority leader, the party "whip" (the latter polls members before key votes and sends them summaries of bills coming up for floor debate), and minority party leaders. The Speaker, even if a member of the opposing party, should try to have a reasonably close relationship with both the president and the president's staff. Finally, the Speaker is next in line to become president after the vice-president.

## SENATE LEADERS

While the Senate does not have a leader who is equivalent to the Speaker, the Senate majority leader is the proverbial "center" of the majority party's communications network. The majority leader must work closely with the

Senate minority leader, as well as with the president (note that the majority party in Congress has been the Democratic party in recent years, but the president has been a Republican in five of the last six presidential administrations). The majority leader does have the right to be recognized first on the floor when debate begins on a bill. Senate majority leaders have varied in their overall legislative effectiveness. Few have matched Lyndon Johnson's legendary abilities displayed during the late 1950s and early 1960s.

## The Committee System

Congress does its legislative work through the system of standing committees and smaller subcommittees. Committees are the "mini-legislatures" whereby the vast volume of legislation can be parceled out in an effective division of labor. Imagine each one of the 20,000 bills in the two-year congressional term being considered by the entire House and Senate! Little would be accomplished. In addition, representatives and senators become "specialists" by serving on a particular committee and acquiring expertise in energy matters, national defense issues, taxation, or agricultural subsidies, among others. Naturally, the freshman representative wants to get on the right committee, one that has prestige and which deals with issues important to his or her constituents back home. A representative or senator from Iowa would probably be more interested in the agricultural committees than in the Public Works and Transportation (House) or Governmental Affairs (Senate) committees.

### CONTROL OVER COMMITTEE ASSIGNMENTS

In the Senate, the Democratic Steering Committee makes the party's committee assignments; the Republicans use their Committee on Committees for their assignments. In the House, the Democrats give this power to the Democratic Steering Committee, which includes the Speaker and other party leaders. House Republicans have formed a Committee on Committees, which includes one member from each state having a Republican representative. However, the final selection is assigned to the executive committee of fifteen members headed by the party's floor leaders.

The actual division of seats on each committee is based upon the percentage of party strength in each house. If 60 percent of the Senate were Democrats, then the 60 percent figure would be carried over to each committee.

### THE ROLE OF SENIORITY

Committee assignments have traditionally been guided by the principle of seniority. This is especially true regarding committee chairmanships. The representative or senator who has served the longest consecutive period of time on a particular committee and is a member of the majority party stands a good chance of becoming chair. Seniority is no longer an automatic procedure, however. For example, House Democrats removed three committee chairmen in 1975, and there have been periodic "revolts" against the seniority principle. Reforms now require that all chairs be approved by secret ballot of each party's rank-and-file.

Some younger members of Congress criticize the seniority practice, arguing that longevity of service is not always associated with legislative competence. But supporters claim that seniority helps avoid political squabbling among competitors for chairmanships, develops expertise and experience, and promotes stability in committee memberships over time.

### COMMITTEE/SUBCOMMITTEE CHAIRS

Legislators who chair committees and subcommittees are influential members of Congress; they can delay or expedite legislation to a significant extent. However, reforms have forced committee chairs to operate in a far less tyrannical manner than was previously the case. Ironically, subcommittee chairs have increased their powers, and are far more likely to delay bills or refuse to hold hearings. The power of the subcommittee has complicated the legislative process by decentralizing authority and diffusing responsibility.

# A BILL'S PASSAGE INTO LAW

More than 20,000 bills may be introduced in Congress during a typical two-year congressional term. Yet only 5 percent to 10 percent of all legislative proposals are typically converted into finished laws. The many legislative obstacles in Congress help explain why this high failure rate exists.

**Who Proposes a Bill?**

The majority of bills are proposed by officials in executive departments and agencies in accordance with presidential wishes. Presidential supporters in Congress can then formally introduce these bills. In addition, legislative ideas can originate with interest groups and even private citizens. Finally, representatives and senators may also draft their own bills.

A bill may be introduced in either house or simultaneously in both houses. Note, however, the constitutional stipulation that all revenue or tax bills must first be submitted in the House of Representatives.

**Different Kinds of Bills and Resolutions**

### PUBLIC BILLS

These bills are measures applicable to the entire nation, such as a defense-spending bill, a new tax measure, or a clean-air bill.

## PRIVATE BILLS

These bills apply to specific individuals. For example, a person may want special permission to become a naturalized citizen.

## JOINT RESOLUTIONS

These are resolutions which require approval by both houses, as well as the president's signature. They are equivalent to a law. Joint resolutions are also used to propose constitutional amendments.

## Introducing a Bill and Referring It to Committee

The formal introduction of a bill involves the assignment of a number by the House or Senate clerk (H.R. 2,000 would be the 2,000th bill introduced in the House during the term; S is the prefix in the Senate). The bill is titled and given a short summary description. The bill is then entered in the *House Journal* and in the *Congressional Record*. This bill now receives its *first reading*. Its *second reading* will occur during floor discussion (if it gets that far); the *third reading* will occur just before a final vote is taken by the House and/or Senate membership.

After the first reading, the Speaker of the House sends the bill to the appropriate committee of jurisdiction. Thus, a bill dealing with new federal price supports for farm crops would be sent to the House or Senate agricultural committees.

The selection of a committee is very important, since one may be more sympathetic to the bill than another. Frequently, several committees can claim jurisdiction over a proposed bill—this has been the case with energy legislation.

In the Senate, the presiding officer of the Senate (in practice, usually the majority leader, or a junior senator appointed by him) refers the bill to the appropriate committee. For example, a bill dealing with benefits for veterans would be sent to the Senate Veterans' Affairs Committee.

## THE COMMITTEE/SUBCOMMITTEE CONSIDERS THE BILL

Woodrow Wilson once wrote that "Congress in its committee rooms is Congress at work." Currently, there are 38 standing or permanent committees in Congress and about 240 subcommittees (smaller committee divisions within each standing committee). Many bills are "killed" or "pigeonholed" in committee.

The committee chair (always a member of the majority party) will delegate the bill to the appropriate subcommittee. Public hearings will be held whereby interested parties, lobbyists from interest groups, and government officials can testify for or against the legislation. Hearings can attract media attention while giving opposing sides a chance to be heard. After these hearings, the subcommittee can take any of the following actions: (1) report the bill favorably with a "do pass" recommendation; (2) refuse to report the bill out, thus killing the bill; (3) report the bill out in an amended or changed format; (4) report the bill unfavorably; (5) report out a "committee bill"— i.e., a completely new bill that the subcommittee has written as a substitute for the original bill.

The full standing committee usually accepts the subcommittee's recommendation. A bill favorably reported out in the Senate is placed on a "calendar" for floor action. In the House, another obstacle to the bill looms—the Rules Committee.

### THE RULES COMMITTEE

This committee is the "traffic cop" of the House. This committee grants a "rule" which allows a bill to go to the House floor at a scheduled time for discussion, debate, and a final vote. A time limit on floor debate may also be included in the rule.

### OPEN AND CLOSED RULES

There are two kinds of rules—"open" and "closed." An open rule permits the bill to be amended on the floor, while a closed rule forbids any amendments. If no rule is forthcoming from the Rules Committee, then the bill has effectively been killed for that congressional session.

In previous years, a very conservative Rules Committee blocked liberal legislation, especially in regard to civil rights. Today, the Speaker of the House has acquired the power to nominate the majority party members and chairperson of this vital committee. Thus, the Rules Committee has become more responsive to the will of the House leadership.

### THE DISCHARGE PETITION

The House may use the discharge method whereby an absolute majority—218 members—sign a petition requesting that the bill be forced out of committee for floor consideration. The Rules Committee may have a bill discharged after seven legislative days. (Other House committees can be subject to a discharge if a bill is not reported out within thirty days after initial referral.) In the Senate, a discharge resolution can be initiated through a simple motion by a member.

## The Bill Is Considered on the Floor of Each House

As a reminder, the second reading of the bill occurs when it reaches the floor. Once the "rule" is approved, actual debate commences. But the nature of the debate differs considerably between the House and Senate. Normal debate per House member is five minutes, given the 435 legislators in the lower chamber. In the Senate, composed of one hundred members, debate is virtually unlimited.

In order to expedite House debate, the Committee of the Whole device is employed. In effect, the House becomes one large committee of itself. Rules are not as strict and floor action is faster, since only 100 House

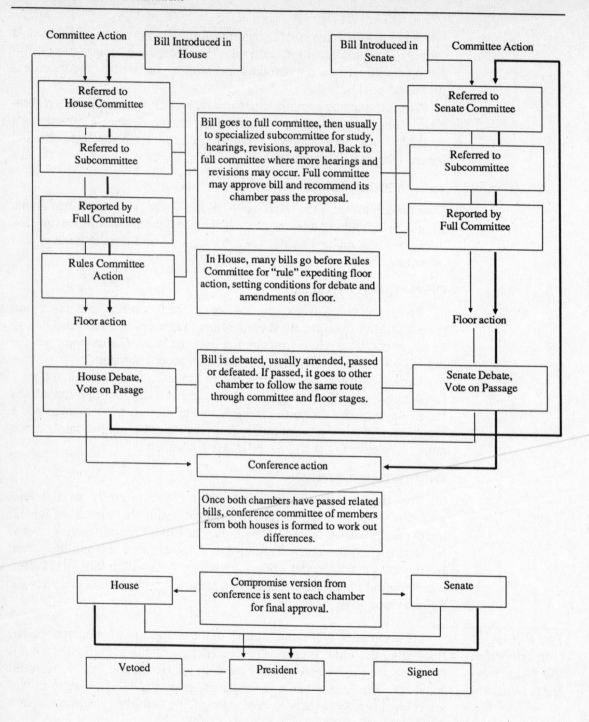

*Fig. 6.1   How a Bill Becomes a Law*
Source: "CQ's Guide to Current American Government," Spring 1992
(Washington D.C.: Congressional Quarterly Inc.), p. 119.

members are required to conduct business, not the normal majority of 218. Debate and voting on each section of the bill proceeds (amendments may also be proposed and voted upon per section) until the entire bill has been covered. The Committee of the Whole is now finished and promptly dissolves itself. The House now goes back into regular session and must approve or reject the Committee of the Whole's action by a vote of the total membership.

In the House, the majority and minority floor leadership agree on how they will divide debating time. At any point, a House member may "move the previous question" or demand that a vote be taken on the bill. If such a motion is approved, only forty minutes of additional debate is permitted.

### House Voting

The House has four different methods for floor votes:

1. voice votes are the most common, the Speaker or presiding officer determining which side—the ayes or nays—has won by sheer volume;
2. standing votes occur if the voice vote is close. All House members in favor, then all members opposed, stand and are counted by the House clerk;
3. teller votes, rare today, have a "teller" from each party who counts members who pass between them, for and against;
4. roll-call votes, also known as a recorded vote, can be demanded by one-fifth of the members present.

Today, the House has a computerized voting system for all recorded votes. Members' votes appear on a large master board above the Speaker's chair. Voting is over when the Speaker locks the system (members are usually allowed fifteen minutes to cast their vote). A tremendous saving of time results from use of this system. By comparison, the Senate uses voice, standing, and roll-call votes, but does not have an electronic voting board. Still, less than ten minutes is typically needed for a roll-call vote in the much smaller Senate. After approval, the bill is engrossed, printed in its final form. Then it is read a third time, voted on, approved, and signed by the Speaker. A House page transports the bill to the vice-president's desk in the Senate. (Remember, the vice-president of the U.S. is the presiding officer of the Senate, according to the U.S. Constitution.)

### Senate Debate

The Senate of the United States is more of a "debating club" in comparison to the House. Debate is unrestricted in the Senate—i.e., senators may speak for as long as they wish. There is no five-minute time limit. Also, senators, once they have the floor, may speak on any topic they choose.

### THE FILIBUSTER

A filibuster is possible in the Senate. It is a means whereby senators may deliberately try to talk a bill to death. The filibuster prevents a final vote on the bill, since all debate must end before the vote can occur. The record for a "one-man" filibuster is the twenty-four hours and eighteen minutes of continuous talking by Senator Strom Thurmond of South Carolina against the passage of the Civil Rights Act of 1957 (the filibuster was unsuccessful). Many other filibusters have been team efforts, in which senators speak one after another in order to delay or obstruct a bill.

A filibuster can be ended by the cloture process, whereby sixteen or more senators sign a petition requesting a cloture vote. If 60 percent of the senators present vote for cloture, then each senator is restricted to one hour of debate. Cloture votes are not easy to attain, as fewer than one-third have been historically successful. Cloture votes are also rare in the Senate, for senators are reluctant to interfere with legislative custom. They also see the filibuster as a weapon of the minority which they may want to use one day. Still, a successful cloture vote means that a vote can occur on the bill. If a majority of the Senate concurs, then the bill has finally been approved.

## Role of the Conference Committee

A conference committee's function is to reconcile different House–Senate versions of a bill. For example, a House student-loan bill which authorizes loan payments for four years and the Senate version which allows two years of loans are not identical. Members of the standing committees who originally debated the bill in both houses will now work together to arrive at one bill. If they cannot arrive at a compromise, the bill dies; if they can, then the conference bill is sent to each floor chamber for a final vote. Rarely does the Congress reject the work of the conference committee. Also, the "conference" bill cannot be amended. It must be approved by both houses. When this happens, the bill is signed by the Speaker of the House and Senate president pro tempore. The bill is sent to the president of the United States for final consideration.

## The President Now Decides

The president has four choices in regard to the bill on his desk. First, he may choose to *sign the bill* and thus turn the proposal into an actual law. Second, the president can *veto the bill*—i.e., reject it outright. The unsigned bill is then sent back to the house where it originated, along with the president's reasons for the veto. Congress can respond by overriding the presidential veto through a two-thirds vote of each house. If this proves impossible, the veto is sustained—i.e., it remains in effect, and the bill is dead for the particular session. Historically, few presidential vetoes are overridden. Third, the president can *keep the bill on his desk* for a period of ten days (Sundays excluded) without signing it or exercising the veto—in this instance the bill automatically becomes law. The fourth choice is the *pocket veto*—the president doesn't act on the bill and Congress adjourns within ten days of the bill's submission to him.

## THE LACK OF AN ITEM VETO

While many state governors have the power of an item veto, presidents do not possess this power under the Constitution. Presidents cannot reject individual sections of a bill—they must accept or reject the entire bill. This lack of an item veto encourages legislators to add riders to a bill—i.e., unrelated provisions which "ride" through the legislative process and which may be repugnant to the president. Recent presidents have urged Congress to approve the item-veto principle. But this is unlikely to occur since Congress would be yielding additional power to the chief executive.

*Throughout most of the nineteenth and early twentieth centuries, Congress was the active and dominant branch of the federal government. But presidents such as Woodrow Wilson, Franklin Roosevelt, Harry Truman, and Lyndon Johnson, among others, gradually took the initiative until the presidency became the center of American political life. Perhaps congressional prestige dropped to its lowest point in the late 1960s and early 1970s. Critics charged that the internal operations of Congress were undemocratic since elderly committee chairmen blocked progressive, liberal legislation. Furthermore, Congress had yielded control over war and the budget to the president. But the Watergate scandal and the Vietnam War diminished the prestige of the presidency. In addition, internal reforms made Congress more open, democratic, and decentralized. Newcomers to Congress were allowed more influence in the legislative process as well.*

*It bears repeating that most voters think favorably of their own representative or senator, but not of Congress as a collective institution. Many Americans perceive Congress as too slow and antiquated when compared to the dynamism of the modern presidency. Nevertheless, Congress has been a major source of political change in American society for more than two centuries. It almost certainly will continue to perform a similar function into the twenty-first century.*

**Selected Readings**

Auerbach, Joel D. *Keeping a Watchful Eye: The Politics of Congressional Oversight* (1990)

Cain, Bruce, John Ferejohn, and Morris Fiorina. *The Personal Vote: Constituency Service and Electoral Independence* (1987)

Dodd, Lawrence C., and Bruce I. Oppenheimer, eds. *Congress Reconsidered.* 5th ed. (1990)

Ripley, Randall B. *Congress: Process and Policy.* 5th ed. (1990)

Smith, Steven S. *Call to Order: Floor Politics in the House and Senate* (1989)

Wormuth, Francis D., and Edwin B. Firmage. *To Chain the Dog of War: The War Power of Congress in History and Law* (1989)

# 7

# *The Presidency*

*In the minds of many Americans, the presidency is the proverbial center of the political system. A large number of citizens do not know who their representatives are in Congress. But they will almost certainly know who the president is and have opinions as to the quality of his performance while in office. A powerful president dominates the news and is the subject of intense scrutiny by news columnists, historians, supporters and opponents in Congress, pollsters, and foreign leaders, among others. In this chapter, we shall examine constitutional perspectives on the presidency, presidential powers and roles, constraints on presidential power, the presidential "character," and the presidential bureaucracy.*

## THE CONSTITUTION AND THE PRESIDENCY

**The Founding Fathers and the Presidential Concept**

The framers of the Constitution accepted the need for a strong leader, but they also did not want the president (the person and the office) to evolve into a tyrant trampling upon individual liberties. Various checks and balances were placed upon the chief executive in an effort to constrain presidential power. None of the framers could have foreseen the degree of power a twentieth-century president would attain. In fact, they believed that the Congress would be the dominant institution of American government.

**Article II of the Constitution**

Article II has a brief description of presidential powers and four short sections which respectively vest executive power in the president, establish his control over foreign affairs through his commander-in-chief role and treaty-making powers, delineate his responsibility to inform Congress about the "state of the Union" and "to take care that the laws be faithfully executed," and cover impeachment procedures by which a president can be removed from office.

## CONSTITUTIONAL QUALIFICATIONS

The Constitution lists only three qualifications that one must possess to be president (Article II, Section 1). A chief executive must be at least thirty-five years old, be a natural-born citizen, and be a resident of the United States for at least fourteen years.

## UNWRITTEN QUALIFICATIONS

There are innumerable unwritten qualifications for the presidency. Nearly all presidents have been white, Anglo-Saxon Protestants. The only Catholic president was John F. Kennedy. There has never been a black, Hispanic, female, or Jewish president of the United States. In the modern era (from 1932 to the present), presidents have been college graduates and men who have had ample political or military experience before assuming the office.

## Constitutional Amendments Relating to the Presidency

There are two constitutional amendments which affect the presidential term and the issue of succession.

### THE TWENTY-SECOND AMENDMENT

The framers originally agreed on a four-year term, believing this would be enough time for a president to gain experience and develop leadership skills. Until Franklin D. Roosevelt held office, no president had served longer than two full terms. In 1951, the Twenty-second Amendment was adopted. In part, it stated:

> No person shall be elected to the office of the President more than twice, and no person who has held the office of President, or acted as President, for more than two years of a term to which some other person was elected President shall be elected to the office of the President more than once.

It is possible for an individual to serve for ten years as president. A vice-president who served two years or less of an unfinished term would then be eligible to serve an additional two full terms or eight years.

### THE TWENTY-FIFTH AMENDMENT

This amendment permits the president to appoint a new vice-president when there is a vacancy in that office (if the vice-president has resigned, died, been assassinated, or impeached). The presidential appointment is subject to congressional approval. Also, if the president is unable to carry out his duties temporarily, the vice-president becomes acting president. If a conflict ensues later between the acting president and the original president over who shall occupy the office, Congress will decide who the president will be by a two-thirds vote of both houses within twenty-one days.

## PRESIDENTIAL SUCCESSION

While the Twenty-fifth Amendment makes it nearly impossible for the line of succession to pass below the vice-president (nine vice-presidents have succeeded to the presidency in American history), there is always the remote possibility that simultaneous vacancies could occur in both the presidential and vice-presidential offices. In this case, the order of presidential succession would be: the Speaker of the House; president pro tem (the presiding officer when the vice-president is absent) of the Senate; secretary of state; secretary of defense; and down through the other cabinet department heads.

## *Presidential Salary*

According to the Constitution, the president's salary is established by Congress and cannot be changed during a term in office. The salary was last set in 1969 by Congress at $200,000. (The president also receives an annual $50,000 expense account, which is taxable.) While the presidential salary seems low by today's standards, his fringe benefits—the White House, a yacht, *Air Force One*, the Camp David hideaway, and extensive medical care, among them—would probably be worth an equivalent of $15 million to $20 million a year for an average wage earner.

It should be noted that former presidents receive a lifetime pension of nearly $100,000 a year. Each widow of a president is allowed a pension of $20,000 a year.

## *Impeachment and Removal from Office*

As described in the Constitution, the House of Representatives can "impeach" a president (and other federal officers) by bringing charges against him for misuse of powers or committing criminal actions. If the Articles of Impeachment are approved by a House majority, the Senate then sits as a jury to determine ultimate guilt or innocence. A two-thirds majority vote by the Senate is required for conviction.

The chief justice of the Supreme Court serves as the presiding judge over the impeachment trial. Only President Andrew Johnson was ever impeached by the House. He avoided conviction in the Senate by a single vote. President Richard Nixon resigned the presidency in 1974 before formal impeachment voting could proceed in the lower chamber.

# THE ROLES AND POWERS OF THE PRESIDENT

## Chief of State

As the chief of state, the president symbolizes the government of the United States and the unity of the nation. He often presides over important ceremonies, such as laying a wreath upon the Tomb of the Unknown Soldier or throwing out the first baseball when the major-league season begins in April. Of course, he frequently greets foreign leaders upon their arrival in Washington.

## Leader in Foreign Policy

The Constitution gives the president the power to appoint U.S. ambassadors and formulate international treaties. Both actions require Senate approval. While a president's ambassadorial appointments are seldom repudiated, the Senate has rejected treaties at least twenty times. The most famous example was President Wilson and the Treaty of Versailles, which established the League of Nations after World War I. A more recent example occurred in 1979, when President Carter's SALT II Treaty (arms-control limitation) was never acted upon by the Senate.

Presidents also use the executive agreement, which is an international understanding with another head of state. Executive agreements, which are far more common than treaties, do not require the advice and consent of the Senate. (The Supreme Court has ruled that executive agreements have the same legal status as treaties.) Executive agreements have covered such areas as the establishment of military bases overseas and resolving financial or international trade disputes. Historically, there have been more than 9,000 executive agreements, compared to some 1,300 treaties. Treaties are considered binding on succeeding presidents, but this is not the case with executive agreements.

## The Commander-in-Chief Role

The Constitution asserts that "The President shall be Commander in Chief of the Army and Navy of the United States, and of the Militia of the several States, when called into the actual service of the United States." In short, the American military is under civilian control, and the top civilian "general" is the president (General MacArthur found this out in April 1951 when he was removed from his Korean command by President Truman for insubordination). Presidents may dispatch troops overseas or use military force as deemed necessary. The president would also give the order to use nuclear weapons against an adversary. As commander in chief, the president can send the armed forces into conflict situations which may lead to full-scale, undeclared wars. (Presidents have ordered troops overseas more than 200 times in American history.) Truman's dispatch of troops to Korea in 1950 and Johnson's commitment of more than a half-million troops to Vietnam from 1965 to 1968 are contemporary examples. Earlier illustrations include Thomas Jefferson conducting a war against the Barbary pirates in the early 1800s, and John Adams ordering the navy to stop French warships from harassing the American merchant fleet in 1798. Neither Adams nor Jefferson sought congressional approval.

However, only Congress has the constitutional right to declare war. (It has done so five times.) In order to check presidential power in the war-making arena, Congress passed the War Powers Act in 1973 (over Nixon's veto), requiring that a president: (a) consult with Congress before sending troops into combat overseas; (b) inform Congress within forty-eight hours after the dispatch of troops as to the reasons behind and implications of this decision; (c) withdraw those combat forces if Congress votes to do so after sixty days have qassed; (d) complete the withdrawal within an additional thirty-day period. In general, presidents have ignored the War Powers Act, and Congress has not forced a president to abide strictly by its provisions (there is also a question about its constitutionality). For example, Congress permitted President Reagan an eighteen-month period during which American troops could stay in Lebanon in 1983 (they were pulled out early after a tragic terrorist bombing occurred, killing 250 U.S. Marines). Conversely, presidents have tried to observe the consultation requirement of the act. President Bush did ask Congress for approval to use force in the Persian Gulf, which he ultimately received in 1990.

Presidents normally have a freer hand in conducting foreign policy, since Congress has traditionally deferred to them, especially in the post–World War II era. The president also has access to better information about foreign nations and leaders from various federal intelligence agencies, such as the Central Intelligence Agency. Finally, in times of international crisis, the public sees the president, not Congress, as the reassuring voice of the nation.

## Chief Legislator

The president plays a vital role in proposing new legislation, while exercising the right to approve or veto laws passed by Congress. Presidents are the only nationally elected government officials (along with vice-presidents). They will frequently try to rally the country behind their legislative agenda through TV speeches, press conferences, newspaper interviews, and radio appeals. Massive public support may influence Congress to vote for the president's legislative programs.

### THE PRESIDENT'S THREE MAJOR ADDRESSES

The president delivers three major addresses which relate to legislative proposals. The State of the Union message is presented annually before a joint session of Congress. In the National Budget message, the president evaluates economic conditions and suggests federal expenditures in different policy areas. The president analyzes economic trends and difficulties in the Annual Economic Report. In addition, the president's staff prepares innumerable legislative recommendations for Congress to consider.

## THE PRESIDENTIAL VETO

The veto power allows the president to reject legislation passed by Congress. There are a number of ways he can exercise the veto:

> a. the president may keep a bill for ten days and neither sign it nor send it back to Congress. If Congress is still in session after the ten days have elapsed, the unsigned bill becomes law;
>
> b. the president may actually veto the bill by means of a written statement noting the objections and delivering the actual bill back to Congress. Congress has the opportunity to override the veto by a two-thirds vote of each house. This is difficult to attain. The vast majority of presidential vetoes are sustained—i.e., they remain in effect. For example, President Carter had only two vetoes overridden out of a total of thirty-one. Franklin Roosevelt, in his twelve years in office, had 626 of 635 vetoes sustained;
>
> c. the president may employ the pocket veto whereby Congress adjourns within ten days after receipt of the bill and the bill goes unsigned. In effect, the president "pockets" the bill without giving Congress the chance of overriding the veto.

## THE ITEM VETO

Presidents, unlike forty-three state governors, do not have the power of an item veto. They have to approve or reject the *entire* bill. They cannot disapprove only certain sections or provisions. Although presidents have asked Congress to consider granting them this privilege, it seems unlikely that Congress will do so since presidential powers would be strengthened significantly.

## PRESIDENTIAL–CONGRESSIONAL RELATIONS

Whether presidents have a hostile or cooperative Congress vis-à-vis their legislative proposals depends upon a number of factors: presidential popularity, presidential communications skills, international and domestic conditions (is the nation at war, or does economic prosperity exist?), and whether or not the president's party controls Congress. However, conflict can occur even when the president's party has voting majorities in both houses. President Carter, a Democrat, had to confront a Democratic Congress which refused to pass many of his proposals, such as tax reform, national health insurance, and a comprehensive energy policy.

**Party Leader**

The president is the national advocate of his party's platform and political philosophy. He is expected to campaign for the party's congressional, state, and local candidates. However, presidents frequently have trouble passing along their popularity to other candidates. In 1986, President Reagan campaigned extensively for Republican senatorial candidates, but seven incumbent GOP senators were nevertheless defeated by their Democratic challengers.

Presidents are also active in raising funds for party candidates, appointing party members as ambassadors, judges, or cabinet department heads, and trying to increase party support in Congress. A president will also be concerned about how policy decisions will affect his party's prospects in forthcoming elections.

**Molder of National Opinion**

A dynamic president who uses television and radio effectively can definitely shape the public's views on key national issues. Some presidents, like John F. Kennedy and Ronald Reagan, were especially skilled communicators whose dramatic press conferences and TV speeches influenced the views of millions of American voters. Other presidents have been less successful due to their personality or historical circumstances (the Grant and Harding administrations were plagued by scandal and corruption). Presidents who try to sell the public unpopular positions may find opinion "backlashing" against them, as was the case with Lyndon Johnson's support for the Vietnam War.

Presidential popularity tends to drop over time. Consequently, many presidents leave office with lower public-approval ratings than when they first entered the Oval Office. One explanation is the "coalition of the minorities" principle, whereby presidents gradually antagonize one group after another due to their decisions. Inevitably, collective disillusionment with presidential policies intensifies dramatically. Another reason is the inevitable gap between what presidential candidates promise during the campaign and what they can actually deliver once in office. Presidents are not all-powerful. They cannot always control events—an oil cutoff, a scandal caused by one of their subordinates, an economic downturn, among others. But they will nevertheless be lambasted by the political opposition and perhaps unfairly blamed by the general public.

**National Economic Manager**

Modern presidents are expected by the public to handle the national economy in a manner that will promote prosperity and abundance for all. This is unrealistic, since the economy can be influenced by private individuals and companies, both at home and abroad. Furthermore, many economic regulatory agencies, such as the Federal Reserve Board, determine interest rates and other monetary policies. They are not subject to *direct* presidential control.

Nevertheless, powerful presidents can forcefully present their economic remedies to the nation. A president who is able to move the nation out of economic recession prior to or during an election year (or take credit for existing prosperity) will be in an enviable political position. Thus, President Reagan benefited from a strong economy in his 1984 campaign against Walter Mondale. Conversely, high levels of unemployment, severe inflation, or a persistent recession will usually doom an incumbent president's chances of reelection. In early 1992, President Bush, aware of the impending November election, proposed several policies intended to shake the American economy out of a prolonged downturn and improve his prospects for reelection.

# CONSTRAINTS ON PRESIDENTIAL POWER

Presidents may be powerful, but their powers are not unlimited. As political scientist Richard Neustadt once put it, presidential power is really the "power to persuade." Presidents must bargain and convince other individuals and institutions in the political system that their policies will be effective. Presidents who imperiously try to "order" other political actors to do their bidding or are perceived as misusing their powers by the courts, the public, Congress, the media, or the bureaucracy will gradually lose their persuasiveness. President Truman once observed that his successor, former army general Dwight D. Eisenhower, would find the presidency to be different from the military. "He'll sit here and he'll say, 'Do this! Do that!' And nothing will happen. Poor Ike—it won't be a bit like the army. He'll find it very frustrating."

## Judicial Constraint

The Supreme Court can apply the judicial review process to all presidential actions. Notable examples have included the Court's ruling voiding President Truman's seizure of the nation's steel mills during the Korean War, and its rejection of President Nixon's claim of executive privilege in withholding the Watergate tapes as criminal evidence in 1974. Although appointed by the president, Supreme Court justices and other federal judges may not always render judicial opinions in accordance with presidential desires.

## Public Opinion as a Constraint

Public opinion can narrow presidents' policy options as well as undercut a chief executive's overall political effectiveness. President Ford's unpopular pardon of Richard Nixon from further prosecution stemming from the Watergate scandal clearly hurt Ford in his race against Jimmy Carter in 1976. In 1980, President Carter, unable to bring the hostages home from Iran and plagued by double-digit inflation prior to election day, saw a majority of voters select his challenger, Ronald Reagan. In normal times, public opinion is usually supportive of the president, but events can transform it into a tidal wave of discontent.

## Congressional Constraint

A recalcitrant Congress can make life miserable for a president, blocking or diluting legislative packages and "interfering" with foreign policy agendas. The authority of Congress to appropriate or withhold money for all federal programs and its right to practice legislative oversight—i.e., investigate and scrutinize the performance of the executive branch—are clear constraints.

### REPRESENTATIVES ARE LOCALLY ORIENTED

Members of Congress see their primary obligation to be one of service to the electorate. Presidential policies which affect their districts or states, such as the closing of key military bases, will be resisted even if these policies benefit the nation as a whole. Representatives can also be reelected many times, presidents just twice. "Lame duck" chief executives in their final year in office (they cannot or will not run again for another four-year term) often lose their political clout with many legislators on Capitol Hill.

### THE LEGISLATIVE VETO

This is another device to control executive power. Provisions for this veto are found in more than 200 laws passed by Congress. The legislative veto permits concurrent resolutions passed by two houses or simple resolutions passed by only one house to confirm, modify, undermine, or reject delegated presidential or executive-branch authority found in prior legislation. The legislative veto was found to be unconstitutional in the 1983 case of *Immigration and Naturalization Service* v. *Chadha*. The Supreme Court ruled that Congress could not reverse an immigration decision made by the attorney general through legislative resolution.

### IMPOUNDMENT

Some presidents have refused to spend appropriated money, claiming economic conditions dictated fiscal prudence. However, Congress has insisted that appropriations are laws which must be fully implemented by the president. The 1974 Budget and Impoundment Control Act stipulated that presidential spending delays or cancellations must be approved by either one or both houses of Congress. (As an example, President Nixon had objected to Congress's funding of water-pollution projects.)

## Media Constraint

The news media—television, radio, magazines, newspapers—can present to the public an image of presidential competence or failure, dynamism or passivity, sincerity or duplicity. The media concentrate their collective attention on the president, so the president's staff will cultivate a favorable presidential "image" through carefully chosen speeches, photo opportunities, and timely media interviews. Ronald Reagan's first term in office had very good media coverage, with journalists rarely criticizing the president for his mistakes. In effect, the media created what has been termed a "Teflon presidency" (blame simply did not "stick" to the president). Televised presidential press conferences can also promote a favorable image, as was the case with John F. Kennedy's showcased wit and charisma during the early 1960s.

Conversely, media exposure of scandal can hurt a president's reputation. The Watergate scandal's role in forcing President Nixon to resign in 1974 was unearthed through the investigative reporting of *The Washington Post*. Even President Reagan's image was tarnished by the heavily publicized Iran-Contra affair during his second term; this scandal suggested that the president had delegated too much authority to subordinates.

## Assisting the President—the Executive Organization

All presidents require assistance in making policy and managing the executive branch of government. The president's circle of advisers is drawn from the EOP or the Executive Office of the President. The EOP currently has nine agencies which have been created to help the president. (In the Bush administration, there have been about 1,600 employees in the EOP.) The most important agencies are the White House Office, the Office of Management and Budget, the National Security Council, and the Council of Economic Advisers. In addition, a president may call on the cabinet—the thirteen secretaries and the attorney general—for policy consultations.

## Components of the EOP

### THE WHITE HOUSE OFFICE (WHO)

The White House Office incorporates the main presidential advisers. A president's closest advisers in the White House Office are usually personal friends who helped him get elected or who have won his trust over the years. Also included are the president's legal counsel, press secretary, appointments secretary, and other clerical staff. Frequently, presidents choose a chief of staff to coordinate WHO activities. The chief of staff usually becomes a close adviser to the president. The selection of expert and dedicated WHO assistants can help a presidential administration succeed. They can prioritize policy objectives, resolve bureaucratic conflicts, assist with presidential speech-making, lobby congressional leaders, and protect the presidential image from a hostile press. Conversely, WHO personnel can handicap a president's effectiveness if they isolate him from important sources of information or are incompetent advisers.

### THE OFFICE OF MANAGEMENT AND BUDGET

The OMB is the largest agency in the EOP. It was originally the Bureau of the Budget, created in 1921 within the Department of the Treasury. (Nixon renamed it the OMB in 1970.) It drafts the president's annual federal budget, which is presented to Congress each January for approval. The director of the OMB can be a powerful figure, such as David Stockman under Reagan, or Richard G. Darman under Bush. The OMB director can also act as a clearinghouse agent for legislative proposals emanating from the executive agencies.

### THE NATIONAL SECURITY COUNCIL

The NSC was created in 1947 and is mandated to advise the "president with respect to the integration of domestic, foreign, and military policies relating to national security." The law requires the president, vice-president, and the secretaries of state and defense to be NSC members. The CIA director and chairman of the joint chiefs of staff have also become important NSC participants. In recent administrations, the national security adviser has been influential, be it Henry Kissinger under Nixon, or Zbigniew Brzezinski under Carter. (See chapter 11 for further details.)

### THE COUNCIL OF ECONOMIC ADVISERS

The CEA was established under the Employment Act of 1946. Three presidentially appointed economists (they can be removed from their positions at any time) analyze the economy and submit their findings to the White House. The CEA's advice is usually incorporated into an annual report. It frequently recommends policies designed to reduce inflation and unemployment.

## THE CABINET

The idea of the cabinet acting as an advisory body for the president has seldom been implemented. The first president, George Washington, had to mediate a quarrel between Jefferson, his secretary of state, and Hamilton, the secretary of the treasury. Abraham Lincoln, once confronted with a cabinet in total disagreement with him, announced the results as "seven nays, one aye—the ayes have it." In the modern era, only Eisenhower used the cabinet extensively.

The problem is that the fourteen cabinet heads are interested mainly in protecting their own departments. The current composition of the President's cabinet is as follows:

| Cabinet Post | Year Established |
|---|---|
| Secretary of State | 1789 |
| Secretary of the Treasury | 1789 |
| Secretary of Defense (Originally the Department of War, created in 1789) | 1947 |
| Attorney General | 1789 |
| Secretary of the Interior | 1849 |
| Secretary of Agriculture | 1889 |
| Secretary of Commerce (Originally the Secretary of Commerce and Labor) | 1903 |
| Secretary of Labor | 1913 |
| Secretary of Health and Human Services (Originally the Secretary of Health, Education and Welfare—renamed Health and Human Services in 1979 when the separate Department of Education was created) | 1953 |
| Secretary of Housing and Urban Development | 1965 |
| Secretary of Transportation | 1967 |
| Secretary of Energy | 1977 |
| Secretary of Education | 1979 |
| Secretary of Veterans Affairs | 1989 |

*Fig. 7.1   Membership of Presidential Cabinet*

These cabinet secretaries may become more concerned with obtaining resources for their departments than with the attainment of presidential goals or objectives. Also, cabinet members are frequently independent-minded, due to their previous successful backgrounds in the corporate and/or political worlds. Thus, they may even oppose presidential policies. Walter J. Hickel, Nixon's interior secretary, and Joseph Califano, Carter's secretary of health, education, and welfare, were both frequently at odds with the White House.

However, a president often employs an "inner or kitchen cabinet" (the latter name is derived from the presidency of Andrew Jackson), consisting typically of the secretaries of state, defense, treasury, and the attorney general, which may serve as a true advisory body. Of course, the precise configuration of the inner cabinet may vary due to the personal preferences of each president.

# *THE VICE-PRESIDENCY*

Historically, the vice-presidency was viewed by many observers as a job of little significance, but also one of potential importance. It was the nation's first vice-president, John Adams, who summed up the office by asserting: "I am nothing, but I may be everything." Woodrow Wilson's vice-president, Thomas R. Marshall, frequently told the story of two brothers who ran away from home. "One ran away to sea, the other became vice-president. Neither has ever been heard from again." The vice-president's only constitutional duty is to preside over the Senate and cast the deciding vote when a tie exists. However, recent presidents have given their vice-presidents important responsibilities. Jimmy Carter kept Walter Mondale informed about and involved in important administrative decisions. Reagan did the same for George Bush. George Bush assigned significant responsibilities to Dan Quayle. The vice-president remains the man who is "one heartbeat away from the presidency." Furthermore, the vice-presidential experience can prepare an individual for the presidential job. Perceptive observers note that thirteen of the nation's forty presidents first served as vice-presidents.

*W*hy have the powers of the presidency grown so much during the last five to six decades? There are two fundamental reasons: (1) a vast national economy and complex industrial society have accelerated public expectations that the president will practice effective oversight responsibilities; (2) the prevalence of wars and America's role as a world leader have also strengthened the presidency. Most Americans view the president as the decisive party who formulates foreign policy and acts first during times of international crisis.

The Constitution lists only three qualifications to be president—be a minimum of thirty-five years of age; be a natural-born citizen; and be a resident of the United States for at least fourteen years. Other constitutional provisions limit the president to no more than two full terms, provide for safeguards in case of presidential disability, and delineate impeachment procedures.

Presidential roles and power have expanded over time. They include serving as: chief of state; foreign-policy leader; commander in chief; chief legislator; party leader; molder of national opinion; and manager of national economic policies. Despite this expansion, presidential powers are still constrained by the courts, public opinion (presidential popularity tends to decline over time), the media, and Congress. Furthermore, the fundamental ability underlying presidential effectiveness is persuasion, not coercion.

*Presidents must rely on their close advisers, other key personnel, and advisory institutions within the Executive Office of the President. In contrast to the EOP, presidents rarely depend upon the cabinet. Finally, the status and responsibilities of the vice-presidents have increased in recent years. Their potential importance should not be overlooked.*

*While the memories of Watergate and Vietnam still haunt many Americans, there seems little doubt that the next generation will continue to look first to the president for national guidance, and even inspiration. Indeed, the forthcoming challenges of the twenty-first century are likely to place an even greater burden on those individuals who will reside at 1600 Pennsylvania Avenue.*

**Selected Readings**

Barber, James David. *The Presidential Character.* 3rd ed. (1985)

Burke, John P., and Fred I. Greenstein. *How Presidents Test Reality* (1989)

Edwards, George C., III. *At the Margins: Presidential Leadership Of Congress* (1989)

Hart, John. *The Presidential Branch* (1987)

Kernell, Samuel. *Going Public: New Strategies of Presidential Leadership* (1986)

Neustadt, Richard E. *Presidential Power* (1980)

Tebbel, John, and Sara Miles Watts. *The Press and the Presidency* (1985)

# 8

## *The Bureaucracy*

*O*ne out of every six Americans works for the "government" in the United States, be it at the federal, state, or local level. This chapter focuses mainly on workers who collectively comprise the federal bureaucracy. (The term "bureaucracy" is derived from the French word bureau, meaning "writing desk" or "office.")

Bureaucrats, or career employees of federal agencies, perform important functions, despite a public image of being lazy, wasteful, ineffective, or inefficient. For example, bureaucrats process FHA (Federal Housing Authority) or VA (Veterans Administration) mortgages and guaranteed loans for college students, maintain national parks, levy fines on industrial polluters, and serve as federal registrars protecting the right to vote.

Every American citizen's life is affected innumerable times by bureaucratic regulations, from the news he or she watches on television to the vitamins/minerals contained in a breakfast cereal, to the safety features found in a modern automobile. This chapter will cover bureaucratic functions, policy-making, personnel, and reforms, in order to better understand the "fourth branch of government," as the bureaucracy is sometimes called.

## THE NATURE OF BUREAUCRACY

**Characteristics of Bureaucracy**    A bureaucracy, a permanent administrative organization, has the following organizational characteristics: written procedures and rules which facilitate communication within the organization; specialization and division of labor where individuals work on specific tasks or jobs for which they have trained; a hierarchical, fixed chain of command where superiors give orders to subordinates; and impersonality, whereby standard rules are followed and all clients are in theory treated alike.

## The Need for Bureaucracies

The need for a large bureaucracy stems from a number of factors. A president cannot hope to enforce and implement multiple public policies without extensive bureaucratic assistance. Second, the broad policy directives of congressional legislation must be followed by specific bureaucratic rules and regulations which will give that law operational meaning. Third, the diversity of the American population and the ongoing technological and economic development of the nation have contributed to the need for increased regulation. Fourth, social welfare, social justice, and national defense concerns have also expanded the bureaucracy.

## Location and Size of Bureaucracies

Federal bureaucrats administer more than 1,000 different domestic and foreign programs. These bureaucrats are found in every city and state and nearly every country in the world.

There are close to 3 million federal employees (plus 2.1 million in the armed forces). Only about 12 percent of federal employees work in Washington, D.C. The rest are dispersed throughout the nation. (California alone has 300,000 federal workers.) For example, the Treasury Department's Internal Revenue Service is located in Washington, D.C. Yet most of the IRS tax work is carried out through regional, district, and local offices.

The largest federal bureaucracy is the Department of Defense, or DOD. The DOD employs over 1 million civilians globally in addition to its 2.1 million members of the armed forces. The VA (Veterans Administration) and Postal Service have 240,000 and 700,000 employees, respectively. Bureaucratic growth in other federal agencies or departments is linked to regulating and managing a complex American economy, overseeing the environment, assuring the quality or safety of consumer goods, and fostering scientific and technological research.

## Bureaucratic Responsibilities

### FUNDAMENTAL BUREAUCRATIC FUNCTIONS

These include providing political continuity, execution or implementation of decisions made by superiors (converting a policy decision into a program of action, then carrying it out), and providing specialized information about problems and policy proposals to Congress and other units of the executive branch.

Bureaucracies ideally separate politics from policy administration. Bureaucrats are obligated to interpret and apply the laws passed by Congress. For example, Congress may pass a Clean Air Act which mandates that major metropolitan areas in the nation comply with clean air standards, as developed and enforced by the Environmental Protection Agency (EPA).

The EPA will subsequently hold hearings on these proposed standards, listen to arguments by those parties opposed to or in favor of these regulations, and then finally issue directives along with penalties for noncompliance (note that agency rulings can be appealed to the federal courts and possibly overturned).

But the primary function of the bureaucracy is to assure continuity in government. Presidents come and go, Congress changes, but the bureaucracy is virtually immortal. The bureaucracy is the "permanent government" in that while there is job turnover, the responsibilities and duties inherent in a bureaucratic position are relatively clear and stable. New employees will perform specified duties much as their predecessors did.

## The Civil Service

There are two types of federal bureaucrats—political appointees and career civil servants. The president appoints the former (more than 2,000 appointments). The remainder belong to the civil service and receive their jobs through a formal, competitive process.

### HISTORY OF THE CIVIL SERVICE

In 1789, there were no career bureaucrats. George Washington and his successor, John Adams, argued that qualified people from the aristocratic, wealthier, and educated classes should handle key administrative positions. Both men also preferred that members of their own party, the Federalists, fill federal posts. Similarly, when Jefferson became president, he removed more than one hundred officials and substituted his own loyal party followers from the Democratic-Republican party.

### THE SPOILS SYSTEM OF ANDREW JACKSON

President Jackson's election in 1828 ushered in an even stronger reaffirmation of the "spoils system" begun by Jefferson ("to the victor belong the spoils"). Jackson dismissed some 200 presidential appointees and close to 2,000 other federal bureaucrats, replacing them with members of his own Democratic party. These people were fired regardless of their actual abilities. Jackson argued that the common man was capable of holding public office and that the party in power should control the bureaucracy. In addition, Jackson was the first president to reorganize the federal bureaucracy on a comprehensive scale.

### THE PENDLETON OR CIVIL SERVICE REFORM ACT OF 1883

Jackson's spoils system eventually led to a bloated, corrupt federal bureaucracy. Reformers urged the creation of a professional civil service based on expertise, not political cronyism. In 1883, two years after President James Garfield was assassinated by a disappointed office-seeker, Charles Guiteau, the new president, Chester A. Arthur, led the fight for civil service reform. The Pendleton Act made merit the basis for hiring personnel in the

| Year | Total Number of Employees | Number Employed in the Washington, D.C., Area |
|------|---------------------------|-----------------------------------------------|
| 1816 | 4,837 | 535 |
| 1821 | 6,914 | 603 |
| 1831 | 11,491 | 666 |
| 1841 | 18,038 | 1,014 |
| 1851 | 26,274 | 1,533 |
| 1861 | 36,672 | 2,199 |
| 1871 | 51,020 | 6,222 |
| 1881 | 100,020 | 13,124 |
| 1891 | 157,442 | 20,834 |
| 1901 | 239,476 | 28,044 |
| 1911 | 395,905 | 39,782 |
| 1921 | 561,142 | 82,416 |
| 1931 | 609,746 | 76,303 |
| 1941 | 1,437,682 | 190,588 |
| 1951 | 2,482,666 | 265,980 |
| 1961 | 2,435,804 | 246,266 |
| 1971 | 2,874,166 | 322,969 |
| 1981 | 2,858,742 | 350,516 |
| 1984 | 2,824,000 | 351,805 |
| 1988 | 2,981,000 | 354,000 |

*Fig. 8.1    Civilian Employees of the Federal Government, 1816–1988*
*Sources: United States Bureau of the Census. Historical Statistics of the United States,*
Colonial Times to 1970, *Bicentennial ed., Part 2, 1102–03; U.S. Office of Personnel*
*Management, Workforce Analysis and Statistics Division, monthly releases.* U.S. Bureau of
the Census, Statistical Abstract of the United States, 1990.
*1988 data rounded to nearest thousand.*

federal work force through competitive examinations. A bipartisan Civil
Service Commission was formed to administer the exams and establish
general hiring policies. Eventually, some 90 percent of the federal work
force would be covered by the merit system.

## CIVIL SERVICE REFORMS UNDER PRESIDENT CARTER

Under President Carter, the Civil Service Reform Act of 1978 replaced the Civil Service Commission with the Office of Personnel Management (OPM) and the Merit Systems Protection Board (MSPB). The OPM duties included enforcing civil service laws, testing applicants, setting pay scales, and appointing personnel.

In order to obtain a civil service job, applicants are required to take a test which demonstrates their competence for the position. The OPM then sends the names of the three top choices to the appropriate agency. Usually, under the "rule of three," one contender will be appointed.

The MSPB hears complaints from federal employees who claim mistreatment at work or job discrimination. Finally, the 1978 act also created the Senior Executive Service, which consisted of 8,500 high-level administrators and managers. The objective of the SES was to reward superior performance with substantial cash bonuses. However, SES members could be transferred or dismissed more easily than other civil servants.

## BUREAUCRATIC JOB ADVANTAGES AND OCCUPATIONS

Job security, along with generous fringe benefits, is a key attraction of a federal job, including liberal pensions upon retirement. Typically diverse federal jobs include white-collar managers, secretaries, clerks, mail carriers, engineers, scientists, doctors, telephone operators, veterinarians, aircraft workers, and plumbers. There are estimated to be more than 15,000 personnel skills in the federal bureaucracy.

## THE HATCH ACT

One disadvantage for federal employees is the legal limitation placed upon their political rights, which other Americans are free to exercise. The 1939 Hatch Act forbids them from actively campaigning for candidates or assuming leadership roles in a political party. The idea behind this law is to create a politically "neutral" bureaucracy and protect employees from political harassment by the party in power.

## FEDERAL EMPLOYEE UNIONS

About one-third of federal employees belong to unions such as the American Federation of Government Employees, the National Association of Government Employees, or the National Federation of Federal Employees. But these groups are not permitted to strike. They must confine their union activities to improving working conditions and representing civil servants at grievance or disciplinary hearings.

## BUREAUCRATIC PAY

Congress regulates the salary and job conditions for federal workers. At the lower and middle grades, civil service pay is equivalent to salaries paid to workers in private firms. Ironically, higher-level salaries are often lower than in private firms. The Civil Service General Schedule contains job grades ranging from GS 1 to GS 18 (the higher the grade, the better the salary). GS 16 to GS 18 grades are applicable only to presidential appointees.

## BUREAUCRATS' BACKGROUNDS

Typically, bureaucratic executives have come from a middle-class background and are male, college-educated, and white. Women, blacks, and Hispanics are underrepresented at the higher levels of civil service management (but this situation is slowly improving). However, in general, federal employees are broadly representative of the American population in terms of social class, religious affiliation, and educational level.

## *Organization of the Federal Bureaucracy*

### CONFUSING BUREAUCRATIC NAMES

Federal bureaucracies operate under a variety of labels which can be both contradictory and confusing. The term "department" is reserved for agencies of cabinet rank. "Agency" often refers to a major unit headed by a single administrator of near-cabinet status, such as the Environmental Protection Agency. But the title "administration" can also have the same connotation—the National Aeronautics and Space Administration or the Veterans Administration. "Commission" usually applies to those agencies which regulate business activities (Securities and Exchange Commission). "Corporation" or "authority" may apply to agencies headed by boards which conduct businesslike activities, such as the Tennessee Valley Authority.

Smaller units within a larger bureaucracy can also reflect inconsistency and confusion. "Bureau" is the name assigned to the major elements in a department, but "service," "administration," "office," "branch," and "division" can be used as well. Major units within the Treasury Department include the Internal Revenue Service, the Bureau of the Mint, and the Office of the Comptroller of the Currency.

### STAFF AND LINE

Any bureaucratic group can be classified as either staff or line agencies. Staff agencies are support organizations whose personnel advise administrators and assist in management. Line agencies directly perform the tasks for which the bureaucracy was formed. Employees within an agency may perform staff or line functions as well.

## THE MAIN DIVISIONS OF A BUREAUCRACY

The executive bureaucracy consists of the fourteen cabinet departments and their subdivisions, the independent agencies, government corporations, and the independent regulatory commissions.

## CABINET DEPARTMENTS

The fourteen cabinet departments are the major service units of the federal government, employing nearly 60 percent of all federal employees. They are line organizations accountable to the president. Each cabinet head, or secretary, is appointed by the president with the consent of the Senate (see chapter 7 for list of cabinet departments). All departments are subdivided into small units, usually called bureaus or agencies, which in turn have their own budget and staff. Bureaus are usually divided on the basis of function, such as the Bureau of the Census in the Commerce Department, or by clientele, such as the Bureau of Indian Affairs in the Department of the Interior.

Cabinet departments vary in size, budget, date of creation, and status. For example, the Department of Defense employs more than a million people and was created in 1789 (originally called the Department of War). The Department of Defense and the Department of Health and Human Services together spend more than 60 percent of all federal outlays. Compare Defense to the Department of Education, established in 1980, with fewer than 5,000 employees, and a much smaller budget. Cabinet departments can also be divided between "inner" and "outer" groups, with the former usually including State, Defense, Treasury, and Justice. Inner cabinet secretaries frequently are close counselors to the president and receive far more media attention than the "outer" cabinet secretaries.

## INDEPENDENT EXECUTIVE AGENCIES (IEA's)

These agencies are organizations with a single main function. Many of these agencies have thousands of employees and billion-dollar budgets. NASA and the Environmental Protection Agency (EPA) are two examples. Like cabinet departments, they are headed by one administrator, but they do not have cabinet status. Smaller, but no less important, examples include the Civil Rights Commission, the Federal Election Commission, and the Small Business Administration. Finally, there are dozens of other IEA's which the public rarely hears about, such as the Migratory Bird Conservation Commission or the American Battle Monuments Commission.

## INDEPENDENT REGULATORY COMMISSIONS (IRC's)

In 1887, Congress created the first independent regulatory commission, the Interstate Commerce Commission, whose original purpose was to regulate the railroads. Subsequently, new commissions were established to supervise other areas of American economic life. For example, the FTC—Federal Trade Commission—tries to protect consumers from false advertising while enforcing the antitrust laws. The FCC—Federal Communications Commission—licenses and regulates television and radio broadcasting. The SEC—Securities and Exchange Commission—guards against fraud in the buying and selling of stocks and bonds. There are eleven such agencies today.

Congress had two reasons for establishing the IRC's. The first was to prevent undue political pressures from interfering with their regulatory assignments. Consequently, IRC's have boards of five to seven members appointed by the president, with Senate approval being necessary. However, commissioners, who serve fixed terms ranging from five to fourteen years (the length depends upon the particular IRC in question), cannot be fired by the president. Also, Congress has required that these boards not be dominated by one political party.

The second reason for creating IRC's was that they could provide closer regulation on a day-to-day basis than Congress. For example, the Food and Drug Administration has the staff and expertise to test new drugs for possible health risks. Congress has neither the time nor the expertise to perform this function.

**Commissions as Quasi-Legislative and Quasi-Judicial Bodies.** These agencies exercise legislative powers when they develop rules and regulations which are equivalent to laws. The IRC's fill in the details of the laws which Congress passes. For example, Congress has stated that railroads must provide "reasonable service" and charge the public "just and reasonable rates." The ICC will publish guidelines and regulations which the railroads must follow in order to accomplish the original congressional goals.

IRC's exercise judicial powers when they handle arguments over regulations procedures. If a railroad wants to increase its freight rates, then it will meet opposition from businesses that do not want to pay the higher rate. The ICC would hold hearings, much like a congressional committee, and then decide the issue.

## GOVERNMENT CORPORATIONS (GC's)

Government corporations combine characteristics of private business firms and federal agencies. However, government corporations differ from private corporations in that Congress decides a GC's purpose, and its personnel are public employees. Three examples are the Tennessee Valley Authority (TVA), the Federal Deposit Insurance Corporation (FDIC), and the Export-Import Bank. The TVA generates electricity and develops flood-control policies; the FDIC protects the savings of bank depositors; and the EIB makes loans to assist the export and sale of American products.

Government corporations are appropriate when the federal government wishes to provide a public service free from executive or legislative interference. Today, there are about sixty GC's.

Each government corporation has a board of directors whose members are appointed by the president and approved by the Senate. GC operations are financed by congressional appropriations and sometimes by their own practices (TVA sells electric power to its customers).

# BUREAUCRACY—INTERACTION WITH THE PRESIDENT, CONGRESS, AND THE PUBLIC

**Bureaucracy and the President**

President Harry S. Truman once told NBC correspondent David Brinkley that he experienced great difficulties in controlling the bureaucracy. John F. Kennedy once complained how difficult it was getting things done through the bureaucracy. Nixon bypassed the State Department bureaucracy by sending his secretary of state, Henry Kissinger, to talk directly to Chinese leaders. Nixon even tried to set up his own counter-bureaucracy within the White House. Other presidents have encountered similar frustrations with the bureaucracy.

Presidents have also tried to reorganize the bureaucracy, but with little success. President Nixon wished to eliminate the Departments of Health, Education, and Welfare; Housing and Urban Development; Labor; Commerce; Transportation; and Agriculture, replacing them with broad-based departments—like Natural Resources and Human Resources. President Reagan came to office promising the abolition of the Energy and Education departments, but failed to do so, actually adding a new Department of Veterans Affairs. In short, reorganization is threatening to established political interests, and thus is consequently resisted.

**Bureaucracy and Congress**

Congress passes laws which the bureaucracy must implement. It also controls the budget of an agency. However, Congress cannot always impose its will on a nonresponsive bureaucracy. For example, in 1978, Congress included a provision in the Airline Deregulation Act of 1978 to protect jobs of fired airline pilots and grant them additional unemployment wages. The Labor Department was supposed to write the regulations necessary to carry out this congressional wish. But, by 1984, more than 5,000 pilots had lost their jobs and no regulations had been written. Opposition from the airlines (they wanted to hire new pilots with lower salaries) and the Reagan administration's objection to new regulations benefiting labor unions contributed to the delay. Bureaucracies are sometimes paralyzed due to outside political pressures and strong interest groups.

### BUDGETS AND THE BUREAUCRACY

Bureaus which maintain close contact with congressional committees or which can appeal to a special-interest or "clientele" group can achieve their budgetary goals. For example, an agency responsible for government-guaranteed mortgages can appeal to realtors and construction firms to ask Congress for a funding increase.

### SUBGOVERNMENTS

Subgovernments, or "iron triangles," consist of heads of bureaucratic agencies, members of congressional committees which have an interest in the agency, and lobbyists for pressure groups. An example of a subgovernment would be farm lobbyists, the Agriculture Department, and the congressional agriculture committees and subcommittees. This "political alliance" can help a bureaucratic agency in resisting presidential calls for cuts in its budget or demands that it be abolished.

## Bureaucracy and the Public

Public complaints about the bureaucracy frequently involve the cost in time and money of filling out endless forms, the existence of too many unnecessary regulations, or irritating delays in bureaucratic performance (typically, late mail delivery or not receiving income-tax refunds or Social Security checks). However, opinion surveys indicate that about two-thirds of the citizenry are generally satisfied with the performance of individual bureaucrats. Most individuals who have personal contact with bureaucrats do not consider them to be personally rude or antagonistic. But the public does view bureaucrats, as a group, as being paid too much for doing too little.

# BUREAUCRATIC CRITICISMS AND REFORMS

## What Are the Main Criticisms of the Bureaucracy?

### RED TAPE

This refers to complicated rules or procedures that must be obeyed if the bureaucratic work is to be accomplished. Red tape can also mean bureaucratic delay or confusion and excessive paperwork. The term derives from the English practice of binding legal and government documents in England with a red-colored tape.

## INFLEXIBLE RULES

Bureaucratic rules are designed to handle routine cases in a standard way. These rules are not designed to handle cases which represent exceptions to those rules.

## THE COST OF COORDINATION

Issues which are complex may require coordination among diverse bureaucracies. Thus, when a new interstate highway is constructed, the Department of Transportation may have to consult with the EPA regarding increased air pollution from auto exhausts. Construction will invariably be delayed and project costs will increase.

Therefore, it is difficult to accelerate bureaucratic performance. Senator Dale Bumpers of Arkansas once described the federal bureaucracy as a "700-pound marshmallow which can be kicked, screamed or cussed at, but it is very reluctant to move."

## TURF BATTLES

Bureaucratic departments and agencies will compete over which one has the responsibility for implementing certain policies. Thus, the State Department and the Defense Department may struggle over how to resolve a foreign policy crisis—whether to favor diplomacy or the use of force. It is inevitable that bureaucracies will see problems from their own perspective or vision of the world.

In addition, not all government programs fall within the clear domain of one bureau. A new weapons system, be it a fighter or missile program, may be claimed by the army, navy, and the air force. Competition is expensive and can lead to unnecessary duplication. But when the DOD has tried to encourage more coordination and standardization, the three services have fought against the idea.

## CONTRADICTORY POLICIES

Government agencies frequently work at cross-purposes. The Department of Agriculture may give subsidies to tobacco farmers, but the Department of Health and Human Services will encourage the public not to smoke. Similarly, the Department of Agriculture teaches farmers how to increase crop yields, but it also pays farmers to produce fewer crops.

## WASTEFUL DUPLICATION

Two or more government agencies will often perform the same function. For example, both the Customs Service and the Drug Enforcement Agency seek to prevent drugs from being brought into the country.

## THE GRACE COMMISSION

In 1984, the Reagan-appointed Grace Commission concluded that bureaucratic streamlining could save more than $400 billion in only three years. The commission recommended reducing federal employees' fringe and pension benefits, adopting efficient accounting procedures, abolishing unnecessary jobs, and eliminating waste and mismanagement in virtually every government bureaucracy. The commission was heavily criticized by Congress and bureaucrats alike. Relatively few of its proposals were actually implemented.

## *Bureaucratic Reforms*

### PRIVATIZATION

Governments have contracted with private firms to furnish public services. Increasingly, some communities have relied on business firms to deliver the mail, not the U.S. Post Office. The federal government has tried privatization to a limited degree. Still, private firms can become "bureaucratized" as well, if their service market is extensive and complicated.

### SUNSET LAWS

A sunset law requires that bureaucracies be reevaluated periodically in terms of their worth, relevance, or effectiveness. If found wanting, the agency is abolished or reorganized. Some thirty states have sunset laws, but there is none at the federal level. Studies reveal that many more federal bureaucratic agencies are created than are ever eliminated. Thus, according to one study, some 250 new agencies have been created during the past two decades, but only about twenty-five have been abolished.

### OMBUDSMAN

Originally founded in Sweden, an ombudsman would be a "citizen advocate" who would receive complaints about bureaucratic performance and possibly take steps to resolve those problems. States and cities do have ombudsmen, and a federal law mandates that all states have ombudsman programs to monitor nursing homes which receive Medicare or Medicaid funding.

### WHISTLE-BLOWERS

Individuals who report corruption or waste in a federal bureaucracy are called "whistle-blowers." A classic case of a whistle-blower was A. Ernest Fitzgerald, a financial analyst in the Pentagon who revealed a $2 billion cost overrun for the Lockheed C5A cargo plane in 1970. Both the defense contractor and the air force had tried to conceal the overrun. Fitzgerald, who lost his job, was eventually reinstated, although at a lesser position. While there have been other whistle-blowers since Fitzgerald, the risks of retaliation from the federal employer do remain.

*B*ureaucracies are essential government structures designed to implement the laws and policies of the Congress and the president. The executive bureaucracy consists of the fourteen cabinet departments and their subdivisions, the independent agencies, government corporations, and the independent regulatory commissions.

Today, federal employees are hired under a merit system, as opposed to the "spoils system" of the past. Civil servants have good job security and decent salaries, although in some cases private-sector compensation may be better. Bureaucrats are broadly representative of the American population.

Finally, while there is a pervasive stereotype of the bureaucrat as an ineffective, lazy, and slow worker, the work of federal employees does involve essential citizen services and important regulatory activities.

Most of the major criticisms of bureaucracies still refer to red tape, inflexible rules, coordination costs, turf battles, contradictory policies, and wasteful duplication. Bureaucratic reforms—privatization, sunset laws, ombudsmen, and whistle-blowers—have had limited impact.

**Selected Readings**

Bryner, George C. *Bureaucratic Discretion: Law and Policy in Federal Regulatory Agencies* (1987)

Goodsell, Charles T. *The Case for Bureaucracy.* 2nd ed. (1985)

Riley, Dennis D. *Controlling the Federal Bureaucracy* (1987)

Rourke, Gary C. *Bureaucratic Politics, and Public Policy* (1984)

Wilson, James Q. *The Politics of Regulation* (1980)

# 9

## *The Judicial System*

*The national government had no court system under the Articles of Confederation. This weakness was remedied by Article III of the Constitution, which specifically provided for one court—the Supreme Court—and authorized Congress to create other courts as deemed necessary.*

*The American judicial system is probably the most powerful in the world. The basis of that power rests with the fact that American courts interpret the law, with the Supreme Court being the final interpreter of the Constitution. Since 1803, the Court has exercised the power of judicial review, the power to declare an act of Congress unconstitutional.*

## THE NATURE OF AMERICAN LAW

The judicial system is an adversarial one in which the courts allow two parties to bring their conflict to court before a judge. In theory, justice is the product of the struggle between these two contending viewpoints.

Federal judges must deal with real cases, not hypothetical ones. All disputes must be "justiciable"—i.e., conflicts must be resolved by legal methods. For example, a case would not go to court involving the question of whether Congress should be abolished. This would be a political question, not a judicial one.

**The Types of Law**

In a democracy, the law both protects and restrains the citizenry. Law may be defined as the principles, rules, and regulations affecting human behavior as established and enforced by government. The five basic types of law are common law, equity, statutory law, constitutional law, and administrative law.

## COMMON LAW

Common law is often termed "judge-made" law, those rules which have been created by judges through their decisions in numerous cases. Common law was derived from twelfth-century England, where judges traveled around the country and rendered decisions designed to remedy wrongs done to individuals.

The colonists brought the body of common law to America. Today, every state in the union bases judicial procedures on English common law, except Louisiana, which uses French or Napoleonic Law as the core of its legal system.

**The Principle of *Stare Decisis*.** The basic principle of common law is *stare decisis*, a term from the Latin meaning "let the decision stand." Judges apply precedents, previous court rulings, to future cases which involve similar situations.

## EQUITY

Equity law permits judges to issue orders preventing possible damage or to direct that some action be taken. Equity is used when simply waiting until a law is violated further would not be wise. For example, assume that a paper factory is polluting a nearby lake by illegally dumping toxic wastes into the water. A judge can issue an injunction, or a "cease-and-desist order," mandating that the factory's owners stop their unlawful actions.

## STATUTORY LAW

At the federal level, this is the legislation passed by Congress. There are two main kinds of statutory law.

**Civil Law.** Civil law represents one major type of statutory law in America. Civil law is concerned with disputes between two private parties, such as divorce. A civil case may also involve an individual's lawsuit against the government, as when an individual is unlawfully injured by an agent of the government.

**Criminal Law.** Criminal law, the second major type of statutory law, involves serious crimes against society, such as murder or armed robbery. Since the government is the enforcer of criminal law, it is the plaintiff (the party that brings the case to court) in all criminal trials; the party which is accused of the crime is termed the defendant. Criminal law violations range from misdemeanors (trespassing) to felonies such as bank robbery. The "state" prosecutes the accused individual in criminal cases. Note that an overwhelming number of all civil and criminal cases involve state law and hence are tried in state courts.

## CONSTITUTIONAL LAW

Constitutional law involves the interpretation and application of the U.S. Constitution, most notably by the Supreme Court, but also by other federal and state courts as well. The U.S. Constitution contains about 6,000 words, with many of its clauses stated in general terms. The precise meaning of constitutional provisions is left to the courts to interpret.

## ADMINISTRATIVE LAW

This body of law refers to those rules and regulations which are issued by bureaucratic agencies. As mentioned in chapter 8, Congress has given authority to these agencies to hold hearings regarding compliance with bureaucratic regulations.

# THE PARTICIPANTS IN THE JUDICIAL SYSTEM

## Litigants

Litigants include both the plaintiff and defendant. Litigants are in court for a number of reasons—typically to right a perceived wrong, change the existing law, sue for damages, or challenge actions of government and corporations. Litigants must have "standing to sue"—i.e., litigants must have a sincere interest in the case and be in danger of suffering an injury or harm from another party—private or public. Standing to sue has been broadened in recent years by "class-action suits," whereby a small group of people can sue so as to represent other people in similar situations. Class-action suits are typically employed in environmental, civil rights, or personal injury cases. Recent class-action suits have involved women who sustained injuries stemming from use of the Dalkon shield, workers becoming ill from prolonged exposure to asbestos insulation, and drivers suffering accidents caused by unsafe automobiles.

## Interest Groups

Interest groups understand the power of the courts to make public policy. They will seek out litigants who have strong cases. For example, the NAACP (National Association for the Advancement of Colored People) chose Linda Brown, a young schoolgirl in Topeka, Kansas, as the plaintiff who would challenge school segregation in 1954. The ACLU (American Civil Liberties Union) is another interest group which chooses cases according to its stated mission of preserving individual freedoms.

## Lawyers

In 1990, there were more than 700,000 practicing lawyers in the United States. Lawyers defend and prosecute individuals, translate policies into legal terminology, or enforce and challenge existing statutes. Formerly, lawyers primarily represented the wealthy classes in American society, but in recent decades public-interest law firms have become concerned about defending the middle and poorer classes of the citizenry. In particular, the federally funded Legal Services Corporation helps the poor.

## *Judges*

Judges are at the center of the judicial process. Ideally, judges are supposed to be "neutral umpires" who weigh the facts of a case and who guarantee that a court hearing is fair to all of the concerned parties. In reality, judges are human beings whose rulings will be influenced by their educational, social, and political backgrounds.

### BACKGROUNDS OF JUDGES AND JUSTICES

Judges serving in the federal judiciary are virtually all lawyers, and predominantly white males. Typically, federal judges have been politically active. In addition, the majority have been in their fifties or sixties, upper-middle to upper class, and Protestant. Consequently, minorities and women have been clearly underrepresented.

# *THE ORGANIZATION OF THE FEDERAL COURT SYSTEM*

## *A Dual Court System*

America's judiciary is a dual system—state/local courts and the federal judiciary. To reiterate, state/local courts handle the vast majority of cases in the nation, including divorces, child-custody disputes, suits between citizens, and traffic violations. Federal courts are concerned only with alleged violations of federal law or the Constitution. They also handle suits between citizens of different states.

The federal court system is composed of three basic levels: (1) district courts; (2) intermediate courts of appeals; (3) the Supreme Court. These are the constitutional courts which exercise the judicial powers found in Article III of the Constitution.

## *Jurisdiction*

Jurisdiction is the authority of a court to hear, try, and decide a case. The federal courts have jurisdiction over cases dealing with constitutional interpretation, questions of admiralty or maritime law, and in which the parties, or litigants, in the case are the United States, a state, or a citizen of a state suing another state. There are different types of jurisdiction:

### EXCLUSIVE JURISDICTION

Cases involving an ambassador, federal crime, infringement of a patent or copyright, or act of Congress can be heard only in a federal court.

## CONCURRENT JURISDICTION

Cases may be tried in either a federal or state court. A case involving citizens of different states is an example. (These cases are known as cases in diverse citizenship.) If the amount of money involved in the lawsuit is more than $50,000, the plaintiff can bring the suit to either court level. If the case is brought before the state court, the defendant can have the case transferred to federal district court.

## ORIGINAL/APPELLATE JURISDICTION

A court which hears a case for the first time has original jurisdiction. A court which is hearing a case on appeal from a lower court has appellate jurisdiction. District courts have only original jurisdiction, the courts of appeals only appellate jurisdiction, and the Supreme Court both original and appellate jurisdiction.

## Selection of Federal Judges

The president appoints all federal judges, provided the Senate confirms them by a majority vote. Presidents prefer judges who are members of their party and who share their political philosophy. Senatorial courtesy is followed whereby senators from the president's party have a veto on judicial appointments from their states. The Senate Judiciary Committee holds hearings on the nominees, with confirmation usually being automatic. In general, federal judges have lifetime appointments. They are subject to impeachment and removal if they are found guilty of criminal offenses while in office.

## U.S. District Courts

District courts are the federal trial courts, handling some 250,000 cases each year (about 80 percent of the entire federal caseload). There are ninety-four U.S. district courts, which are located in judicial districts in the nation and territories (one each in the District of Columbia, Guam, Puerto Rico, and the Virgin Islands). A large state, like California, has several district courts (it has four). Every state has at least one. District courts are the only federal courts which have grand juries (which indict individuals after determining there is enough evidence to justify a criminal trial) and jury trials to try defendants.

The number of judges in each district ranges from one to twenty-seven, depending upon population. Single judges typically hear a case, but three-judge panels are used in some instances (voting-rights cases or antitrust actions). Typical cases which will be tried in these courts for the first time (original jurisdiction) include federal crimes, such as tampering with the mail; counterfeiting; interstate theft; bank robbery; kidnapping; tax evasion; and treason. Civil cases involving more than $10,000, in which the U.S. government is a party, and bankruptcy cases filed in accordance with federal statutes are also typical.

## U.S. Courts of Appeals

Established by Congress in 1891, these courts were designed to relieve the burden of so many cases being handled by the Supreme Court. Today, most losing district court litigants appeal their cases to a United States Court of Appeals. (An average of 10 percent to 15 percent of all district-court cases are appealed.) However, appeals from federal administrative agencies, such as the Federal Trade Commission, can reach these courts as well. Currently, there are thirteen of these courts, one in each of eleven judicial circuits (regions), one for the District of Columbia, and a thirteenth court called the United States Court of Appeals for the Federal Circuit (it specializes in customs and patent appeals). The range of judges for each circuit is anywhere from three to twenty-four, with panels of three judges usually hearing cases.

These courts do not retry cases, but review records of the lower-court proceedings and evaluate arguments about legal questions raised in those cases. They have only appellate jurisdiction. Appeals-court justices can uphold the lower court decision or modify part of its ruling. An appeals court can remand (send back) a case to the trial court for additional review. The Courts of Appeals review about 35,000 cases a year.

## U.S. Supreme Court

The Court currently consists of nine members—the chief justice and eight associate justices (originally it had six, but was expanded to ten during the Civil War)—who are appointed for life by the president, with Senate

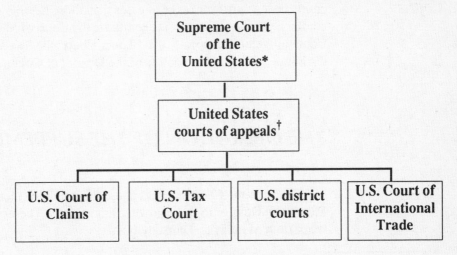

*Fig. 9.1   The Federal Court System*
*(connecting lines indicate the path of appeals)*
*\*The United States Supreme Court may also hear appeals from the highest court in each of the states, from the Court of Military Appeals, and from three-judge district courts.*
*†The United States courts of appeals may also hear appeals concerning decisions of federal regulatory agencies.*

confirmation. The Supreme Court is the court of last resort on all questions of federal law, due to its power of judicial review as first established in the 1803 case of *Marbury* v. *Madison*. It has both original and appellate jurisdiction.

### ORIGINAL JURISDICTION

The Court's original jurisdiction (Article III, Section 2) pertains to cases involving ambassadors of foreign nations and those in which a state is a party to a dispute. Examples of the latter have included an argument between California and Arizona over the control of water from the Colorado River, and a conflict between Maryland and Virginia over oyster-fishing rights. Fewer than five cases a year come to the Supreme Court due to original jurisdiction. The vast majority of cases before the Court fall under appellate jurisdiction.

### APPELLATE JURISDICTION

Under appellate jurisdiction, only cases which are appealed from lower courts are heard by the Court. Although more than 4,500 cases are filed with the Supreme Court each year, the Court reviews only an average of 300.

## Legislative or the Special Courts

Congress also has created legislative courts which serve a particular purpose and are staffed by individuals with fixed terms in office. These courts hear a narrower range of cases than those heard by the constitutional courts. Examples of legislative courts are the Court of Military Appeals, the Court of Veteran Appeals, the Claims Court, the Tax Court, the various territorial courts, and the courts of the District of Columbia.

# THE OPERATION OF THE SUPREME COURT

## Term

The Supreme Court's term is approximately nine months, from the first Monday in October to the following June or July. The Court is "open" each week from Monday to Thursday.

## Selection of Justices

The formal process involves presidential nomination and Senate confirmation. However, presidents realize that a Supreme Court appointment can influence public policy for decades to come. They are careful to select nominees who are competent, ethical, and, most important, share their own political values. Thus, President Reagan, a political conservative, selected conservative justices. Similarly, President Bush appointed Clarence Thomas, a black conservative, to the Court in 1991.

The Senate Judiciary Committee questions Supreme Court nominees carefully in open hearings which can sometimes be intensely critical. (Charges of sexual harassment against Clarence Thomas in 1991 led to widely publicized hearings about the morality of the nominee.) If the committee approves the nominee, the full Senate debates the nomination and ultimately votes to confirm or reject. (Thomas was narrowly confirmed by a vote of 52 to 48.) In the twentieth century, the Senate has rejected only ten out of forty-nine nominees.

## How Cases Reach the Court

About half the cases appealed to the Court are disposed of quickly by returning the case to a lower court. The Court usually perceives these "disposed cases" as: (a) not containing significant constitutional challenges; (b) it agrees with the lower-court ruling. Most cases reach the Court by a writ of certiorari ("to be made more certain"), an order by the Court to send up the case record because there is a claim that the lower court mishandled the case. The second method of reaching the Court is the appeal, a petition by one of the parties to a case requesting the Court's review of the lower court's decision. Most cases that do reach the Court come from the federal Courts of Appeals and the highest state courts.

### WHICH CASES ARE HEARD BY THE COURT

The Court does not issue advisory opinions—it must wait for a case. Interest groups frequently use test cases to challenge the constitutionality of an issue. Lawyers can file briefs explaining why their clients' cases deserve Court review. Poor appellants can file pauper petitions. A good example was the case of Clarence E. Gideon, who, while in a Florida prison serving time for burglary, petitioned the Court on the grounds that he had been denied a lawyer during his trial. Subsequently, the Court ruled in *Gideon* v. *Wainwright* that Gideon's right to have an attorney, as provided for in the Sixth Amendment, had been violated.

The Court decides which cases should be heard based on the "rule of four"—i.e., if four of the nine justices agree. Certiorari or appeal is then granted.

### HOW A CASE IS DECIDED

The Court decides about three-fourths of all reviewed cases without oral arguments. The Court issues a ruling and an unsigned written opinion termed a *per curiam* opinion which explains the decision. In the remainder of the cases, attorneys for the litigants submit briefs which argue the case's merits. Each side is permitted half an hour to present its case orally and answer questions from the justices. After these oral arguments, justices will meet in a closed conference, discuss the case, and eventually vote. The chief justice, if agreeing with the majority, will write the majority opinion or assign another justice to do so. If the chief justice is not with the majority, the senior justice may write the opinion. The final opinion may take months to be formulated. Other justices can write a concurring opinion which agrees with the majority opinion, but for different legal reasons. Dissenting opinions disagree with the majority decision. These opinions are important because they serve as precedents to be followed in similar cases in the future. Minority opinions can also become the majority's reasoning in a future case.

## THE ACTUAL DECISION

The final decision is announced in open court, with all decisions being published in the *United States Reports*. Cases can be decided by a mere 5-to-4 majority vote.

## THE DECISION'S IMPLEMENTATION

Lower courts are supposed to follow Supreme Court rulings. Government agencies and businesses must implement Court decisions. For example, state legislatures had to rewrite the death-penalty laws after the Court's *Furman* decision. (In the 1972 *Furman* v. *Georgia* decision, the Court ruled in a 5-to-4 vote that the death penalty as imposed by existing state laws was unconstitutional. The laws arbitrarily discriminated against minorities and the poor in that these groups were far more likely to be sentenced to death by judges and juries.) Local school boards had to formulate desegregation strategies after *Brown*.

Outright defiance of Supreme Court rulings is rare. Delay and evasion are the more common strategies, such as prayer still being practiced in the public schools or some communities resisting desegregation's implementation.

# HISTORICAL EVOLUTION OF THE SUPREME COURT

The Supreme Court has evolved through several distinct eras. The eras represent the changing political climates of the nation, as presidents have appointed new justices and public attitudes have changed toward the Court as well.

**The Marshall Era**

Chief Justice John Marshall instituted the idea of giving a single opinion for the entire Court, improved the Court's image, and built the judicial foundation for a powerful national government. He also wanted to protect private property through support for a strong national government.

**Taney Court**

From 1836 to 1864, the Taney Court developed the constitutional basis for state police powers. It could not resolve the slavery issue, and became infamous due to the Dred Scott decision, which held that a Negro could not be a citizen.

**Civil War and Reconstruction**

During this era, the Court tried to overturn Reconstruction statutes of Congress, so Congress repealed its appellate jurisdiction. Congress also reduced the size of the Court to seven members. Under President Grant, Congress reinstated the Court's size to nine justices.

**Era of Corporate Power**

From 1875 to 1937, the Supreme Court was sympathetic to the growth of corporate power; consequently, it limited national government and states' regulatory statutes. However, with the New Deal, FDR initiated extensive governmental measures to alleviate the Great Depression. Subsequently, FDR tried unsuccessfully to "pack the Court" (expand it to fifteen). However, after 1937 the Court began to uphold economic and social legislation favored by the federal government.

**Warren Court— 1953–1969**

The Court was dominated by a liberal majority, led by Chief Justice Earl Warren, who had been appointed by President Eisenhower (Eisenhower, a political conservative, later regretted selecting Warren). Its constitutional rulings benefited the disadvantaged, strengthened civil liberties in regard to self-incrimination, reaffirmed the right to counsel and speedy trials, changed the nature of legislative reapportionment, and promoted the historic desegregation policy incorporated in *Brown* v. *Board of Education* (1954).

**Burger Court**

Warren E. Burger replaced the retiring Earl Warren in 1969. As a Nixon appointee, Burger presided over a Court that became increasingly conservative. The Burger Court was less protective of the rights of alleged criminals and underprivileged individuals. Still, this Court preserved many of the civil rights and civil liberties gains implemented by the Warren Court. The Burger Court was supportive of a woman's right to an abortion (*Roe* v. *Wade*) and against laws which discriminated economically against women in the work force. But it also ruled that a woman who was on pregnancy leave from work was ineligible for temporary disability or sick-pay benefits. Additionally, the Burger Court required school busing to eliminate school segregation and upheld affirmative-action programs. Ironically for President Nixon, it was the unanimous decision of the Burger Court which forced him to turn over the secret White House Watergate tapes, thus eventually leading to his resignation in 1974.

**Rehnquist Court**

William H. Rehnquist became chief justice in 1986 upon Burger's retirement. Rehnquist had dissented from many of the Burger Court's majority rulings and, as chief justice, appeared to support greater state authority over the citizen. With the addition of Reagan Justices O'Connor, Scalia, and Kennedy, and Bush appointees Souter and Thomas, a conservative bloc appeared to constitute a voting majority by 1991. The retirement of liberal Thurgood Marshall further strengthened the conservatives. Only Justices Blackmun and Stevens could be counted on in the liberal bloc.

The Rehnquist Court has gradually eroded previous liberal decisions on the issues of criminal rights, abortion, and affirmative action. Most observers expected that *Roe* v. *Wade*'s pro-abortion ruling would eventually be overturned by the conservative Rehnquist Court.

# CONSTRAINTS ON JUDICIAL POWER

### Congress and the Courts

Congress can impeach judges or reject judicial appointments. Congress can also increase the number of judges, allowing a president to appoint more judges who share his judicial philosophy. For example, in 1978, Congress created positions for 152 new federal district and appellate judges, giving President Carter a chance to appoint more than 40 percent of the federal bench.

Congress can pass amendments or change a law that the Court had declared unconstitutional. The Twenty-sixth Amendment, giving eighteen-year-olds voting rights, was passed after the Supreme Court had ruled that Congress could not lower the voting age through regular legislation. In 1978, the Supreme Court ruled that a Tennessee dam's river location was endangering a tiny fish called the snail darter, an action in violation of the Endangered Species Act. In 1979, Congress passed legislation reversing the Court's ruling.

A powerful weapon of congressional control is the power of Congress to decide areas of jurisdiction for the lower courts and to redefine Supreme Court appellate jurisdiction. During the 1950s, Congress was hostile to Supreme Court rulings on civil rights, and proposed legislation which would have curtailed Court jurisdiction in this policy area.

### Public Opinion and the Court

The Supreme Court is sensitive to public opinion, especially changing political moods during different historical eras. Opinion not only restrains the Court, it may energize it. The Court must be sure to maintain its legitimacy before the people.

# *JUDICIAL ACTIVISM VS. JUDICIAL RESTRAINT*

*Position #1—
The Courts Are
Too Powerful
or Judicially
Active (the
Judicial-
Restraint
Position)*

Critics of the judiciary argue that courts go too far in policy-making. The courts have developed policies for school busing, abortion, nuclear power, affirmative action, environmental pollution, educational reforms, corrections, ad infinitum. Critics argue that since federal judges are not elected, they are the least democratic public officials to be found among the three branches. Courts should not go beyond the "referee" principle. Judicial restraint should be practiced, while leaving policy decisions to the executive and legislative branches of government.

*Position #2—
The Courts
Must Be
Judicially
Active*

Advocates of judicial activism argue that the courts frequently must make policy in order to meet pressing social needs and to help those who are weak economically or politically. For example, state legislatures and the Congress allowed segregated public schools to exist for many decades. Even if courts do make policy, these policies can be overturned by executive or legislative actions. For example, when the Supreme Court ruled the federal income tax illegal, Congress initiated the Sixteenth Amendment legitimizing such a tax. The amendment was ratified in 1913.

*The founders saw the importance of an independent judiciary as a bulwark against the potential political excesses of the executive and legislative branches. The courts have also evolved into protectors of those citizens who lack political influence or economic power.*

*It should be noted that the courts seldom attack the fundamental principles of American society. Collectively, they can be constrained by other institutions, as well as by public opinion. In short, most case decisions will reflect the basic values of American society at a particular point of time or within the context of a specific historical era.*

*The American judicial system is an adversarial one, in which legally resolvable issues, not "political questions," are handled. Litigants must have "standing to sue." The five types of law are common, equity, statutory, constitutional, and administrative. The two major legal divisions of law are civil and criminal.*

*Structurally, America's judiciary is a "dual" system, consisting of both federal and state courts. Federal courts may have either original or appellate jurisdiction, depending upon the nature of the case. The Supreme Court is at the apex of the federal judicial pyramid, although it agrees to hear only a small percentage of cases appealed from the lower courts. Since the 1930s, the Court has generally moved to protect civil liberties and civil rights. Finally, the debate over judicial activism versus judicial restraint continues.*

**Selected Readings**

Abraham, Henry J. *The Judiciary: The Supreme Court and the Governmental Process.* 7th ed. (1987)

Baum, Lawrence. *American Courts: Process and Policy.* 2nd ed. (1990)

Carp, Robert A., and Ronald Stidham. *Judicial Process in America* (1990)

O'Brien, David M. *Storm Center: The Supreme Court in American Politics.* 2nd ed. (1990)

Posner, Richard A. *The Federal Courts: Crisis and Reform* (1985)

Woodward, Bob, and Scott Armstrong. *The Brethren: Inside the Supreme Court* (1979)

# 10

## *Civil Liberties and Civil Rights*

*T*he Bill of Rights was added to the original Constitution as a collective guarantee that the liberties of citizens—including such basic freedoms as speech, press, and religion—could not be arbitrarily infringed upon by the ruling power of the federal government or the wishes of a tyrannical majority. The Fourteenth Amendment established the due-process clause as a further reaffirmation of these freedoms.

Civil liberties can create conflicts among competing interests in society. The accused may desire a fair trial, but the press may desire maximum coverage. Citizens in a community may wish to censor sexually explicit publications, but others will believe in freedom of speech. These and innumerable other disputes will demand resolution.

Civil liberties are not the same as civil rights. Civil liberties are the individual rights that are guaranteed by the Constitution, as exemplified in the Bill of Rights. They are the citizen's legal and constitutional protections against the government. Civil rights involve the protection of individuals and groups against discrimination based upon race, national origin, religion, or sexual orientation. Their struggle for civil rights is ultimately to gain access to public facilities, better job opportunities, legal equality, or other societal services denied to them. Civil rights are largely derived from federal or state statutes, and from the "equal protection clause" of the Fourteenth Amendment.

The content, application, scope, and extension of civil liberties and civil rights have been interpreted by the judiciary and particularly the Supreme Court. The Court has delivered many important rulings affecting black

*Americans, women, Hispanics, native-American Indians, and other minor-*
*ities. This chapter will be concerned with many of these decisions and their*
*significance.*

## CIVIL LIBERTIES

Civil liberties are closely linked to the principle of limited government. They represent freedoms which governmental authority cannot normally suppress. However, these freedoms are relative, not absolute. For example, while the Constitution provides for free speech, an individual cannot, to use the words of Supreme Court Justice Oliver Wendell Holmes, "yell fire in a crowded theater when there is no fire." The civil liberties contained in the Bill of Rights, originally applicable only to the federal government, were eventually extended to state governments.

**The Incorporation of the Bill of Rights**

The original intent of the Bill of Rights was to restrain the new federal government, not to place restrictions on the existing states. The "incorporation" of the Bill of Rights into the Fourteenth Amendment's *due-process clause*—"No State shall . . . deprive any person of life, liberty, or property, without due process of law"—by the courts meant that constitutional rights of individuals could not be infringed upon by state governments. The incorporation process began with the case of *Gitlow* v. *New York* in 1925, when the Supreme Court ruled that freedom of speech could not be impaired by the states. Today, virtually the entire Bill of Rights has been incorporated.

**The First-Amendment Freedoms— Religion, Speech, Press, Assembly, and Petition**

### FREEDOM OF RELIGION

The First Amendment states that "Congress shall make no law respecting an *establishment of religion* or prohibiting the *free exercise* thereof." These two "clauses" have respectively strengthened church–state separation and the freedom to practice whatever one's religious beliefs may be.

### ESTABLISHMENT CLAUSE

This clause implies a "wall of separation" (a phrase originating with Thomas Jefferson) between church and state. There is no state religion in America. Government may not show favoritism toward one religion over another—it must be impartial toward all. These fundamental views were articulated further by the Supreme Court in the 1960s through its "three-part test." To determine if a law or government policy violated the clause, the following points required evaluation: (1) the law must have a secular purpose; (2) the law must not advance or interfere with religion; (3) the statute must not result in "excessive entanglement" of church and state.

Subsequently, the Supreme Court has found most types of public assistance to church-supported schools unconstitutional (exceptions: textbook loans and bus travel, since they were "neutral" activities assisting children's welfare, not religious values) and invalidated the use of a state-written prayer in the public schools (*Engel* v. *Vitale*, 1962). However, it has ruled in favor of schools giving "released time" to students so they can participate in religious activities, provided that these do not occur on public school grounds.

### FREE-EXERCISE CLAUSE

In America, government cannot force any individual to believe in or practice a particular religion. But the Free-Exercise Clause does not constitute a license for the perpetration of harmful or antisocial religious practices. For example, the courts would not allow a religious ritual of human sacrifice. Nor would the courts allow a sick child to be denied a needed blood transfusion due to religious dogma. In another case, the Supreme Court banned polygamy, even though the Mormon Church approved of it.

The Supreme Court has usually protected an individual's religious beliefs (or absence of them), if deemed legitimate, from state intrusion. The Court ruled that Jehovah's Witnesses did not have to salute the American flag (their religion's beliefs interpreted the salute as a violation of the biblical commandment against idolatry), that the Amish were not required to send their children to any kind of school after the eighth grade (modern education conflicted with the agrarian life-style of the Amish, so their children could stop attending school altogether), and that an atheist did not have to take a public oath of office (expressing a belief in God) to keep his government job. Similarly, a conscientious objector can legally avoid military service due to his or her religious beliefs. But it is important to remember that "free exercise" is not absolute. Thus, an Orthodox Jewish chaplain in the U.S. Air Force could not wear his yarmulke (skullcap) since it violated the military's dress code. The chaplain had asserted that wearing a yarmulke was essential to his functioning as a total Orthodox being.

## Freedom of Speech and the Press

The First Amendment asserts that "Congress shall make no law abridging the freedom of speech, or of the press." But government can issue restrictions on freedom of expression when circumstances warrant. A discussion of some of these limits follows.

### LIBEL AND SLANDER

No one has the right to write (libel) or verbalize (slander) *deliberately* false, malicious statements about someone's character or reputation. A reporter (and his or her paper) who did so could be sued in court by the aggrieved plaintiff. The tabloid *National Enquirer* was brought to court by Carol Burnett, the entertainer, after the paper had alleged that she had been seen inebriated in public (Ms. Burnett won and collected monetary restitution). But one must demonstrate conclusively that libelous statements are false—true statements void the possibility of collecting damages.

## SYMBOLIC SPEECH

An illegal act cannot be justified under a freedom-of-speech umbrella. An individual who burns his draft card to protest foreign policy is still violating the law. However, the courts have approved symbolic speech in some situations. For example, in 1965, court approval was awarded to high-school students who wore black arm bands to protest the Vietnam War. Burning the American flag as a form of political protest has also been ruled constitutional.

## "CLEAR AND PRESENT DANGER" TEST

Speech cannot lead to an immediate and recognizable harm to people and/or property. For example, a speaker who urged his audience to commit crimes (with audience members doing so shortly after the speaker had finished) would have violated the acceptable boundaries of free speech. Similarly, members of a subversive hate group who advocated the violent overthrow of the U.S. government would be guilty of sedition, as mandated by the Smith Act of 1940. Thus, in 1950, the Supreme Court upheld the conviction of eleven members of the American Communist party under the anti-sedition provisions of the Smith Act.

## PRIOR RESTRAINT

Can the government censor a newspaper story before it is published—i.e., practice the concept of prior restraint? The Supreme Court has normally ruled the practice unconstitutional on the grounds that a free press is vital to the preservation of democracy. A famous 1971 case of prior restraint involved the Pentagon Papers, top-secret documents relating to the real reasons behind America's involvement in Vietnam. When the documents were "leaked" to *The New York Times* and parts of it were printed, the Nixon administration sought a court injunction to stop further publication on national security grounds. But the Court rejected this plea, asserting that the public's right to know superseded governmental secrecy.

A similar situation applies to "gag orders," which are court orders that prevent the press from writing stories about a criminal case before that case is tried in a courtroom. Formerly, judges used gag orders to guard defendants against adverse pre-trial publicity. But Supreme Court decisions have since voided these "orders" as but another kind of prior restraint.

## SHIELD LAWS

Are reporters protected from revealing confidential sources of information under the First Amendment's freedom-of-press provision? In the 1972 case of *Branzburg* v. *Hayes*, the Supreme Court ruled that reporters were not exempt from supplying information to a grand jury as part of a criminal investigation. Special exemptions for the news media would have to be furnished by congressional or state law. Since the Branzburg ruling, about thirty states have passed their own "shield laws," which grant reporters limited immunity from divulging confidential information in nonfederal cases.

## THE ISSUE OF OBSCENITY

Can governments legally censor books, movies, magazines, plays, records, artwork, or other forms of expression which are considered obscene? The problem arises over how to define what is or what is not obscene, since moral sensitivities differ among disparate communities or even regions of the nation. While the Supreme Court has admitted that there is no universal definition of obscenity (Justice Potter Stewart once stated that he could not define obscenity, but he knew it when he saw it), it has decided that each community can judge for itself whether a literary or cinematic work violates standards of morality. The Court has also reiterated that a literary or video work, to be considered obscene in its entirety, must appeal exclusively to "prurient interests," depict sexual conduct in an offensive manner, and lack literary or artistic merit.

| | |
|---|---|
| **Freedoms of Assembly and Petition** | The right of the people to assemble *peaceably* in groups and voice their grievances is again broadly permitted, but far from absolute. A balance between freedom and order must be struck. For example, a group will usually not be allowed to hold a protest demonstration if it interferes with city traffic or blocks entrances to public buildings. A march near a school which disrupts normal learning activities can be prohibited. Governments can formulate and enforce reasonable laws which control the time, place, and organization of the assembly. |
| **Protecting the Accused— Amendments Four, Five, Six, and Eight** | A significant portion of the Bill of Rights is devoted to protecting citizens who are accused of crimes from being subjected to illegal government procedures or coercion. In the United States, an individual is presumed innocent until proven guilty. The civil liberties of the accused are designed to strengthen these important principles. |

## THE FOURTH AMENDMENT'S SEARCH-AND-SEIZURE PROVISIONS

The Fourth Amendment requires that the police must have a search warrant before entering a person's home, apartment, trailer, or other place of residence. The warrant must be issued by a judge after authorities have established "probable cause" (meaning that good reason exists to believe a crime has occurred or that evidence will be found at the particular location). The warrant usually describes the place to be searched and what type of evidence is to be seized.

Most searches are conducted without a warrant. Examples of warrantless searches include the following: (a) the individual voluntarily agrees to a search; (b) searches which follow a lawful arrest; (c) searches of all parts of a car if probable cause is shown (the car and its owner could be long gone before an officer returned with a warrant); (d) a person may be arrested in a public place on the grounds that a crime was about to be committed by him or her; (e) police may stop a person's car and test that driver for signs of intoxication; (f) a warrant is not needed to seize evidence in "plain view"—i.e., stolen firearms, even if the original warrant specifies that the search is for illegal drugs.

**The Exclusionary Rule.** Evidence which is improperly obtained cannot be used as evidence in a court of law. This is the exclusionary rule, a rule which was eventually applied to the states by the 1961 Supreme Court case of *Mapp* v. *Ohio*. The exclusionary rule is controversial, with opponents claiming that it can interfere with the prosecution and conviction of truly guilty people. In recent years, the Supreme Court has relaxed the rule somewhat, allowing the police to use evidence which would have "inevitably" been found through legal methods and establishing a "good-faith" exception (evidence can be used if the police believed they had a constitutionally valid warrant even though it is later found to be defective in some way).

**Wiretapping and Electronic Surveillance.** The framers of the Constitution could not have imagined the sophisticated eavesdropping equipment of the twentieth century—sensitive microphones, VCR's, telephone "taps," and more. The Supreme Court for many years ruled wiretapping to be legal, then reversed itself, stating that it violated the Fourth Amendment. But today, after congressional legislation (the 1968 Omnibus Crime Control Act) and further judicial review, wiretapping is permitted if certain procedures are followed. Law enforcement personnel must first secure a warrant from a local, state, or federal judge authorizing electronic "bugging" before the actual surveillance can begin.

## THE FIFTH AMENDMENT: SELF-INCRIMINATION, GRAND JURIES, DOUBLE JEOPARDY

**Self-Incrimination.** The Fifth Amendment states that no person "shall be compelled in any criminal case to be a witness against himself." In other words, a citizen does not have to say anything which could lead others to believe he or she is guilty of the alleged offense. The famed "Miranda Rules" stem from the Fifth Amendment—i.e., an arresting officer must inform the suspect that he or she has the "right to remain silent, for anything you say may be used against you in a court of law." Similarly, a defendant's refusal to testify at his or her trial is not an indication of guilt, and the judge will so remind the jury.

**Grand-Jury Indictments.** Members of a federal grand jury, numbering between sixteen and twenty-three, may issue a true bill of indictment, a statement that there is enough evidence (or not enough evidence) to justify a petit or jury trial for an alleged federal crime (after listening to a prosecutor). Grand juries are supposed to prevent unwarranted criminal trials, but they usually issue indictments (a minimum of twelve juror votes is needed) in 90 percent or more of the cases they hear. Grand juries are also criticized because their sessions are held in secret and their members hear only the prosecution's arguments. More than half of the states have abolished grand juries, relying on an affidavit of "information" whereby a prosecutor files formal charges and swears to their validity.

**Double Jeopardy.** The Fifth Amendment also states that no person should be "twice put in jeopardy of life or limb." The rationale for double jeopardy is that it prevents the state from repeatedly prosecuting a citizen in court until it finally achieves a guilty verdict. An individual may not be tried again for the *exact same crime* once found innocent of that crime in a court of law. Note that double jeopardy does not prevent a new trial for a citizen who is found guilty. Also, an individual could be tried twice—one time in a federal court, then again in a state court—for a crime which involved an alleged violation of both state and federal laws, such as selling narcotics.

## THE SIXTH AMENDMENT: THE RIGHT TO COUNSEL AND A SPEEDY TRIAL

The Sixth Amendment states that "In all criminal prosecutions, the accused shall enjoy the right . . . to have the Assistance of Counsel for his defense." The right of a citizen to have an attorney for his or her defense originally applied only to federal offenses. In 1963, the Supreme Court ruled in *Gideon* v. *Wainwright* that this right applied to all state felony trials (the Court later extended the right to include misdemeanor cases in which a person might have to serve a jail sentence). Subsequently, thousands of prisoners across the country who had been denied counsel were released.

In addition, the Sixth Amendment enjoins that "In all criminal prosecutions, the accused shall enjoy the right to a speedy and public trial . . ." The objective is to minimize trial delays and possibly limit the amount of time a citizen must stay in jail (if he or she cannot afford bail). Federal law has clarified the "speedy" term, mandating that no more than one hundred days should pass between arrest and the start of a federal criminal trial.

Finally, the amendment states that a person accused of a federal offense must be tried by impartial jurors. Jurors are usually selected from a community list of registered voters. A federal jury is composed of twelve members and may convict only if all twelve jurors agree on a guilty verdict. By comparison, several states use only six-member juries. But a unanimous verdict is also required for these juries.

**Plea Bargaining.** Note that a majority of people accused of crimes never have a jury trial. Plea-bargaining procedures are used whereby the accused, in exchange for admitting guilt, is charged with a lesser crime. Plea bargaining has been declared constitutional so long as the plea is voluntarily made and understood fully by the defendant. Although plea bargaining has been criticized as a mockery of justice, the judiciary has accepted it as a method of reducing the vast backlog of cases and consequently saving both time and money.

## THE EIGHTH AMENDMENT: EXCESSIVE BAIL AND CRUEL AND UNUSUAL PUNISHMENT

The Eighth Amendment states that "Excessive bail shall not be required, nor excessive fines imposed . . ." and forbids "cruel and unusual punishment."

**Excessive Bail, Fines.** Bail is a specified amount of money, set by the court, which serves as a guarantee that an individual will appear for his or her trial at a designated time in the future. Bail allows the individual to prepare a defense outside of a jail cell and is based on the assumption that the "presumed innocent citizen should not stay incarcerated. However, bail is not a guaranteed right—the Constitution states only that it should not be excessive. A judge may deny bail altogether if he feels the accused may flee or is dangerous to society. This "preventive detention" policy has been declared constitutional by the courts.

**Cruel and Unusual Punishment.** In recent years, the death penalty has been challenged on the grounds that it constitutes "cruel and unusual punishment." The Supreme Court has disagreed, stating that the death sentence does not violate the Constitution if applied equitably. But the Court has cautioned that lower courts must carefully consider "mitigating factors"—the defendant's age and prior police record, the use of alcohol or drugs, the precise circumstances of the murder—before imposing a death sentence. Many states have rewritten their death-penalty statutes, with some eliminating automatic imposition of the penalty once a defendant has been convicted, and others providing a "two-step" process—a trial to determine guilt or innocence, followed by a separate hearing to decide if death is warranted. Despite opposition to the idea of capital punishment, the number of annual executions in the United States has gradually increased during the last decade. (In 1991, there were close to 2,500 people on death row in the United States.)

## Conclusions

Despite imperfections in America's civil liberties system, even critics would concede that the scope of protection accorded the accused is extensive. Furthermore, the Supreme Court has strengthened democracy by expanding these individual freedoms through numerous decisions. In a comparable way, the Court has assisted the civil rights struggle, especially since 1954. We now turn to that topic.

# CIVIL RIGHTS

## The Struggle for Black Equality and Racial Desegregation

The American civil rights movement began with the struggles of black Americans to abolish the abhorrent practice of slavery, establish legal equality, and end school desegregation.

### SLAVERY AND THE CIVIL WAR

The establishment and perpetuation of slavery in the South was a contributing factor leading to the Civil War. The infamous Dred Scott decision (1857) ruled that all blacks, slave or free, were not citizens and therefore had no right to sue in a federal court. The decision also held that Congress had no power to control the spread of slavery in the new territories. Dred Scott polarized the nation further, and seemingly invalidated the series of political compromises between slave and free states which had forestalled a final political rift.

Once the war had begun, Lincoln's Emancipation Proclamation (1863) freed the slaves in the rebellious states. In 1865, the Thirteenth Amendment permanently abolished the institution of slavery. The Fourteenth Amendment (1868) asserted that all persons born or naturalized in the nation were citizens. Its key provision on civil rights stated that no state shall "deny to any person within its jurisdiction the equal protection of the laws." The Fifteenth Amendment (1870) asserted that a state could not deny the right to vote on "account of race, color, or previous condition of servitude."

## THE CIVIL RIGHTS CASES AND *PLESSY* v. *FERGUSON*

The three postwar constitutional amendments did not establish racial equality. Indeed, in the Civil Rights Cases of 1883 the Supreme Court overturned the Civil Rights Act of 1875, which had forbidden racial discrimination and separation in public accommodations (hotels, theaters, and so on). The Court reasoned that the 1875 law had applied only to governmental acts of discrimination, not private wrongs. In *Plessy* v. *Ferguson* (1896), the Court ruled that the "separate but equal" doctrine was constitutional, in that separate facilities (in this case, railway cars in Louisiana) for the races, so long as they were equivalent in quality, did not violate the equal-protection clause of the Fourteenth Amendment. This decision would sanctify legal segregation for the next fifty-eight years, with "Jim Crow" laws spreading throughout the South. Blacks were segregated from whites in virtually every societal aspect—schools, transportation, parks, public restrooms, hospitals, prisons, and even in cemeteries. (Violence toward blacks was all too common as well.) However, the NAACP—the National Association for the Advancement of Colored People—was created in 1909 and led the fight to overturn this entrenched segregation pattern. The NAACP's legal goal was to show that "separate but equal" actually meant unequal educational opportunity and citizenship. The organization's efforts centered on the federal courts.

## COURT RULINGS LEADING TO *BROWN* v. *BOARD OF EDUCATION OF TOPEKA*

In 1938, the Supreme Court began to chip away at the separate-but-equal doctrine in *Missouri ex rel. Gaines* v. *Canada*. The Court ruled that a Missouri law forbidding admission of a qualified black student to an all-white law school (there was no law school of equal quality for blacks in the state) was unconstitutional. In 1950, the Court decided that a separate University of Texas law school for blacks was not equal in terms of prestige or reputation to the University of Texas law school attended solely by whites (*Sweatt* v. *Painter*). The judicial stage was set for the historic *Brown* v. *Board of Education of Topeka* decision.

**The *Brown* Decision.** On May 17, 1954, the Court held that educational segregation based on race was unconstitutional, a violation of the equal-protection clause of the Fourteenth Amendment. Chief Justice Earl Warren stated in his opinion that segregation implied racial inferiority:

> Does segregation of children in public schools solely on the basis of race, even though the physical facilities and other "tangible factors" may be equal, deprive the children of the minority group of equal educational opportunities? We believe that it does.

. . . . To separate them from others of similar age and qualifications solely because of their race generates a feeling of
inferiority as to their status in the community that may affect their
hearts and minds in a way unlikely ever to be undone. . . . We
conclude that in the field of public education the doctrine of
"separate but equal" has no place. Separate educational facilities
are inherently unequal. Therefore, we hold that the plaintiffs and
others similarly situated for whom the actions have been brought
are, by reason of the segregation complained of, deprived of the
equal protection of the laws guaranteed by the Fourteenth
Amendment.

## FROM 1954 TO THE PRESENT

In 1955, the Supreme Court ordered that public schools desegregate
"with all deliberate speed" and that the lower federal courts oversee this
process. However, the desegregation of some 2,200 public-school systems
in the South and border states could not be accomplished overnight. Civil
rights organizations, such as the NAACP, had to fund numerous lawsuits to
force an end to school segregation. States like Delaware, Maryland, and
Kentucky rapidly complied with the Court's ruling. But resistance mounted
in other Deep South states and Congress. (Some 101 southern congressmen
signed the Southern Manifesto, a document claiming that the *Brown* decision
was unlawful and suggesting the passage of a constitutional amendment
overturning *Brown*.) In Arkansas (1957), Mississippi (1962), and Alabama
(1963), violence at Little Rock's Central High School, the University of
Mississippi in Oxford, and the University of Alabama in Tuscaloosa, respectively, had to be quelled by National Guard or federal troops sent by
Presidents Eisenhower and Kennedy.

Other states tried nonviolent methods of resistance to desegregation—
from "freedom of choice" plans allowing students to select the school they
wished to attend, to providing tuition grants so students could attend private
schools. However, the Warren Court ruled these schemes unconstitutional.

## THE CIVIL RIGHTS ACT OF 1964

The segregation pattern was not shaken massively until passage of the
Civil Rights Act of 1964. (In 1964, 98 percent of black children attended
all-black schools.) Title VI of this statute linked a cutoff of federal aid to
any local or state government that continued the practice of racial discrimination. Southern schools began to desegregate rather than lose badly
needed federal funding. Within eight years, the number of totally segregated
public schools in the South had declined substantially.

## NORTHERN SEGREGATION AND FORCED BUSING

In northern public schools, segregation was due mainly to residential housing patterns—i.e., what was called *de facto* ("in fact") rather than *de jure* ("by law") segregation sanctioned by government. The Supreme Court ruled that busing of black children to white schools (or whites to black schools) to achieve integrated school districts was constitutional if those school districts had *intentionally* segregated the races. Busing's goals were to improve the quality of black education, reduce the psychological stigma of segregation, and facilitate harmonious black–white race relations. In some cities, busing was effective; in others, such as south Boston, busing was violently resisted. Frequently, busing resulted in "white flight" to the suburbs. Hence, inner-city schools, with far fewer whites, remained black-majority institutions.

*The Modern Civil Rights Movement— Challenging Discrimination in Public Accommo- dations, Employment, Housing, and Voting*

## PUBLIC ACCOMMODATIONS

The *Brown* decision did not end discrimination in public accommodations. But it sparked a new round in the civil rights revolution. In Montgomery, Alabama, the city's blacks engaged in a year-long boycott (1955–1956) of the city's buses, after a black woman, Rosa Parks, had refused to sit in the rear of a bus. The boycott's leader was the Reverend Dr. Martin Luther King, Jr., who borrowed the nonviolent protest techniques used by Mahatma Gandhi against the British in India. In Greensboro, North Carolina, four black college students engaged in a sit-in at a segregated Woolworth's lunch counter, encouraging similar sit-ins around the country. But civil rights activists in Birmingham, Alabama, and Neshoba County, Mississippi, were attacked or murdered. The federal government responded with five separate civil rights laws during the 1957–1964 period, the most dramatic being the passage of the Civil Rights Act of 1964. The act prohibited racial discrimination in transportation lines, hotels, restaurants, sporting arenas, and other areas. Discrimination in public accommodations was now considered an illegal restriction of interstate commerce.

## DISCRIMINATION IN EMPLOYMENT

The Civil Rights Act of 1964 also outlawed employment discrimination on the basis of race, color, religion, national origin, sex, and age. The act covered employers who had at least fifteen employees on their payrolls.

## THE CIVIL RIGHTS ACT OF 1991

In 1991, Congress passed legislation which extended for the first time punitive damages to victims of employment discrimination based on race, sex, or physical disability. Both Republicans and Democrats argued that racial minorities and women deserved greater protection against bias in hiring, promotion, and general workplace relations. The law was aimed at countering a series of 1989 Supreme Court rulings which had made it more difficult for workers to bring and win job-discrimination lawsuits.

## HOUSING

The Civil Rights Act of 1968 banned discrimination on the basis of race, color, religion, national origin, or sex in the sale or rental of housing. However, the act has not initiated widespread changes in housing ownership or occupancy. Economic reasons and persistent discrimination have left the central cities mainly black, the suburbs white.

## VOTING RIGHTS

The Voting Rights Act of 1965 abolished literacy tests which were used by southern states to block the vast majority of black citizens from voting. The act empowered the attorney general to send federal registrars into southern counties. The law was extended in 1970 and 1975 to include other minorities. In 1982, its provisions were renewed for another twenty-five years.

The Voting Rights Act led to a dramatic increase in national black voter registration (more than 12 million by 1990) and black elected officials (in 1960 there were fewer than 300; by 1988 there were more than 7,000). Many of America's largest cities elected black mayors. In 1984, the Reverend Jesse Jackson became the first serious black presidential candidate. Renewed efforts to register more black voters resulted in Jackson's successes in the early 1988 presidential primaries and caucuses.

## OVERALL BLACK GAINS SINCE 1954

The civil rights revolution is far from over. However, since 1954, there have been accomplishments. De jure segregation has been abolished. Public accommodations have been totally desegregated. Black electoral power in many large cities—Washington, New York, Los Angeles, Detroit, Atlanta, Chicago, and Philadelphia—is impressive. Educationally, the median number of years spent in school by blacks is now comparable to that of whites.

In two other areas—black family income and unemployment—there has been less progress. The gap between white and black median family incomes has not been closed. Black unemployment, prior to the severe recession of 1991, was double that of whites. For black Americans, the struggle for full equality will continue.

# THE STRUGGLE FOR WOMEN'S EQUALITY

**Early History**

In the early 1800s, women had few political rights and were the victims of an oppressive, protective paternalism. They were considered legally subservient to their husbands, could not own their own property, or even be admitted to the public schools. Menial jobs with long hours and low wages were their lot. By the middle of the nineteenth century, women became politically organized, first becoming involved in the struggle to abolish slavery, then with the suffrage movement after the Civil War. Led by Susan B. Anthony and Elizabeth Cady Stanton, the suffragettes fought successfully for the passage of the Nineteenth Amendment in 1920, guaranteeing that "the right of the citizens of the United States to vote shall not be denied or abridged by the United States or by any State on account of sex." The struggle for equality would intensify again during the 1960s.

# THE CONTEMPORARY STRUGGLE AGAINST SEX DISCRIMINATION

**Women and the Workplace**

By the 1960s, millions of women were entering the labor market. In 1990, more than half of all women with children under six were either working or seeking employment. But their wages lagged behind those paid to men. Women earned only about seventy cents for every dollar working men received for doing the same kind of work. (Many women have lower-paying jobs due to less education or experience, a reflection of marriage demands and child-rearing.) Accordingly, women demanded that they should be paid equivalent salaries to men in those jobs which involved similar skills and effort.

**Discrimination in Employment and Education**

The Civil Rights Act of 1964 prohibited sexual discrimination in hiring, firing, or promoting an individual. (The 1991 Civil Rights Act allowed women to sue small- and medium-sized businesses for damages stemming from on-the-job sexual harassment or other acts of job bias.) The Education Amendments of 1972 prevent schools and colleges from discriminating against women in the areas of admissions, financial aid, and even women's athletic programs.

**Discrimination in Credit**

Prior to the Equal Credit Opportunity Act of 1974, single women were usually refused loans by banks or denied credit cards. The theoretical assumption was that women would marry, become pregnant, and consequently renege on their debts. Even when loans were given to married couples, a woman's income was not counted as part of the family's total income base. The loan was recorded only in the husband's name. Consequently, widowed or divorced women frequently had no credit history. The act eliminated these abuses.

## Discrimination and the Supreme Court

During the 1970s, the Burger Court was active in invalidating state laws which discriminated against women in jury selection (Florida and Louisiana had drawn prospective juries only from lists of male voters), child support (Utah had required divorced fathers to support their daughters only to age eighteen, but sons to twenty-one, the assumption being that women would marry earlier), and employee pension plans (women retirees could not receive less pension money per month than male retirees). The Court also approved state statutes which prohibited the Jaycees and Rotary from barring women members (business contacts at these clubs were important to both men and women). The overall thrust of the Burger Court (and the Rehnquist Court) has been to abolish the stereotype that "a woman's place is only in the home" and that men are the only "breadwinners" in the family. This attitude was implied in Justice William Brennan's 1973 opinion in *Frontiero* v. *Richardson* (a law treating men and women in the military differently was overturned):

> There can be no doubt that our nation has had a long and unfortunate history of sex discrimination. Traditionally, such discrimination was rationalized by an attitude of "romantic paternalism" which, in practical effect, put women not on a pedestal, but in a cage.

## Discrimination and Employment Leaves

A discrimination issue for the 1990s is the granting of job leave for new mothers, either with some funding or the guarantee of job security upon returning to work. Nearly one hundred foreign nations do provide assistance to women on maternity leave. In the United States, women's groups have lobbied for a federal law mandating a four-month unpaid leave for a mother or father of a newborn child. Such a bill was passed by Congress in 1990, but it was vetoed by President Bush.

## The Equal Rights Amendment

Led by such feminists as Gloria Steinem and Betty Friedan (author of *The Feminine Mystique*), the demand for women's equality was incorporated into the Equal Rights Amendment, submitted to the states by Congress in 1972. The ERA read as follows:

> Equality of rights under the law shall not be denied or abridged by the United States or any state on account of sex.

Opponents of the ERA charged that the amendment would force women to be drafted, lead to unisex bathrooms, and undermine traditional marital and family values. Defenders saw the ERA as an important guarantee of equality. The proposed amendment never received the thirty-eight-state vote necessary for ratification, and politically "died" in 1982. However, the public still supports the concept. Several states have also passed their own equal-rights amendments. Recently, women's groups have urged that another ERA be submitted to Congress.

## Women in the Military

Women who serve in the military (they comprise 11 percent of all military personnel) have fought for equality in career opportunities, promotions, and combat duty. (Congress opened all of the service academies to women in 1975.) The law has prohibited women from combat duties (but women did play an active role in Panama in 1989 and the Persian Gulf in 1991). There is also the question of whether both men and women should be forced to register for the draft, although current federal statutes mandate only male draftees.

## Abortion and the Right to Privacy

A final, vital issue for many American women is the right to an abortion. Currently, the 1973 Supreme Court decision in *Roe* v. *Wade* remains the national policy, asserting that a woman has a constitutional right to an abortion during the first trimester, the second trimester can involve state regulation to protect the mother's health, and the state could ban abortions altogether during the third trimester of pregnancy. The Court based the *Roe* decision on the right of privacy implied in the Fourteenth Amendment's due-process clause. Since the decision, there have been approximately 1,500,000 abortions performed in the nation.

Pro-abortion groups are worried that the Rehnquist Court may eventually overturn *Roe*. In particular, the Court's ruling in *Webster* v. *Reproductive Health Services* (1989), which upheld the state of Missouri's right to impose new regulations and restrictions on abortion, troubled many pro-choice (abortion supporters) women. (The Webster ruling barred public hospitals from performing abortions and banned the use of public funds in advising women to have these operations.) Conversely, pro-lifers—those adamantly opposed to abortion—welcomed the Webster ruling. The controversy over abortion, like other aspects of the women's movement, promised continuing political and legal conflict. In 1992, the Supreme Court was scheduled to hear new cases challenging *Roe*.

# THE CIVIL RIGHTS STRUGGLE OF OTHER GROUPS—HISPANICS, NATIVE AMERICANS, ASIAN AMERICANS, THE DISABLED, THE ELDERLY, AND GAYS

**Hispanic Americans**

About 8 percent of the American population is composed of Hispanic Americans. Mexicans number about half of the Hispanic population, followed by Puerto Ricans, Cubans, and refugees from Central and South America. Collectively, Hispanics are the fastest-growing minority group in the nation. Demographers suggest that they will surpass black Americans in total numbers in two or three more decades. Like blacks, they have experienced considerable discrimination in voting, housing, jobs, and education.

About one-third of Hispanics live at or below the poverty line. Unemployment is a serious problem. Many are exploited by employers, being paid substandard wages in urban sweatshops or as rural farm workers. Educationally, Hispanics experience significant illiteracy, high drop-out rates from school, and fewer numbers of college graduates than other minorities. In the past, Hispanic children also have attended underfunded and segregated schools. Politically, there are relatively few Hispanic elected officials (most are at the local level), due to Hispanics lagging behind white and black Americans in both voter registration and voter turnout. Furthermore, the diverse nationalities comprising the Hispanic population have, until recently, inhibited political unity and organized interest-group activity. A notable exception has been Cesar Chavez, who organized migrant farm workers in California during the 1960s. However, Hispanics have now started some important political organizations, such as LULAC—League of United Latin American Citizens—and the Mexican American/Puerto Rican Legal Defense and Education Fund. All of these groups are active in fighting discrimination through the federal courts.

**Native Americans (Indians)**

When America was discovered by European explorers, there were probably 10 to 15 million Indians or Native Americans living in the New World. Today, there are about 1.5 million Native Americans residing on American soil. Concentrated in the western states and Alaska, slightly less than half of the total Native American population lives on government reservations where low income, high mortality rates, and other health problems are common.

The federal government's policy toward Native Americans has vacillated from treating them as citizens of separate, independent nations to attempting complete assimilation (civilizing the Indians and bringing them into white society). Congress has granted Indian tribes the right to develop their own constitutions, determine tribal membership, and handle their own systems of justice. Still, Native Americans were not awarded the full rights of American citizenship by Congress until 1924. Despite being citizens, Indians were denied the right to vote for decades by some states.

Native Americans became more politically militant in the 1960s, when groups such as the National Indian Youth Council and the American Indian Movement (AIM) began protesting federal policy toward their ancestral lands, past treaties, and ownership of mineral resources. In 1972, Indian groups marched on Washington, protesting the policies of the BIA—the Bureau of Indian Affairs. In the two decades since, Native Americans have intensified their political efforts in order to right historic wrongs and to restore fully their civil rights.

## Asian Americans

While most Asian Americans today have greater median incomes than either Hispanics or Native Americans, they also can document previous acts of discrimination. Historically, the nineteenth and twentieth centuries witnessed Chinese and Japanese immigrants enduring prejudice in schooling, employment, and property ownership. The most egregious case occurred in 1942, when, as a reaction to the Japanese attack on Pearl Harbor, President Franklin Roosevelt signed an executive order placing 120,000 Japanese Americans living on the Pacific Coast into internment camps in seven western states. These citizens were forced to sell their property at a loss. They remained interned until 1945. (Some of the younger men served in segregated Japanese American army combat units in the European campaign.) In 1988, Congress authorized compensation of $20,000 to each of the 60,000 camp survivors. Despite these setbacks, Japanese Americans today have the highest median number of years of schooling and family income of any ethnic group in the nation.

The most recent wave of Asian immigration has been that of the Vietnamese, who escaped their country after communist forces were victorious in 1975. More than a million refugees came to America. Despite encountering some community prejudice, the Vietnamese have been reasonably successful in America. Less than one-third of Vietnamese families depend upon welfare. A good many have become owners of small and mid-sized businesses.

## The Elderly and Disabled

As Americans live longer, the elderly—that sector of the population over sixty-five—have developed into a potent political force (they have high voter turnout rates as well). Organizations supporting the interests of the elderly include the Gray Panthers and the American Association of Retired Persons. The elderly have fought for legislation abolishing age discrimination in employment, better medical benefits, and extension of Social Security benefits.

The disabled have also demanded more equitable treatment from society. They have acquired wheelchair ramps for better access to public buildings, demanded handicapped parking spaces, and sought opportunities to learn through special-education programs. In 1990, the Americans with Disabilities Act was passed, guaranteeing the rights of all handicapped citizens.

**Gay and Lesbian Rights**

Estimates are that homosexuals comprise about 10 percent of the U.S. adult population. This large minority group, commonly called "gays," has fought against discrimination, based largely on life-style, in hiring, housing, and public accommodations. In addition, the growing problem of AIDS, or acquired immune deficiency syndrome, a fatal disease affecting mainly homosexual males, intravenous drug users, and recipients of blood transfusions, has intensified public hostility and thus complicated the struggle for gay and lesbian rights. Furthermore, thirty states have various forms of anti-homosexual laws. In 1986, the Supreme Court ruled constitutional a Georgia law making private homosexual relations between consenting adults a crime. Conversely, over 100 American cities have laws prohibiting discrimination against gays. Recent Gallup polls have found that a majority of Americans favor equal job opportunities for gays.

Gay organizations, such as the Gay Liberation Front, have lobbied for homosexual rights vis-à-vis federal hiring procedures, membership in the military, easing of immigration policies, and even hiring in private law firms. Gay groups have gradually acquired considerable political power, especially in such cities as San Francisco, Houston, New York, Denver, and Washington, D.C. Gay organizations have also successfully pressured Congress to appropriate additional funds for AIDS research and treatment.

# AFFIRMATIVE ACTION AND CIVIL RIGHTS

All of the previously discussed civil rights legislation prohibiting discrimination does little to overcome the effects of *past* discriminatory practices. The federal government's answer has been the policy of *affirmative action*, mandating that most employers, both public and private, make an earnest effort to hire and/or promote minority workers—women, blacks, Hispanics, and so on. True equality of opportunity is now the goal. However, critics assert that this policy is tantamount to *reverse discrimination*, whereby blacks or women are hired on the basis of their race or sex, not their actual merit or qualifications. The Supreme Court has wrestled with this controversy in a number of important rulings.

**Regents of the University of California *v.* Bakke**

In 1979, Alan Bakke, a qualified white male, applied to the university's medical school at Davis. But sixteen of the one hundred seats for the entering freshman class were assigned to nonwhite students, with several less qualified than Bakke. Bakke claimed reverse discrimination, arguing that the college policy constituted a violation of the Fourteenth Amendment's Equal Protection Clause. The Supreme Court, while ordering Bakke to be admitted, also ruled that rigid racial quotas were inappropriate for university admission–affirmative action programs (but race could be used as *one of several eligibility criteria* in affirmative-action decisions).

**United Steelworkers *v.* Weber *(1979)***

In this case, Brian Weber, a white steelworker, was rejected from a training program primarily aimed at increasing the number of blacks in the work force. Weber charged reverse discrimination, but the Supreme Court ruled that the training programs, although founded on quotas, were constitutional since they corrected racial imbalances in employment.

**United States *v.* Paradise *(1987)***

This case involved the Alabama Department of Public Safety, which had discriminated in the hiring and promoting of black state police officers. The Supreme Court supported a lower-court decision which had ordered one black trooper promoted for each white trooper promoted. Past discrimination toward black officers had to be overcome through equitable treatment now and in the future.

While a more conservative Rehnquist Court has recently demonstrated less support for some affirmative-action programs, the philosophy supporting affirmative action does not appear to be in immediate judicial danger. However, scholarly studies suggesting that affirmative-action programs have not appreciably narrowed racial discrimination in hiring practices may influence Supreme Court justices to rethink the validity of these programs at some point in the near future.

*Civil liberties guarantee individual freedoms of speech, religion, press, assembly, and petition against governmental interference. Similarly protected are the rights of the accused—no double jeopardy, protection against self-incrimination, bail, the right to counsel, among others—which collectively are a further reflection of the "innocent until proven guilty" principle of jurisprudence. However, civil liberties are not absolute. They can be limited by government, especially if the abuse of liberty leads to a "clear and present danger."*

*The original Bill of Rights affected only the federal government. It required the process of incorporation to apply these rights to state governments as well. The incorporation process started with the case of Gitlow v. New York (1925), the first time that the due-process clause of the Fourteenth Amendment was applied to state law.*

*Civil rights involve the protection of both groups and individuals against state discrimination based on the suspect criteria of race, national origin, or sex. The historic, generational struggle over civil rights has involved blacks, women, Hispanics, Native Americans, and other minorities. Black Americans fought the institution of slavery, then segregation. In 1954, the* Brown *decision finally overturned the "separate but equal" doctrine. Voting inequality and discrimination in housing, public accommodations, and employment have also been subjects of concern for black Americans. The federal government has passed civil rights acts and other laws designed to rectify these ills. In the women's civil rights struggle, the right to vote and "liberation" from a traditional societal stereotype occupied the earlier phases of the movement. Modern issues of concern for women include comparable worth, abortion, service in the military, the ERA, and educational equality, among others. Other minorities have also sought equality of opportunity, especially through such contemporary policies as affirmative action.*

## Selected Readings

Brigham, John. *Civil Liberties and American Democracy* (1984)

Cornell, Stephen. *The Return of the Native: American Indian Political Resurgence* (1988)

Cushman, Robert F. *Cases in Civil Liberties.* 5th ed. (1989)

Faux, Marian. *Roe v. Wade: The Untold Story of the Landmark Supreme Court Decision That Made Abortion Legal* (1988)

Kessler-Harris, Alice. *Out to Work: A History of Wage-Earning Women in the United States* (1982)

Kluger, Richard. *Simple Justice: A History of Brown v. Board of Education and Black America's Struggle for Equality* (1976)

Levy, Leonard W. *The Establishment Clause: Religion and the First Amendment* (1986)

Williams, Juan. *Eyes on the Prize: America's Civil Rights Years, 1954–1965* (1987)

Witt, Elder. *The Supreme Court and Individual Rights.* 2nd ed. (1988)

# 11

# Public Policy

*One definition of politics (see chapter 1) is the story of "who gets what, when, and how." In other words, the various political institutions which have been previously covered in this book are all concerned, directly or indirectly, with establishing public policies—laws, regulations, or decisions. Policies represent the final "authoritative allocation of values." But governmental inaction can also represent a negative form of policy.*

*The two general categories of public policy covered concisely in this chapter—domestic and defense/foreign—impact heavily upon every citizen of the United States, both economically and socially. But even more important, the effectiveness of governmental policies will determine if the pressing problems of American society will ultimately be resolved or not.*

## THE POLICY-MAKING PROCESS

**Three Fundamental Policy-Making Factors**

Every policy is shaped by both public and private actors and their interests, a framework of beliefs or attitudes toward a policy proposal, and the formal rules and institutions ingrained into the democratic political process. These factors are implicit in each of the policy-making stages described as follows.

What steps do governmental leaders take in order to develop a policy solution in answer to a pressing national problem? The policy-making process can be compartmentalized into five steps or stages.

## AGENDA-BUILDING

The problem must be recognized as a "problem" by governmental leaders and placed on the "set of issues" being considered at a particular point in time. For example, the problem of equal pay for working women was not on the political agenda back in the 1940s and early 1950s because most women stayed at home to raise families. However, the entrance of millions of women into the work force in the 1960s, 1970s, and 1980s gradually turned this potential problem into a recognizable, serious issue for the public, concerned interest groups, Congress, the president, and the judiciary.

## POLICY FORMULATION

Policy formulation refers to creating an "action plan" involving ways of solving a particular problem. Who develops this plan? Participants may include executive, legislative, and interest-group representatives. However, it is rare that only one formulation proposal is developed or that it receives unanimous support from all concerned parties. Conflicting proposals or reformulation of original plans is the norm. For example, the nation's growing reliance on imported oil is criticized by energy experts. But those same experts come up with different action plans to reduce oil imports, such as promoting solar power, or building more nuclear power plants, or even giving oil companies bigger tax breaks to encourage domestic drilling. While these and other energy proposals are discussed and debated, the original problem only grows worse. Today, the nation imports close to 50 percent of its oil from foreign sources. In the early 1970s, the nation imported about one-third.

## POLICY ADOPTION

Policy adoption means that the formulation plan or plans have been converted into a concrete government response, usually in the form of a law passed by Congress. But the mere passage of a law does not mean that the problem is solved. For example, Congress has appropriated millions of dollars to prosecute the "war against drugs" in America. Yet, all indications are that the drug problem in America is worsening, rather than improving.

## POLICY IMPLEMENTATION

Implementation, or the "carrying out" of a policy, is essential to its effectiveness. When the Supreme Court ruled segregation unconstitutional (see chapter 10), other institutions and personnel had the responsibility of making integration a reality. Similarly, when Congress passes legislation mandating specific clear-air standards in America's large metropolitan areas, it is the EPA (Environmental Protection Agency) which must enforce those standards. Implementation can fail because of poor communication between policy formulators and implementers, inadequate resources to perform the implementation process (a cut in EPA funding would mean fewer inspectors), and attitudes toward the policy by the implementers (bureaucrats could disagree with the wisdom of the policy).

### POLICY EVALUATION

Policy evaluation involves judging what the operational consequences of a particular policy have been over time. A well-intentioned policy could create more harm than good. A classic case was Prohibition during the 1920s, when the manufacture and sale of alcoholic beverages were forbidden. But this attempt to legislate social morality led to bootlegging, crime, and illegal "bathtub gin." Prohibition was eventually repealed by the Twenty-first Amendment. A more recent example involved the decision to construct a national interstate highway system in the 1950s. However, while the construction of the system helped the economy and assisted individual mobility, it also led to traffic congestion and an increase in air pollution over the next three decades. Typically, it may take years of evaluation to determine the ultimate success or failure of a complex public policy.

## TYPES OF DOMESTIC AND FOREIGN POLICIES

Public policy can be divided into three broad categories—domestic, foreign, and defense.

### Domestic Policy

Political scientists perceive three types of domestic policy: regulatory, distributive, and redistributive.

### REGULATORY POLICY

Regulatory policies exert federal controls over individuals and corporations. Typical policies would cover the protection of consumer rights and the environment.

### DISTRIBUTIVE POLICY

These policies involve direct government benefits to individuals, groups, and business firms. Examples would include federal subsidies (payments) to the nation's farmers, or federal support for health research to pharmaceutical laboratories.

### REDISTRIBUTIVE POLICY

Redistributive policies confer social benefits such as jobs or money to specific groups. Typically, people think of welfare payments to the poor as falling within this category. AFDC—Aid to Families with Dependent Children—is a cash-grant system which uses income from affluent taxpayers to provide for individuals who cannot support themselves, most notably single mothers with children.

## Foreign Policy

Foreign policies can be either regulatory or distributive, vis-à-vis other nations. Trade sanctions directed at a nation would be aimed at modifying (or regulating) its behavior. Thus, in 1991, the United States and other Western nations placed an economic boycott against Iraq in hopes that these pressures would force Iraq to withdraw from Kuwait. A distributive foreign policy is exemplified by a foreign-aid program to a specific nation, such as American aid to Egypt or Israel.

## Defense Policy

Defense policies deal with military or national security matters. Defense policy can fall into either the strategic or structural subcategory.

### STRATEGIC DEFENSE POLICY

This type of defense policy will deal with the utilization and location of military units overseas. For example, with the dissolution of the Soviet Union in 1991, defense experts called for the withdrawal of most, if not all, American troops stationed in Western Europe.

### STRUCTURAL DEFENSE POLICY

Structural defense policy is distributive in the sense that it deals with how defense resources—manpower, weapons, funds—will be allocated. For example, a congressional decision to close military bases in a particular state or region of the nation will mean a loss of defense dollars. Another example would be the Defense Department's decision to build a new tactical fighter for the air force. The defense company receiving the government contract would obviously make a good profit. Also, the federal contract, worth billions of dollars, would benefit the economy of the community where the corporation was located.

# DOMESTIC POLICY-MAKING— THE ECONOMY

Until the Great Depression, the prevailing economic philosophy in America was that of laissez faire, meaning that the federal government could aid corporations through subsidies or tax breaks, but also had to refrain from intervening in or closely regulating the marketplace. The collapse of the national economy after the stock market crash in 1929 changed this thinking forever. FDR's New Deal programs bequeathed a legacy of active governmental management of the economy. Consequently, today the federal government relies on monetary and fiscal policies in its efforts to create stable prices, low inflation, low unemployment, and high productivity.

## Monetary Policy

Monetary policy refers to government controls over the amount of money in circulation and the cost of credit. The "monetarist" school of economics is led by economist Milton Friedman, who argues that the national money supply should be carefully correlated with the rate of economic growth. The principal institution coordinating monetary policy is the Federal Reserve System, often called the "Fed."

### THE FEDERAL RESERVE SYSTEM (FRS)

Established in 1913, the FRS is composed of twelve regional banks and the Federal Reserve Board (FRB). More than 6,000 private banks are members of the system. The FRB is directed by a seven-member board of governors who are presidentially appointed to fourteen-year, staggered, nonrenewable terms in office. The FRB chairman has a four-year renewable term (all FRB appointments are confirmed by the Senate). The FRB is relatively independent of presidential or congressional controls.

### THE FED'S OPERATION

Banks which are members of the FRS can borrow from one of the twelve regional banks. But the Fed can regulate the economy through these loans. The Fed can: (a) raise or lower member banks' deposit requirements (this determines how much money is available for loans to citizens or businesses); (b) increase or decrease the discount (interest) rate charged to member banks (the cost of private loans will go up or down); (c) buy or sell government bonds and securities, thus contracting or expanding the money supply. So, the Fed increases the supply of money when economic growth is sluggish or unemployment is high (more money available will encourage purchases and investments, helping business growth and the creation of jobs), or decreases the money supply when the economy is experiencing hyper-inflation (too much money is chasing too few goods). For example, in December

1991, the Fed tried to fight a lingering recession by cutting the discount rate by a full percentage point. The hope was that lower interest rates would bolster a sagging economy.

## Fiscal Policy

Fiscal policy involves managing the economy through changes in government spending, borrowing, and tax rates. Its intellectual roots can be traced to the ideas of British economist John Maynard Keynes. Keynes reasoned that depressions occurred because individuals stopped spending and investing, thereby causing reductions in productivity, jobs, and wages. Under these circumstances, government would have to increase its spending (even if it had to borrow funds) to assure maximum production and high employment. (Keynesian economics is personified in the Employment Act of 1946, which made the government responsible for managing the economy and destroyed forever the laissez faire approach.) Conversely, periods of inflation should be countered by the government's raising tax rates to reduce the amount of money in circulation.

### SUPPLY-SIDE ECONOMIC THEORY

A different fiscal approach became popular in the 1980s during the presidency of Ronald Reagan. Supply-side economics stressed that tax cuts would encourage people to save, leading to an accumulation of investment capital and improved national productivity. This renewed economic activity would, over time, yield substantial government tax collections, covering any revenue lost through the original tax-cut process. Unfortunately, the theory did not work—economic growth was modest and personal savings actually declined. Furthermore, government budget deficits soared during the Reagan years, creating a problem which continues to plague the nation and the Bush administration.

## The Federal Deficit

When the federal government spends more than it takes in through tax receipts, the government is said to run a deficit. In the 1992 fiscal year, the federal deficit was estimated at $362 billion. The total of all past deficits equals the gross national debt, which in fiscal year 1992 was expected to exceed $4 trillion. While national deficits are not new, the growth of debt in the past was closely related to the ability of the economy to repay that debt. What was disturbing about the deficits of the 1980s was that the nation's gross national product (the monetary value of all goods and services produced annually; often expressed as GNP) was not growing fast enough to offer any hope of repayment. Furthermore, deficits shifted massive debt to future generations, who would be burdened with the bills for current public services. The growing interest on the national debt, amounting to more than $300 billion in fiscal year 1992, also prevented needed dollars from flowing into the private sector for productive investment by businesses and households.

Why have deficits grown larger? To reduce the federal deficit, political leaders either have to raise taxes and/or cut government spending. Neither option is popular with the voters. Raising taxes hurts the individual's pocketbook, breeding political resentment toward officeholders; cutting spending may harm programs which are popular with different constituencies, such as farm subsidies. In short, everyone favors reducing the deficit in principle, but no one wants to "pay the political piper" by having to sacrifice income or self-interest.

Another reason is the inherent difficulty of cutting the federal budget. Much of the budget is devoted to programs which are politically uncontrollable or deemed economically essential—Social Security, federal retirement programs, interest on the national debt, or Medicare. One estimate is that spending on discretionary programs accounts for only a little more than 20 percent of the entire budget. The amount spent on national defense is a controllable budgetary item, but severely cutting military preparedness is considered a risky option in a world of innumerable threats to the nation's security.

## THE GRAMM-RUDMAN-HOLLINGS ACT

In 1985, Congress tried to grapple with the deficit through the Gramm-Rudman-Hollings Act. The act created a schedule of reduced deficits so that the federal budget would eventually be balanced by 1993. Each year, if necessary, automatic cuts in both domestic and defense programs would allow deficit reductions to occur (some programs were exempt from cuts, such as Social Security). However, the act's effectiveness has been diluted by congressional reliance on "creative bookkeeping" (example: the cost of the savings-and-loan bailout was kept "off budget" so the billions of dollars involved would not be added to the deficit) and delaying expenditures until the next fiscal year. Congress has also postponed the final target date for a "zero deficit" from 1993 to 1996.

## THE DEBATE OVER A BALANCED-BUDGET AMENDMENT

Another proposed solution for the deficit was to add a constitutional amendment mandating that Congress match tax revenues and government's projected spending each fiscal year. The amendment would have two escape clauses—Congress could waive the balanced budget requirement in wartime or through a two-thirds vote in both the House and Senate. Proponents argued that the amendment would by law eliminate future deficits. Opponents asserted that the amendment would eliminate the oft-needed economic stimulus of government spending and render fiscal policy approaches null and void. In general, momentum for a balanced-budget amendment seemed to wane in the early 1990s.

*Federal
Taxation
Policy—the
Problem of
"Fairness"*

Benjamin Franklin once observed that nothing is certain in life "except death and taxes." While most Americans do not like to pay taxes, they accept the idea that taxes are the "price we pay for civilization" (a quote attributed to Supreme Court Justice Oliver Wendell Holmes). But in recent years, citizens have charged that the American tax system is unfair. Tax cheating and evasion were becoming more common among all classes of taxpayers. As a result, Congress changed the tax laws in 1986 and again in 1990.

## PROGRESSIVE AND REGRESSIVE TAXATION

A progressive tax is based upon the idea that the higher one's income, the more taxes one is supposed to pay. But critics have long charged that the wealthy do not pay their fair share of taxes, due to countless loopholes and tax shelters in the law. Defenders of tax breaks for the wealthy argue that the American economy requires private capital. Wealthy people must be encouraged to invest extra money acquired through tax savings. For example, high-income citizens can buy municipal bonds, and accumulate tax-free interest. But the average wage earner must pay taxes on any interest he or she accrues in a typical savings account.

Critics also point to the Social Security payroll tax being regressive— i.e., the tax falls more heavily on poorer citizens than the wealthy. Since all taxpayers pay the same percentage of their annual income for Social Security, proportionately far more dollars are paid by low-income wage earners. (In 1992, the percentage paid by employees was 6.2 percent, up to a cap of $55,500 of annual income; an additional 1.45 percent was paid for the Medicare program, up to a $130,200 cap.)

## THE 1986 TAX REFORM ACT AND 1990 AFTERMATH

In 1986, Congress tried to simplify the tax process, by lowering tax rates and reducing tax brackets from fourteen to four. Many tax deductions were abolished or limited (one example: a business person's lunch was reduced to 80 percent deductibility instead of the former 100 percent figure). Millions of poor people no longer had to pay any taxes whatsoever. However, the act did not resolve the issue of fairness. Four years after the act, studies revealed that the upper-middle-income class was still paying a higher tax rate than the wealthy. Also, many large corporations remained undertaxed. The resulting furor led Congress and President Bush in 1990 to tinker again with the tax laws. While the progressivity of the income tax was apparently improved, new federal taxes on cigarettes, alcohol, wine, beer, gasoline, and airplane tickets were clearly regressive (the poor and middle-class taxpayers would spend a greater proportion of their income on these taxes than the wealthy).

# DOMESTIC POLICY—SOCIAL WELFARE PROGRAMS

As with economic policy, the federal government did not become massively involved in social policy until the onset of the Great Depression in the 1930s. Since that time, there have been two general kinds of government programs: (1) public-assistance programs that provide benefits to the poor, commonly called "welfare"; (2) social insurance and regulation programs which try to meet the needs of the general public.

*Assisting the Poor*

## WHY ARE PEOPLE POOR?—CONSERVATIVE AND LIBERAL VIEWS

Political conservatives argue that people are poor because they are lazy, come from broken homes, or cannot discipline themselves to plan for the future. Conservatives oppose welfare programs on the grounds that they destroy the incentive to work, reward indolence, and create a cycle of dependency. Conversely, political liberals argue that society has failed to train or educate the poor properly. Government also has the obligation to ensure a decent standard of living for all Americans. Finally, racial and sexual discrimination is another cause of poverty.

## WHO ARE THE POOR?

Between 30 and 35 million people in America are classified as poor (the exact number can vary, depending upon current economic conditions in the nation). One in every eight families falls below the government's official poverty line, which in 1991 was an annual income of slightly over $13,000 for a family of four. The demographic characteristics of the "poor" include minority-group members (blacks, Hispanics, Native Americans); the elderly, many of whom are on fixed incomes; the young (especially black teenagers), who have high unemployment rates; rural families on farms; and households headed by a woman.

## THE HOMELESS

A new development worsening the plight of the poor during the 1980s and into the 1990s was the tragedy of the "homeless"—millions of Americans who slept on the streets or in shelters because they had no place to live. While the homeless consisted in part of drug addicts or mentally ill people, many middle-class parents who had lost their jobs became part (along with their children) of the estimated 3 million homeless. The lack of low-cost public housing made the problem even worse. While conservatives saw the homeless as societal derelicts who were responsible for their own condition, liberals wanted to spend more tax dollars on job retraining programs, subsidized housing, mental health, and drug-rehabilitation centers.

## MAJOR PROGRAMS TO ASSIST THE POOR

These programs include Aid to Families with Dependent Children (AFDC), Medicaid, the Food Stamp Program, and Supplemental Security Income (SSI).

**AFDC.** This program, the most expensive and heavily criticized by welfare reformers, represents a redistributive policy whereby money is reallocated from affluent members of society to those individuals who are incapable of supporting themselves. Begun in 1935 as ADC—Aid to Dependent Children—the program was not seen as "welfare" since women with young children were not expected to have jobs, especially given the surplus of labor available during the Great Depression. Today, AFDC provides cash benefits from local, state, and federal sources (the last contributes slightly more than half of all benefits) to more than 11 million individuals, of whom nearly 7 million are children. AFDC extends aid to children whose fathers no longer provide financial support due to death, divorce, disability, or desertion. Opponents of AFDC argue that the system encourages fathers to leave their families, since only then can cash benefits be received. Consequently, a 1988 AFDC reform labeled "workfare" mandated that able-bodied adults not involved in child care seek job training or gainful employment.

**Medicaid.** Medicaid is another federal/state program designed to help the poor pay for their medical bills. It was created in 1965 as an amendment to the Social Security Act. In fiscal year 1991, the federal government spent $52.5 billion on the program. Medicaid benefits can vary from state to state, although they usually cover hospital, doctor, and lab costs. Some states have Medicaid funds to cover additional expenses such as dental care, drugs, or stays at nursing homes. Unfortunately, Medicaid does not apply to some 40 million Americans who cannot afford regular medical care or insurance and who are also ineligible for Medicaid's benefits.

**Food Stamps.** The food-stamp program had its roots in FDR's New Deal, but the modern assistance program originated in the early 1970s. It is administered by the Department of Agriculture. Coupons are given to welfare recipients and are redeemed for food in local supermarkets. The cost of the program was around $20 billion for fiscal year 1991. Nearly ten out of every one hundred Americans receive food stamps today (almost 24 million in all). The food-stamp program is usually credited with improving the health and nutrition of the very poor.

**Supplementary Security Income (SSI).** Created in 1974, SSI's objective was to establish a minimum national income level for the elderly, blind, and disabled. SSI eligibility, as for AFDC, is a means test. Recipients must show that they are truly poor, with low incomes and few assets. The cost of SSI to the federal government in fiscal year 1991 was more than $15 billion, and it served nearly 5 million Americans.

*Social-Insurance/Regulation Programs*

In addition to helping the poor, the federal government has formulated public policies directed at the needs of every American, irrespective of income. Two specific examples are social-insurance and social-regulation programs.

### SOCIAL-INSURANCE PROGRAMS

A nationally planned social-insurance program began in the United States in 1935 when Congress passed the Social Security Act, establishing unemployment insurance and retirement benefits. (It was subsequently expanded to cover the disabled and their survivors.) Under Social Security, employees and employers contribute through payroll taxes to a trust fund, with the worker receiving benefits once retirement age is reached, normally at age sixty-five (payroll taxes also cover the Medicare and unemployment-compensation operations). If the insured worker were to die, benefits would go to his or her spouse and children. Well over 90 percent of all workers in the United States are covered by the Social Security system, and recipients number more than 40 million. However, Social Security is not a personal savings account. Benefits upon retirement are determined by Congress and could be lowered if the system faces financial emergencies, as was the case in the 1980s. Finally, it is almost certain that Social Security taxes will be increased periodically to fund the program.

### MEDICARE

Created in 1965, Medicare is also funded by payroll taxes, with funds being directed into the Health Insurance trust account administered by the Social Security Administration. Part A of Medicare is mandatory health insurance. Medicare Part B is a voluntary medical insurance program to cover physicians' fees and is funded by premiums subtracted from the Social Security checks of participating retirees.

### SOCIAL-REGULATION PROGRAMS

An important policy concern for the federal government has been to protect citizens from dangerous social and economic hazards stemming from modern industrial society. Numerous federal agencies have been formed to ensure the purity of food, the quality of our air and water, the safety of drugs and consumer products, the honesty of advertising, and healthy working conditions. For example, the Occupational Safety and Health Administration was created in 1970 to enhance workplace safety. OSHA has regulated the handling of toxic chemicals in factories and issued standards that lower the risk of worker exposure to dangerous materials, such as asbestos, lead, and cotton dust. While the costs of regulation may result in higher prices for the consumer, advocates of social regulation insist that saving human lives takes priority.

### THE SAVINGS-AND-LOAN SCANDAL

Advocates of regulatory policy point to the S&L banking disaster. The federal government during the Reagan years deregulated its traditionally close supervision of S&L's, allowing these banks to compete for funds against other investment institutions. The result was mismanagement, speculative and failed real estate loans, and fraud by many leading bank executives. Between 1989 and 1991, more than 400 banks collapsed, and a government estimate was that by the end of the 1990s another 2,000 might go under. The "bailout" would probably cost the government and the American taxpayers anywhere from $200 billion to $600 billion to pay off depositors. The lesson was that deregulation could backfire, unless careful monitoring followed its implementation.

# FOREIGN AND DEFENSE POLICY

America's political leaders must carefully plan the nation's foreign and defense policies. These policies are closely linked to the nation's survival and the quality of its way of life. Even with the December 1991 official disintegration of the Soviet Union, America's main international adversary of the last forty-five years, other threats to the nation's security remained. While the experts considered the Cold War to be over, terrorism, nuclear proliferation, civil wars, international drug trafficking, and trade conflicts all remained potentially dangerous. In addition, the need to have a strong defense seemed more apparent than ever. From late 1990 to early 1991, the United States, with its allies, had sent in hundreds of thousands of American troops and assembled an awesome collection of planes and naval vessels in the Persian Gulf after the Iraqi invasion of Kuwait. A short but decisive war had broken Iraqi resistance, restored Kuwait's sovereignty, and assured a steady supply of imported oil to the West at reasonable prices. But who could be sure that future Saddam Husseins were not waiting for their moment on the international stage? America's position of world leadership might be altered by the post–Cold War era, but it was certain that a return to a past policy of isolationism made little sense. A very brief summary of how America had reached its position of world leadership may prove helpful.

*America's
Foreign Policy
History—from
Isolationism to
World
Leadership*

## FROM ISOLATIONISM TO WORLD WAR II

As a very young nation, the United States needed time to develop its economy and political system. Fighting in costly wars could destroy the nation's internal development. The wisdom of Washington's Farewell Address admonition to avoid "entangling alliances" was heeded by succeeding generations of Americans. President James Monroe's "Doctrine" of 1823, warning Europe to stay out of the Western Hemisphere, was a reaffirmation of isolationism. This pattern persisted, despite the Spanish-American War of 1898 and World War I (note America's refusal to become a member of the League of Nations after World War I). For most of the 1920s and 1930s, the United States was preoccupied with internal problems, such as Prohibition and the Great Depression. The American people were determined to stay neutral, even with German and Japanese military forces on the march in Europe and Asia. But the Japanese attack on Pearl Harbor (December 7, 1941) brought the United States into World War II. The nation was unified and committed to the war effort for the next four years. With the surrender of Japan and Germany in 1945, the United States became the preeminent power in the international system. True to its historical pattern, America looked forward to an era of peace when it could again forget about world politics. However, the start of the Cold War compelled the nation to abandon any hope of a return to isolationism.

## THE SOVIET UNION, CONTAINMENT, AND THE COLD WAR

Wartime friendship between the United States and the Soviet Union rapidly dissolved into a permanent pattern of enmity as the Soviets expanded their power into Eastern Europe and threatened American interests in Europe, Asia, and the Middle East. In 1947 the United States devised the policy of containment, a long-term strategy of checking perceived Soviet expansionism by economic (the Marshall Plan, which aided Western Europe), diplomatic (the forming of alliances with other nations), and military (the Korean War in 1950) means. Throughout the 1950s, Cold War crises periodically erupted in such places as Indochina, Suez, Hungary, Lebanon, Quemoy and Matsu, and Cuba. Both nations nearly went to nuclear war during the Cuban Missile Crisis of 1962. However, America's will and military might forced the USSR to remove those missiles. But containment also led the United States into the Vietnam War in 1965; it was a war which was eventually lost a decade later at the cost of $150 billion and 58,000 American lives. By the mid-1970s, both nations had adopted a policy of *détente*, a relaxation of tensions which led to agreements on arms control, trade and cultural exchanges, and even a joint space flight.

## REAGAN, GORBACHEV, AND THE END OF THE COLD WAR

By the middle of the 1980s, the Soviet Union was confronting major economic difficulties, a result of spending too much on defense while neglecting the social welfare needs of its people. The USSR had felt compelled to match the massive American defense buildup begun by Ronald Reagan's administration in 1981. (Ironically, Reagan had justified the additional $1.5 trillion increase on defense by claiming that the USSR would soon achieve military superiority over the United States.) In 1985, Mikhail Gorbachev, a new and youthful Soviet leader, decided to reverse the arms race and concentrate on improving his nation's economy. Under his twin themes of *glasnost* (open discussion) and *perestroika* (economic restructuring), Gorbachev attempted to introduce democracy and a mild form of capitalism into the Soviet Union. Gorbachev also withdrew Soviet troops from Afghanistan, allowed Eastern Europe to leave the Soviet empire, and negotiated new arms-control agreements with Europe and the United States. But the Soviet economy worsened, and opposition to Gorbachev's other policies increased among Communist party hardliners and elements of the Soviet military. In August 1991, Gorbachev was placed under house arrest by these plotters, who tried to seize control of the nation. Although the coup was short-lived, it was Boris Yeltsin, the president of Russia, and not Gorbachev, who emerged as the hero of the resistance. In the months that followed, the republics of the Soviet Union declared their independence. Under Yeltsin's prodding, the Soviet Union dissolved and formed a new commonwealth. Gorbachev resigned his office in December 1991.

## A NEW WORLD ORDER AND AMERICAN FOREIGN POLICY

Containment has been successful. But the post–Cold War era means that America's foreign and defense policies will have to adjust to the new international realities. Ironically, the defeated powers from World War II— Germany and Japan—are now major competitors, with higher GNP growth rates than America's. A United States of Europe looms on the horizon, further complicating America's trade relationships. Even the new commonwealth inside the old USSR still possesses more than 27,000 nuclear warheads, a formidable military capability. Finally, the United States is, or may soon be, withdrawing many of its troops from overseas bases in Europe, the Philippines, South Korea, and possibly Japan.

What should America's defense policies be in the post–Cold War era? Should the nation drastically reduce the size of its armed forces or cut back on new weapons systems, such as the next-generation submarine, bomber, or fighter aircraft? Perhaps even more fundamental is how much should be spent on defense. Can defense cuts be used to fund social programs—i.e., the so-called "peace dividend"? All of these questions and many more must be considered and analyzed by the institutions and individuals concerned with defense and foreign policy analysis, formulation, implementation, and evaluation.

*Foreign and Defense Policy: Major Actors and Institutions*

## THE PRESIDENT

The president is the key foreign-policy maker, with his powers drawn from constitutional provisions, historical precedent, and institutional advantages. The Constitution designates the president as the commander in chief of the armed forces; this grant of power has allowed the chief executive to involve the nation in more than 125 undeclared wars. Other important constitutional powers extended to presidents include the making of treaties and the appointing of ambassadors, ministers, or consuls. The president has two distinct advantages in the foreign policy arena: (1) access to unlimited information about foreign nations and leaders from a variety of intelligence sources (CIA, State, Defense); (2) his acknowledged ability to rally public and congressional support behind new foreign/defense initiatives.

## THE NATIONAL SECURITY COUNCIL (NSC)

Established in 1947, the National Security Council consists of the president, the vice-president, the national security advisor, the secretaries of defense and state, the CIA director, the chairman of the joint chiefs of staff, and other officials invited by the president. The NSC advises the president on foreign policy and formulates policy options for him to consider. The NSC is headed by the national security adviser (NSA), whose particular policy role can vary in each presidential administration. An extremely influential NSA was Henry Kissinger, in the Nixon administration; he opened a dialogue with the People's Republic of China and negotiated an end to the Vietnam War. An NSA can also clash with the secretary of state over policy options. This happened in the Carter administration when NSA Zbigniew Brzezinski differed with Secretary of State Cyrus Vance over the best method of gaining the release of American hostages in Iran. A third role was followed by President Bush's NSA, Brent Scowcroft, who kept a low-profile, but nevertheless influential, position in the policy-making process.

## THE DEPARTMENT OF STATE

The secretary of state is "sometimes" (see above, regarding the NSA) the president's chief foreign policy spokesman. James Baker played this role in the Bush administration. State coordinates relations with the 200 independent nations around the world through its network of embassies and consulates (intelligence personnel are also part of the network). The core of state is its 4,500 career diplomats who comprise the Foreign Service. Foreign Service personnel are knowledgeable about the culture and language of the nations to which they are assigned. Logically, state is organized along geographic and functional lines, such as the Bureau of African Affairs or the Bureau of Refugee Programs. In short, state can furnish valuable information to the president and his advisers regarding what kind of policy should be directed toward other nations.

### THE DEPARTMENT OF DEFENSE (DOD)

Created in 1947, the DOD's organizational goal was to unite the disparate military services—army, navy (the marine corps is housed within the navy department), and air force—under a civilian secretary of defense, thereby achieving a coherent defense strategy for the nation. The DOD, the largest organization in the United States government, contains more than 1 million civilian employees and 2 million military personnel. Its annual budget in fiscal year 1992 was nearly $300 billion.

A key part of DOD is the joint chiefs of staff (JCS), which is composed of a chairman (Colin Powell in the Bush administration) and the heads of the four services. The JCS advises the secretary of defense and the president on military strategy and budgetary needs. In the post–Cold War era, competition among the rival services for budgetary resources should intensify more than usual.

### THE CENTRAL INTELLIGENCE AGENCY (CIA)

Congress created the CIA in 1947. The "director" of the CIA is appointed by the president and confirmed by the Senate (in 1992, the job was held by Thomas Gates). The CIA has three major functions: (1) coordinating all foreign policy information from state, defense, and other intelligence agencies; (2) analyzing and evaluating this data; (3) informing the president and the NSC as to the policy significance of its data assessments. In addition, the CIA operates a global intelligence network, accumulating potentially valuable information from both overt and covert methods.

### CONGRESS

Traditionally, Congress has deferred to the president regarding the handling and execution of foreign policy. After the Vietnam War, Congress tried to reassert its will in foreign relations, passing the War Powers Act in 1973 over President Nixon's veto. Briefly, the War Powers Act limits the president's power to keep U.S. combat troops overseas indefinitely. Conceivably, Congress could vote to bring the troops home after sixty days, with an additional thirty days granted for withdrawal. However, Congress has never invoked this provision of the War Powers Act. The act also calls upon presidents to consult with Congress regarding the onset of hostilities, which President Bush did prior to the combat phase of the Persian Gulf war in 1991.

Congress still has important powers in the foreign and defense policy process—confirmation of presidential nominees by the Senate (some are defeated, such as John Tower's 1989 bid for DOD secretary in the Bush administration); ratification of treaties (the Senate never ratified SALT II during the Carter years); control over appropriations; and the oversight or investigation power. For example, Congress exhaustively probed CIA activities in the 1970s and explored the causes and implications of the Iran-Contra scandal in 1987 and 1988 by calling key witnesses and experts to testify before the appropriate committees.

## PUBLIC OPINION AND THE MEDIA

In general, the mass public does not possess detailed information about foreign policy or military-related issues. However, the public's general mood toward a foreign-policy event can be shaped through media reports. For example, the public clearly perceived the leader of Iraq, Saddam Hussein, as an evil dictator due to newspaper and television coverage which communicated that image. Consequently, support for the 1991 Persian Gulf war was overwhelming. Conversely, negative media reporting during the Vietnam War resulted in public opinion turning against the war, forcing an eventual withdrawal of American troops. Similarly, media stories of outrageous spending on military equipment (the $1,000 Thermos bottle for bomber pilots) shaped public opinion and led to congressional calls for a reform of the defense procurement process.

## Two "Intermestic" Foreign and Defense Policies

Foreign and defense policies are "intermestic," affecting both international and domestic objectives. Two specific policies—American relations with Japan, and the proverbial "guns vs. butter" dilemma—illustrate the intermestic concept.

### AMERICAN-JAPANESE RELATIONS

American-Japanese relations were increasingly strained in the early 1990s. Significant segments of the American public, Congress, and business community viewed Japan as an unfair trading partner. The growing perception, whether totally true or not, was that Japan could sell its autos, computers, or electronic equipment freely on the American market, but U.S. goods were systematically excluded from Japan's consumer market of 120 million people. The result was a one-sided balance of trade, whereby Japan accumulated an annual $41 billion trade surplus with the United States in 1991.

Japan "bashers" called for increased protectionist policies toward Tokyo, involving strictly enforced, reduced quotas on Japanese auto imports and higher tariffs on other Japanese products. Japan countered that such moves would harm relations with the United States and would not eliminate the real reasons for the trade imbalance—a declining American economy, superior Japanese workers, and a higher savings rate in Japan (17 percent to 20 percent in Japan; 4 percent to 5 percent in America), which subsidized more efficient and higher-quality controls in industrial production.

Critics of protectionism toward Japan noted the intermestic repercussions of this policy. Internationally, radical leaders in Japan who disliked the United States might use protectionism as a way of eventually gaining political power. By claiming that America was trying to strangle Japan economically by boycotting its products, Japan's new leaders could retaliate by asking American military forces to withdraw from bases on Japanese soil. Also, Japan might quickly rearm, encouraging those latent forces of militarism still present in Japanese society. Domestically, protectionism could hurt the American economy since Japanese firms and investments create jobs for millions of employed Americans while simultaneously underwriting part of the federal deficit. It is not entirely improbable that Japanese investments could be shifted over time to Europe, Asia, the Middle East, Africa, and Latin America. Like it or not, the American economy's stability is increasingly dependent upon foreign capital (conversely, so is the Japanese economy). In conclusion, objective analysts stressed that the two nations needed each other, a fundamental fact that should not be forgotten by policy-makers in Washington and Tokyo.

## "GUNS vs. BUTTER"

As previously implied, defense budgets inevitably raise the question as to whether too many or too few resources are being devoted to military preparedness. The overall size of the defense budget (the "guns" side of the equation) is determined not only by the severity and number of international threats confronting American security at a particular point in time. Defense spending also has its domestic dimension. The presence of military bases around the nation helps local economies in terms of employment and production of goods and services. Members of Congress facing the closing of military bases in their districts will protest vehemently. Furthermore, defense corporations which receive fewer federal contracts for military hardware will not only have profits reduced, but they are likely to let workers go, again adversely affecting the economy. In short, there are strong incentives to avoid severe cuts in defense spending.

The "butter" side of the debate refers to the diversion of defense dollars (after cutting back on various defense items, from weapons to personnel) to social welfare programs—perhaps more shelters for the homeless, increasing expenditures on medical research, financing a national health plan, building mass-transit systems, or cleaning up the environment. Advocates of this approach stressed the "peace dividend" idea, claiming that with the end of the Cold War there was no longer a need to spend $300 billion or more on national defense. Furthermore, part of the billions saved could be used to reduce the federal deficit. However, in the early 1990s, it appeared that the peace dividend was largely illusory. Defense advocates, while agreeing to a smaller military in terms of personnel, argued that expensive weapons research and development had to proceed if America were to retain its technological edge, as demonstrated in the 1991 Persian Gulf war by the devastating effectiveness of Tomahawk cruise missiles, laser-guided bombs, the radar-invisible Stealth fighter, and the Patriot missile system. In short, national policy-makers, confronting a complex interplay of both domestic and international favors, cannot avoid a continuing "guns vs. butter" debate each fiscal year.

*P*ublic policy represents governmental solutions to social, political, and economic problems which beset American society. (Government inaction or delay is also a kind of negative policy decision.) The policy process involves five stages: (1) agenda-building; (2) formulation; (3) adoption; (4) implementation; (5) evaluation (note that evaluation of policy effectiveness may take considerable time). Every domestic or foreign policy process will be affected by the interests, beliefs, and attitudes of the involved decision-makers and the democratic rules which underlie the entire process. Finally, domestic policy may be regulatory (OSHA and workplace safety), distributive (farm subsidies), or redistributive (the AFDC program). Foreign policy can be either regulatory (trade sanctions) or distributive (foreign aid). Defense policy can involve strategic principles (troop withdrawals) or structural choices (location of military bases).*

*Domestic economic policies can rely on the monetarist approach advocated by Milton Friedman (controlling the money supply and interest rates), or the fiscal approach of John Maynard Keynes (changing government spending, borrowing, and tax rates). The monetarists utilize the Federal Reserve Board to expand or restrict the money supply through its loan policies toward member banks. Neither economic approach has been able to resolve the problem of a growing federal deficit, a result of excessive government spending vis-à-vis lower tax receipts, unrealistic public and congressional expectations, and a largely uncontrollable federal budget. One deficit solution, the well-intentioned Gramm-Rudman-Hollings Act, has been misapplied by Congress. Another "solution," the proposed balanced budget amendment with its many attendant problems, has little chance of being adopted in the foreseeable future.*

*Domestic tax policies are viewed as unfair and unnecessarily complex by many Americans. Tax reforms have not yet resolved the dual problems of "progressivity" or "regressivity." Domestic social welfare policies which aid the poor have helped millions of American citizens, even though their necessity remains a point of contention between liberals and conservatives.*

By contrast, social-insurance (Social Security and Medicare) and regulation programs (OSHA) have acquired greater legitimacy.

American foreign and defense policies have been formulated against the background of a fundamental shift from isolationism to full-scale internationalism, especially after World War II. A new, post–Cold War era will mean that American leaders will have to reassess different threats and the appropriate level of defense spending needed to preserve the nation's security. Increasingly, these policy decisions will be complicated by the "intermestic" variables surrounding such decisions, as suggested by our concise look at American-Japanese relations and the proverbial "guns vs. butter" dilemma.

## Selected Readings

Chisman, Forest, and Alan Pifer. *Government for the People—The Federal Social Role* (1988)

Crabb, Cecil V., Jr., and Pat M. Holt. *Invitation to Struggle: Congress, the President, and Foreign Policy.* 4th ed. (1992)

Derian, Jean-Claude. *America's Struggle for Leadership in Technology* (1990)

Greider, William. *Secrets of the Temple: How the Federal Reserve Runs the Country* (1987)

Heilbroner, Robert, and Peter Bernstein. *The Debt and the Deficit: False Alarms/Real Possibilities* (1989)

Ishihara, Shintaro. *The Japan That Can Say No* (1990)

Mueller, John. *The Obsolescence of Major War* (1990)

Nathan, James, and James Oliver. *United States Foreign Policy and World Order.* 4th ed. (1989)

Phillips, Kevin. *The Politics of Rich and Poor: Wealth and the American Electorate* (1990)

Starling, Grover. *Strategies for Policy-Making* (1988)

# *Glossary*

---

**Administrative Law**  The body of law which deals with the legality of rules and procedures as set forth by governmental bureaucracies.

**Affirmative Action**  Government and private policies which strive to hire minorities in order to make up for previous patterns of discrimination.

**Agenda-Building**  A latent societal deficiency which is recognized as a "problem" by public officials or private individuals, thus requiring a policy solution.

**Bail**  An amount of money which serves as a guarantee that an individual will appear in court for his or her trial at a specified time.

**Balancing the Ticket**  The principle which guides a presidential nominee's selection of a vice-presidential running mate, whereby the V.P. nominee has contrasting personal and political traits in order to maximize the ticket's appeal to as many voters as possible.

**Biased Sample**  A sample which does not faithfully represent the population; hence, the poll results will be inaccurate.

**Bicameral**  Refers to a legislature composed of two houses, or chambers.

**Block Grants**  Federal grants-in-aid which are directed at broad policy areas, such as crime or community development. Generally, the states and localities have greater discretion in determining how the funds may be allocated than is the case with categorical grants.

**Bureaucracy**  A large, complex administrative organization based on a hierarchical structure, with written rules and regulations; its purpose is to implement policy.

**Cabinet Departments**  Collectively, the fourteen executive departments which administer the policies of the federal government.

**Categorical Grants**  Federal grants-in-aid which are directed at a specific state or local governmental project.

**Checks and Balances/ Separation of Powers**  The system of ambition checking ambition, whereby political power is fragmented and divided among the three branches of government.

**Civil Liberties**  Those rights guaranteed to the individual by the Constitution and, more specifically, the Bill of Rights.

**Civil Rights**  The right of citizens not to be discriminated against due to their race, sex, or national origin.

**Civil Service**  Term applied to federal employees who are hired according to the merit principle.

**"Clear and Present Danger"**  Unlawful speech which leads to an immediate and obvious harm to other individuals and/or property.

**Cloture**  The Senate rule which terminates a filibuster, requiring sixteen or more senators to sign a petition, then a three-fifths vote of approval, then a one-hour debate limitation per senator.

**Coalition of Minorities**  The public-opinion phenomenon which seems to engulf most presidents over time—i.e., disillusionment with presidential policies by many groups in American society collectively produces a drop in presidential popularity.

**Commander-in-Chief Role**  The presidential role which places him in control of the American armed forces, as stipulated in the Constitution. Much to the distress of Congress, presidents have used this constitutional privilege in numerous military interventions overseas, with some leading to full-scale wars.

**Comparable-Worth Doctrine**  The doctrine espoused by women's groups which asserts that women should be paid equivalent salaries to those of men when similar job responsibilities and skills are involved.

**Confederation**  A political system in which the states have ultimate power and the central government is relatively weak.

**Conference Committee**  A joint House-Senate committee whose purpose is to reconcile different versions of a bill.

**Connecticut Compromise**  Also known as the Great Compromise, which provided for representation in the House to be based on population, and for the Senate to have equal representation for each state.

**Containment**  A foreign policy directed against the Soviet Union and its allies after World War II, calling for a variety of economic, diplomatic, and even military means to block communist expansion around the globe.

**Cooperative Federalism**  Federalism which views the relationship between the states and the federal government as a "marble cake"—i.e., one of overlapping powers and responsibilities.

**Dealignment**  The process whereby voters and public officials experience a decline in loyalty and attachment to the two major political parties.

**De Facto Segregation**  Segregation "in fact" or racial separation that has occurred through natural residential patterns or by private, non-political, means.

**De Jure Segregation**  Segregation which is sanctioned by law and the power of government.

**Delegate Orientation**  Representatives or senators whose votes on bills are closely linked to voter preferences in their districts or states.

**Delegated Powers**  Powers specifically listed in the Constitution as belonging to Congress, such as the power to declare war or to borrow money.

**Détente**  A "relaxation of tensions" between the United States and the Soviet Union which occurred in the mid-1970s.

**Direct Democracy**  A type of democracy in which all the citizens participate in political life and decision-making (e.g., New England Town Meeting).

**Direct Lobbying**  The lobbying technique which involves face-to-face interaction between lobbyist and legislator.

**Distributive Policy**  Policies which allocate direct benefits to individuals, groups, or business firms.

**Double Jeopardy**  The Fifth Amendment admonition that an individual may not be tried twice for the exact same crime once he or she is found innocent of that crime.

**Dual Federalism**  The doctrine, now outmoded, that the federal-states relationship was akin to a "layer cake," in that powers and responsibilities of the two levels of government could be clearly separated.

**Due-Process Clause**  Constitutional guarantee, found in the Fifth and Fourteenth amendments, that government will not deprive any person of life, liberty, or property by any unfair, arbitrary, or unreasonable action. Due process applies to both federal and state governments.

**Economic Interest Groups**  Interest groups whose main motivation is to win monetary or job-security benefits for their memberships.

**Electoral College**  The 538 electors—men and women—who actually elect the president in their respective states after the popular votes have been cast. A majority—270—is needed for victory.

| | |
|---|---|
| **Equal-Time Provision** | The FCC requirement that radio or TV broadcasters make air time available to all candidates running for public office. |
| **Establishment Clause** | Refers to the First Amendment's prohibition against a "state religion" and the "wall of separation" between church and state. |
| **Executive Agreement** | A presidential agreement with another head of state. It has the power of law but does not require Senate approval. |
| **Exit Polls** | Polls which are based on questioning individuals after they have left the voting booth on election day. The responses can allow TV networks to make early predictions regarding candidate winners or losers. |
| **"Faithless Elector"** | An elector in the Electoral College who decides to change his or her vote, despite being previously pledged to a specific presidential candidate. |
| **FEC** | The Federal Election Commission, created in 1974 in order to enforce campaign finance laws. |
| **Federal Deficit** | An economic condition in which government spending far exceeds collected revenues. |
| ***Federalist Papers*** | The collection of articles written by Madison, Hamilton, and Jay which defended the new Constitution against the anti-Federalists during the ratification period. |
| **Federal Union** | A political system in which there is a constitutional division of powers between the national government and the states, provinces, or sub-regions. |
| **Filibuster** | A lengthy debate, which can occur only in the Senate, intended to "talk a bill to death" by preventing a floor vote from occurring. |
| **Fiscal Economic Policy** | Economic management techniques which rely on changes in government spending and borrowing. The altering of tax rates is also included. |
| **Fiscal Year** | The federal government's twelve-month period, running from October 1 through September 30, during which the budget and other financial policies are formulated and implemented. |
| **Formal Party Organization** | Refers to party leaders who organize and operate party structures at the federal, state, and local levels of government. |
| **Free-Exercise Clause** | The First Amendment's guarantee that every individual is entitled to pursue his or her own religious beliefs free from government interference. |
| **Glasnost** | A Russian term meaning "openness," or Gorbachev's policy intended to promote democratic discussion among Soviet citizens. |
| **Government** | The institutions and processes which are responsible for developing decisions and rules for all of society. |
| **Governmental Interest Groups** | Interest groups which represent foreign governments or America's state and local governments in Washington, D.C. |

| | |
|---|---|
| **Government Corporation** | A governmental body created by Congress which performs a public service but which is structured like a private business firm (e.g., the TVA). |
| **Gramm-Rudman-Hollings Act** | A 1985 law which tried to attack the budget deficit through mandated reductions so that a "zero deficit" would be attained by 1993. |
| **Grand Jury** | A jury which decides if there is enough evidence against the accused to warrant a petit, or trial, jury. If so, an indictment will be issued. |
| **Gross National Debt** | The sum of all annual federal deficits, which currently is estimated at over $4 trillion in fiscal year 1992. |
| **"Guns vs. Butter"** | The continuing debate in American politics over whether more resources should be devoted to social-welfare programs rather than to national defense. |
| **Hatch Act** | The 1939 act which prohibits federal employees from engaging in partisan political activity in order to promote a "neutral" civil service. |
| **House Speaker** | Created by the Constitution, the Speaker is chosen by a vote of his majority party. He is the presiding officer of the House, and second in line to become president (after the vice-president). |
| **Impeachment** | The procedure by which a president, or any federal official, may be removed for misconduct in office. The House brings formal charges against the accused; the Senate acts as the jury. A two-thirds vote of the Senate is necessary for conviction and subsequent removal from office. |
| **Implied Powers** | Powers which are logically deduced through court interpretation or congressional action and stem from the delegated powers granted Congress by the Constitution. These powers are directly related to the "necessary and proper" elastic clause. |
| **Impoundment** | A presidential refusal to spend money which has already been appropriated by Congress. A 1974 law has limited this presidential practice. |
| **Incorporation** | The process by which the Bill of Rights was applied to the states as well as to the federal government. |
| **Independent Regulatory Commission** | Agency which possesses administrative, legislative, and judicial powers all directed at regulating an important aspect of the national economy. |
| **Independent Voter** | A voter whose allegiance to the main political parties is relatively weak or virtually nonexistent. |
| **Indirect Lobbying** | Lobbying directed at public opinion or the grass-roots membership of the interest group. |
| **Interest Aggregation** | The function of a political party which combines conflicting, disparate views of groups and individuals into policy compromises. |
| **Interest Group** | A collection of individuals who share common attitudes and try to influence government for specific policy goals. |

**Intermestic**  A term which recognizes that many public policies contain consequences for both international relations and domestic politics.

**Isolationism**  A traditional American foreign policy orientation which calls for non-alignment and neutrality in world affairs.

**Item Veto**  A power granted to many state governors, but not to the president. This type of veto allows sections of a bill to be rejected by the executive, while permitting the remainder of the bill to become law.

**Keynote Address**  The first major speech at a national nominating convention, whereby the speaker intends to extol the virtues of his or her own party, attack the opposing party, and rally the party faithful for the upcoming campaign.

**Laissez-Faire Economic Policy**  An economic doctrine, popular in the nineteenth and twentieth centuries (prior to 1932), which asserted that government should not interfere in the marketplace or unnecessarily regulate big business.

**Legislative Veto**  A congressional device to curb executive power through the use of a concurrent resolution (by one or both houses). The concurrent resolution is not subject to presidential veto. However, the legislative veto was ruled unconstitutional in the 1983 case of *Immigration and Naturalization Service* v. *Chadha*.

**Libel**  Purposeful, malicious, and knowingly false written defamation of an individual's character or reputation.

**Line Agency**  An agency that carries out government programs and provides various kinds of services.

**Literary Digest**  The magazine which in 1936 incorrectly predicted Landon's win over Roosevelt due to unwittingly creating a "biased" sample through surveys mailed primarily to wealthier classes of voters.

**Lobbyist**  A paid representative of an interest group who tries to influence the policy decisions and views of a public official.

**Material Benefits**  Tangible benefits such as better salaries or improved working conditions which an interest group may provide to its members.

**Media "Circles"**  Refers to the respective levels of media influence, from the most powerful (e.g., the Big Three networks, *The New York Times*, etc.) to the outer circle of local news.

**Media "Concentration"**  Refers to media corporations which, according to some authorities, have disproportionate power, thus possibly endangering the American tradition of diversity of thought and expression.

**Minor Political Party**  A political party which for reasons of ideology, economic protest, issues, or factionalism challenges the two major parties.

**Monetary Economic Policy**  An economic approach which seeks control over the money supply and the cost of credit, primarily through the Federal Reserve System.

**"Negative Campaigning"** Campaigning designed to raise questions about a candidate's opponent by focusing on character deficiencies, especially through political commercials.

**Non-Economic Interest Groups** Issue-oriented groups which typically include public interest, consumer, and environmental varieties.

**Ombudsman** An official who would help citizens resolve their problems with bureaucratic agencies.

**Oversight Function** The power of Congress to investigate the performance of executive agencies or to hold hearings on major problems facing American society.

**Partisan Identification** The relatively strong influence of the family in transmitting parental political party affiliation to children.

**Partisan Orientation** Representatives or senators whose votes on bills are heavily influenced by their respective party leaders.

**Party Identification** The degree to which citizens view themselves as loyal to the Republican or Democratic parties.

**Party in the Electorate** Voters who identify with a political party or are influenced by party loyalty at election time.

**Party in the Government** The appointed or elected officeholders in the legislative and executive branches of government.

**Party Platform** A written document, approved at the national convention, which delineates where the party "stands" on the important political issues of the day. A "plank" is one specific issue in the platform.

**"Peace Dividend"** Alleged savings from the defense budget which can be applied to social programs.

**Perestroika** A Russian term meaning "restructuring," which Gorbachev used to promote his policies of economic change in the Soviet Union.

**Petit Jury** A jury which decides upon the ultimate innocence or guilt of an individual.

**Plea Bargaining** A legal tactic which allows the defendant to plead guilty in exchange for a lesser sentence.

**Policy Adoption** A policy's action plan is "converted" into an actual law or decision.

**Policy Evaluation** The stage of the policy process which assesses whether a policy's operational consequences have resulted in a successful resolution of the original problem.

**Policy Formulation** A stage of the policy process in which an "action plan" is devised.

**Policy Implementation** The stage of the policy process in which the policy's operational intent is "carried out" by the appropriate administrators or bureaucrats.

**Political Action Committee**   Committee established by corporations, labor unions, or other groups which distribute funds to election campaigns.

**Political Efficacy**   The perception or feeling that an individual's voting act can truly make a difference in public policy, the functioning of government, and the quality of his or her own life.

**Political Party**   A group of people who voluntarily band together for the purpose of winning political offices and then making public policy.

**Political Power**   The ability to influence the behavior of others so that they are compelled to take actions that they might normally wish to avoid.

**Political Socialization**   The life-long process by which an individual learns and develops his or her attitudes toward political issues, leaders, and government.

**Politico Orientation**   Representatives or senators whose votes on bills are a "blend" of both the trustee and delegate orientations.

**Politics**   The authoritative allocation of values, or "who gets what, when, how."

**Poll "Tracking"**   The polling technique whereby voting groups are surveyed almost continuously during a campaign, in order to detect rapid shifts in opinions and attitudes.

**"Power to Persuade"**   The real basis of presidential power, in that a president must convince others that his policies and decisions are in their best interests.

**Presidential Nominating Caucus**   Literally, a meeting of party members and one way of selecting national convention delegates rather than through a primary. The method, as used in Iowa, involves a series of meetings at various political levels—local, county, and state—culminating in the final selection of delegates to the national nominating convention.

**Presidential Primary**   A nominating election, whereby voters can directly express their preference for a nominee and/or select delegates to the national convention.

**Privatization**   A proposed remedy for bureaucratic inefficiency, whereby services normally run by government would be handed over to private-sector firms, such as mail delivery.

**Progressive Tax**   A tax which requires that higher-income citizens pay more taxes than lower-income citizens.

**Protectionism**   In international trade, a policy of erecting tariffs or quota barriers to raise the price of imports while protecting domestic industries.

**Psychological Variables**   Voter perceptions relating to the sense of party identification; a candidate's issue positions; and the candidate's personality, style, or image. Any or all of these variables can influence the final voting decision.

**Public Agenda**   The list of those issues publicized heavily by the media in order to attract the attention of the public.

**Public Policy** The actual "output" of government, or what a government does or does not do about a societal problem.

**Purposive Benefits** Benefits won by an interest group but which are extended to individuals in society who are not members of the group (e.g., clean air).

**Realignment** A shift in the party loyalties of the electorate so that the previous minority party becomes the majority party for a lengthy period of time.

**Redistributive Policy** A reallocation of public funds from middle-class and wealthy taxpayers to individuals who cannot support themselves or who are in need of other forms of governmental assistance.

**Registration** The process, intended to prevent voter fraud, by which a voter's name, address, place of residence, etc., are recorded at the local registrar's office, thus making him or her eligible to vote.

**Regressive Tax** A tax which disproportionately affects lower-income taxpayers, such as the Social Security payroll tax.

**Regulatory Policy** Policy which protects the general population from actual or potential economic, health, or environmental hazards.

**Representative Democracy** A democracy in which the people elect representatives who in turn make political policies and decisions.

**Residency Requirements** A citizen must usually have lived in a locality for at least thirty days prior to an election in order to vote in local, state, and congressional races.

**Rules Committee** The "traffic-cop" committee in the House which schedules bills for floor action, allocates the length of time for debate, and decides whether the bill can be amended on the floor (open or closed rule).

**Sample** In polling procedures, a representation or mirror of the much larger population's qualities or attributes.

**Self-Incrimination** The Fifth Amendment protection which states that an individual cannot be compelled to testify against himself or herself.

**Senior Executive Service** Established during the Carter presidency, the SES consists of top civil servants who would be rewarded for effective job performance through bonuses but also would be more easily dismissed or demoted.

**Seniority System** A congressional tradition by which the member of the majority party with the longest continuous service on a committee automatically assumes that committee's chairmanship.

**"Separate but Equal"** The 1896 doctrine which asserted that segregation of the black and white races was constitutional so long as separate facilities (in this case, trolley cars) were comparable in quality.

**Shield Laws** State laws designed to protect reporters from disclosing confidential news sources against their will.

**Single-Member District System**    The type of electoral system in the United States whereby there can be only one winner per office—he or she is the individual who receives a plurality of the votes.

**Slander**    Verbal or oral defamation which wrongfully disparages an individual's character or reputation.

**Social Contract**    The philosophical concept that the rulers and the ruled have mutual obligations—the ruled pledge support for the government, the rulers protect the people's life, liberty, and property.

**Sociological Factors**    Factors including a voter's socioeconomic background and group affiliations, which, interacting with psychological factors, can collectively explain the voting decision.

**"Soft" Money**    Money used by state and local parties to encourage voter turnout and which is not regulated by federal law.

**"Solid South"**    The label attached to the former states of the Confederacy whose voters consistently voted for Democratic presidential candidates until the late 1960s. Thereafter, southern voters have gravitated toward conservative Republican presidents, while still backing congressional Democrats.

**Speaker of the House**    The Speaker is the presiding officer of the House and assigns bills to committees and influences the legislative process to a considerable degree.

**Spoils System**    "To the victor belong the spoils"—i.e., the presidential tendency prior to 1883 to fill government positions with party supporters and friends regardless of their particular expertise.

**Staff Agency**    An agency that collects and distributes information for policy-makers in the government.

**Standing Committees**    Permanent structures that evaluate proposed legislation within their respective areas of expertise. Along with their smaller divisions, known as subcommittees, they can kill or pass along bills for final debate to each chamber floor.

**Strategic Defense Policy**    Policy which deals with the utilization and location of overseas military units.

**Structural Defense Policy**    Distributive defense policy which is concerned with the allocation of defense resources, including manpower, weapons, and funding.

**Subgovernment**    A "policy" alliance which is composed of a bureaucratic agency, congressional committee, and interest group.

**Suffrage**    The right to vote.

**Sunset Laws**    Laws which mandate that agencies which are no longer necessary or which are ineffective be abolished.

**Supply-Side Economics** An economic theory based on the premise that reductions in federal taxes and spending will increase the private sector's productivity.

**"Switchers"** Voters who change party loyalties periodically, rather than staying exclusively with the candidates of one party.

**Three-Fifth's Compromise** Constitutional Convention agreement which considered slaves to be worth three-fifths of a white male voter for purposes of representation in the House of Representatives.

**Trustee** Representatives or senators whose votes on a bill are mainly reflections of their own judgment rather than a mere extension of their constituents, as in the delegate orientation.

**Unitary Government** A political system in which the central government has supreme power and in which the states/localities derive all their power from that governmental level.

**Veto** A presidential power which is used to reject a bill passed by Congress. In Latin, literally "I forbid."

**War Powers Act** Legislation passed in 1973 authorizing Congress to bring American combat troops home after sixty days, despite presidential opposition. The act also called for close congressional-presidential consultation prior to the beginning of combat operations.

**Watchdog Role** The role of the media centering on protecting the public from political, social, or economic excesses by exposing those individuals responsible for them.

**Whistle-Blower** Bureaucrat who reveals waste or corruption in his or her agency or department.

**Yellow Journalism** A type of journalism attributed to William Randolph Hearst at the turn of the century, intended to promote newspaper sales through sensational, exaggerated news stories. The opposite of objective reporting favored by most contemporary newspaper editors.

# Appendix A

---

## THE DECLARATION OF INDEPENDENCE
## (July 4, 1776)
## The Unanimous Declaration of the Thirteen
## United States of America

When, in the Course of human events, it becomes necessary for one people to dissolve the political bands, which have connected them with another, and to assume, among the powers of the earth, the separate and equal station to which the Laws of Nature and of Nature's God entitle them, a decent respect to the opinions of mankind requires that they should declare the causes which impel them to the separation.

We hold these truths to be self-evident, that all men are created equal, that they are endowed by their Creator with certain unalienable Rights; that among these are Life, Liberty, and the pursuit of Happiness. That to secure these rights, Governments are instituted among Men, deriving their just powers from the consent of the governed, that whenever any Form of Government becomes destructive of these ends, it is the Right of the People to alter or to abolish it, and to institute new Government, laying its foundation on such principles and organizing its powers in such form, as to them shall seem most likely to effect their Safety and Happiness. Prudence, indeed, will dictate that Governments long established should not be changed for light and transient causes; and accordingly all experience hath shown, that mankind are more disposed to suffer, while evils are sufferable, than to right themselves by abolishing the forms to which they are accustomed. But when a long train of abuses and usurpations, pursuing invariably the same Object, evinces a design to reduce them under absolute Despotism, it is their right, it is their duty, to throw off such Government, and to provide new Guards for their future security. Such has been the patient sufferance of these Colonies; and such is now the necessity which constrains them to alter their former Systems of Government. The history of the present King of Great Britain is a history of repeated injuries and usurpations, all having in direct object the establishment of an absolute Tyranny over these States. To prove this, let Facts be submitted to a candid world:

He has refused his Assent to Laws the most wholesome and necessary for the public good.

He has forbidden his Governors to pass Laws of immediate and pressing importance, unless suspended in their operation till his Assent should be obtained; and when so suspended, he has utterly neglected to attend to them.

He has refused to pass other Laws for the accommodation of large districts of people, unless those people would relinquish the right of Representation in the Legislature: a right inestimable to them and formidable to tyrants only.

He has called together legislative bodies at places unusual, uncomfortable, and distant from the depository of their Public Records, for the sole purpose of fatiguing them into compliance with his measures.

He has dissolved Representative Houses repeatedly, for opposing with manly firmness his invasions on the rights of the people.

He has refused for a long time, after such dissolutions, to cause others to be elected; whereby the Legislative Powers, incapable of Annihilation, have returned to the people at large for their exercise; the State remaining in the meantime exposed to all the danger of invasion from without, and convulsions within.

He has endeavoured to prevent the population of these States; for that purpose obstructing the Laws for Naturalization of Foreigners; refusing to pass others to encourage their migrations hither, and raising the conditions of new Appropriations of Lands.

He has obstructed the Administration of Justice, by refusing his Assent to Laws for establishing Judiciary Powers.

He has made Judges dependent on his Will alone, for the tenure of their offices, and the amount and payment of their salaries.

He has erected a multitude of New Offices, and sent hither swarms of officers to harass our People, and eat out their substance.

He has kept among us, in times of peace, Standing Armies, without the Consent of our legislatures.

He has affected to render the Military independent of and superior to the Civil Power.

He has combined with others to subject us to a jurisdiction foreign to our constitution, and unacknowledged by our laws; giving his Assent to their acts of pretended legislation:

For quartering large bodies of armed troops among us:

For protecting them, by a mock Trial, from Punishment for any Murders which they should commit on the Inhabitants of these States:

For cutting off our Trade with all parts of the world:

For imposing Taxes on us without our Consent:

For depriving us, in many cases, of the benefits of Trial by Jury:

For transporting us beyond Seas to be tried for pretended offenses:

For abolishing the free System of English Laws in a neighboring Province, establishing therein an Arbitrary government, and enlarging its Boundaries, so as to render it at once an example and fit instrument for introducing the same absolute rule into these Colonies:

For taking away our Charters, abolishing our most valuable Laws, and altering, fundamentally, the Forms of our Governments:

For suspending our own Legislatures, and declaring themselves invested with Power to legislate for us in all cases whatsoever.

He has abdicated Government here, by declaring us out of his Protection, and waging War against us.

He has plundered our seas, ravaged our Coasts, burnt our towns, and destroyed the lives of our people.

He is at this time transporting large Armies of foreign Mercenaries to compleat the works of death, desolation, and tyranny, already begun, with circumstances of Cruelty and perfidy scarcely paralleled in the most barbarous ages, and totally unworthy the Head of a civilized nation.

He has constrained our fellow Citizens taken Captive on the high seas to bear Arms against their Country, to become the executioners of their friends and Brethren, or to fall themselves by their Hands.

He has excited domestic insurrections amongst us, and has endeavoured to bring on the inhabitants of our frontiers, the merciless Indian Savages, whose known rule of warfare is an undistinguished destruction of all ages, sexes and conditions.

In every stage of these Oppressions We have Petitioned for Redress in the most humble terms: our repeated Petitions have been answered only by repeated injury. A Prince whose character is thus marked by every act which may define a Tyrant, is unfit to be the ruler of a free People.

Nor have We been wanting in attention to our British brethren. We have warned them from time to time of attempts made by their legislature to extend an unwarrantable jurisdiction over us. We have reminded them of the circumstances of our emigration and settlement here. We have appealed to their native justice and magnanimity, and we have conjured them by the ties of our common kindred to disavow these usurpations, which would inevitably interrupt our connections and correspondence. They too have been deaf to the voice of justice and of consanguinity. We must, therefore, acquiesce in the necessity which denounces our Separation, and hold them, as we hold the rest of mankind, Enemies in War, in Peace Friends.

We, therefore, the Representatives of the United States of America, in General Congress, Assembled, appealing to the Supreme Judge of the world for the rectitude of our intentions do, in the Name, and by the Authority of the good People of these Colonies, solemnly publish and declare, That these United Colonies are, and of Right ought to be Free and Independent States; that they are Absolved from all Allegiance to the British Crown, and that all political connection between them and the State of Great Britain is, and ought to be, totally dissolved; and that as Free and Independent States, they have full Power to levy War, conclude Peace, contract Alliances, establish Commerce, and to do all other Acts and Things which Independent States may of right do. And for the support of this Declaration, with a firm reliance on the Protection of divine Providence, we mutually pledge to each other our Lives, our Fortunes, and our sacred Honor.

*[Names omitted]*

# Appendix B

## INDEX GUIDE TO THE CONSTITUTION

**PREAMBLE**

**ARTICLE I.** The Legislative Department.

Organization of Congress and terms, qualifications, appointment, and election of Senators and Representatives.

Procedure in impeachment.

Privileges of the two houses and of their members.

Procedure in lawmaking.

Powers of Congress.

Limitations on Congress and on the States.

**ARTICLE II.** The Executive Department.

Election of President and Vice-President.

Powers and duties of the President.

Ratification of appointments and treaties.

Liability of officers to impeachment.

**ARTICLE III.** The Judicial Department.

Independence of the judiciary.

Jurisdiction of national courts.

Guarantee of jury trial.

Definition of treason.

**ARTICLE IV.** Position of the States and territories.

Full faith and credit to acts and judicial proceedings.

Privileges and immunities of citizens of the several States.

Rendition of fugitives from justice.

Control of territories by Congress.

Guarantees to the States.

**ARTICLE V.** Method of amendment.

**ARTICLE VI.** Supremacy of the Constitution, laws, and treaties of the United States.

Oath of office—prohibition of a religious test.

**ARTICLE VII.** Method of ratification of the Constitution.

**AMENDMENTS**

| | |
|---|---|
| I. | Freedom of religion, speech, press and assembly; right of petition. |
| II. | Right to keep and bear arms. |
| III. | Limitations in quartering soldiers. |
| IV. | Protection from unreasonable searches and seizures. |
| V. | Due process in criminal cases. Limitation on right of eminent domain. |
| VI. | Right to speedy trial by jury, and other guarantees. |
| VII. | Trial by jury in suits at law. |
| VIII. | Excessive bail or unusual punishments forbidden. |
| IX. | Retention of certain rights by the people. |
| X. | Undelegated powers belong to the States or to the people. |
| XI. | Exemption of States from suit by individuals. |
| XII. | New method of electing President. |
| XIII. | Abolition of slavery. |
| XIV. | Definition of citizenship. Guarantees of due process and equal protection against State action. Apportionment of Representatives in Congress. Validity of public debt. |
| XV. | Voting rights guaranteed to freedmen. |
| XVI. | Tax on incomes "from whatever source derived." |
| XVII. | Popular election of Senators. |
| XVIII. | Prohibition of intoxicating liquors. |
| XIX. | Extension of suffrage to women. |
| XX. | Abolition of "lame duck" session of Congress. Change in presidential and congressional terms. |
| XXI. | Repeal of 18th Amendment. |
| XXII. | Limitation of President's terms in office. |
| XXIII. | Extension of suffrage to District of Columbia in presidential elections. |

# Appendix C

## THE CONSTITUTION OF
## THE UNITED STATES OF AMERICA

### Proposed by Convention September 17, 1787
### (effective March 4, 1789)

We the People of the United States, in Order to form a more perfect Union, establish Justice, insure domestic Tranquility, provide for the common defence, promote the general Welfare, and secure the Blessings of Liberty to ourselves and our Posterity, do ordain and establish this CONSTITUTION for the United States of America.

**Article I**

**Section 1.** All legislative Powers herein granted shall be vested in a Congress of the United States, which shall consist of a Senate and House of Representatives.

**Section 2.** The House of Representatives shall be composed of Members chosen every second Year by the People of the several States, and the Electors in each State shall have the Qualifications requisite for Electors of the most numerous Branch of the State Legislature.

No Person shall be a Representative who shall not have attained to the Age of twenty-five Years, and been seven Years a Citizen of the United States, and who shall not, when elected, be an Inhabitant of that state in which he shall be chosen.

Representatives and direct Taxes shall be apportioned among the several States which may be included within this Union, according to their respective Numbers, which shall be determined by adding to the whole Number of free Persons, including those bound to Service for a Term of Years, and excluding Indians not taxed, three-fifths of all other Persons. The actual Enumeration shall be made within three Years after the first Meeting of the Congress of the United States, and within every subsequent Term of ten Years, in such Manner as they shall by Law direct. The Number of Representatives shall not exceed one for every thirty Thousand, but each State shall have at Least one Representative; and until such enumeration shall be made, the State of New Hampshire shall be entitled to chuse three, Massachusetts eight, Rhode Island and Providence Plantations one, Connecticut five, New York six, New Jersey four, Pennsylvania eight, Delaware one, Maryland six, Virginia ten, North Carolina five, South Carolina five, and Georgia three.

When vacancies happen in the Representation from any State, the Executive Authority thereof shall issue Writs of Election to fill such Vacancies.

The House of Representatives shall choose their Speaker and other Officers; and shall have the sole Power of Impeachment.

**Section 3.** The Senate of the United States shall be composed of two Senators from each State, chosen by the Legislature thereof, for six Years; and each Senator shall have one Vote.

Immediately after they shall be assembled in Consequence of the first Election, they shall be divided as equally as may be into three Classes. The Seats of the Senators of the first Class shall be vacated at the Expiration of the second Year, of the second Class at the Expiration of the fourth Year, and of the third Class at the Expiration of the sixth Year, so that one-third may be chosen every second Year; and if Vacancies happen by Resignation, or otherwise, during the Recess of the Legislature of any State, the Executive thereof may make temporary Appointments until the next Meeting of the Legislature, which shall then fill such Vacancies.

No Person shall be a Senator who shall not have attained to the Age of thirty Years, and been nine Years a Citizen of the United States, and who shall not, when elected, be an Inhabitant of that State for which he shall be chosen.

The Vice-President of the United States shall be President of the Senate, but shall have no vote, unless they be equally divided.

The Senate shall choose their other Officers, and also a President pro tempore, in the absence of the Vice-President, or when he shall exercise the Office of the President of the United States.

The Senate shall have the sole Power to try all Impeachments. When sitting for that purpose they shall be on Oath or Affirmation. When the President of the United States is tried, the Chief Justice shall preside: And no person shall be convicted without the Concurrence of two thirds of the Members present.

Judgment in Cases of Impeachment shall not extend further than to removal from Office, and disqualification to hold and enjoy any Office of honor, Trust, or Profit under the United States: but the Party convicted shall nevertheless be liable and subject to Indictment, Trial, Judgment, and Punishment, according to Law.

**Section 4.** The Times, Places and Manner of holding Elections for Senators and Representatives, shall be prescribed in each State by the Legislature thereof; but the Congress may at any time by Law make or alter such Regulations, except as to the Places of Chusing Senators.

The Congress shall assemble at least once in every Year, and such Meeting shall be on the first Monday in December, unless they shall by Law appoint a different Day.

**Section 5.** Each House shall be the Judge of the Elections, Returns and Qualifications of its own Members, and a Majority of each shall constitute a Quorum to do Business; but a smaller number may adjourn from day to day, and may be authorized to compel the Attendance of absent Members, in such Manner, and under such Penalties, as each House may provide.

Each House may determine the Rules of its Proceedings, punish its Members for disorderly Behaviour, and, with the Concurrence of two-thirds, expel a Member.

Each House shall keep a Journal of its Proceedings, and from time to time publish the same, excepting such Parts as may in their Judgment require Secrecy; and the Yeas and Nays of the Members of either House on any question shall, at the Desire of one fifth of those Present, be entered on the Journal.

Neither House, during the Session of Congress, shall, without the Consent of the other, adjourn for more than three days, nor to any other Place than that in which the two Houses shall be sitting.

**Section 6.** The Senators and Representatives shall receive a Compensation for their Services, to be ascertained by Law, and paid out of the Treasury of the United States. They shall in all Cases, except Treason, Felony, and Breach of the Peace, be privileged from Arrest during their Attendance at the Session of their respective Houses, and in going to and returning from the same; and for any Speech or Debate in either House, they shall not be questioned in any other Place.

No Senator or Representative shall, during the Time for which he was elected, be appointed to any civil Office under the Authority of the United States, which shall have been created, or the Emoluments whereof shall have been increased, during such time; and no Person holding any Office under the United States shall be a Member of either House during his continuance in Office.

**Section 7.** All Bills for raising Revenue shall originate in the House of Representatives; but the Senate may propose or concur with Amendments as on other bills.

Every Bill which shall have passed the House of Representatives and the Senate, shall, before it become a Law, be presented to the President of the United States; If he approve he shall sign it, but if not he shall return it, with his Objections, to that House in which it shall have originated, who shall enter the objections at large on their Journal, and proceed to reconsider it. If after such Reconsideration two-thirds of that House shall agree to pass the bill, it shall be sent, together with the Objections, to the other House, by which it shall likewise be reconsidered, and if approved by two-thirds of that House, it shall become a Law. But in all such Cases the Votes of both Houses shall be determined by Yeas and Nays, and the Names of the Persons voting for and against the Bill shall be entered on the Journal of each House respectively. If any Bill shall not be returned by the President within ten Days (Sundays excepted) after it shall have been presented to him, the Same shall be a Law, in like Manner as if he had signed it, unless the Congress by their Adjournment prevent its Return, in which Case it shall not be a Law.

Every Order, Resolution, or Vote to which the Concurrence of the Senate and House of Representatives may be necessary (except on a question of Adjournment) shall be presented to the President of the United States; and before the Same shall take Effect, shall be approved by him, or being disapproved by him, shall be repassed by two-thirds of the Senate and House of Representatives, according to the Rules and Limitations prescribed in the Case of a Bill.

**Section 8.** The Congress shall have Power To lay and collect Taxes, Duties, Imposts and Excises, to pay the Debts and provide for the common Defence and general Welfare of the United States; but all Duties, and Excises shall be uniform throughout the United States;

To borrow money on the credit of the United States;

To regulate Commerce with foreign Nations, and among the several States, and with the Indian Tribes;

To establish an uniform rule of Naturalization, and uniform Laws on the subject of Bankruptcies throughout the United States;

To coin Money, regulate the Value thereof, and of foreign Coin, and fix the Standard of Weights and measures;

To provide for the Punishment of counterfeiting the Securities and current Coin of the United States;

To establish Post Offices and post Roads;

To promote the Progress of Science and useful Arts, by securing for limited Times to Authors and Inventors the exclusive Right to their respective Writings and Discoveries;

To constitute Tribunals inferior to the Supreme Court;

To define and punish Piracies and Felonies committed on the high Seas, and Offenses against the Law of Nations;

To declare War, grant Letters of Marque and Reprisal, and make Rules concerning Captures on Land and Water;

To raise and support Armies, but no Appropriation of Money to that Use shall be for a longer Term than two Years;

To provide and maintain a Navy;

To make Rules for the Government and Regulation of the land and naval forces;

To provide for calling forth the Militia to execute the Laws of the Union, suppress Insurrections and repel Invasions;

To provide for organizing, arming, and disciplining the Militia, and for governing such Part of them as may be employed in Service of the United States, reserving to the States respectively, the Appointment of the Officers, and the Authority of training the Militia according to the discipline prescribed by Congress;

To exercise exclusive Legislation in all Cases whatsoever, over such District (not exceeding ten Miles square) as may, by Cession of particular States, and the acceptance of Congress, become the Seat of the Government of the United States, and to exercise like Authority over all Places purchased by the Consent of the Legislature of the State in which the Same shall be, for the Erection of Forts, Magazines, Arsenals, Dock-yards, and other needful Building;—And

To make all Laws which shall be necessary and proper for carrying into Execution the foregoing Powers, and all other Powers vested by this Constitution in the Government of the United States, or in any Department or Officer thereof.

**Section 9.** The Migration or Importation of such Persons as any of the States now existing shall think proper to admit, shall not be prohibited by the Congress prior to the Year one thousand eight hundred and eight, but a tax or duty may be imposed on such Importation, not exceeding ten dollars for each Person.

The privilege of the Writ of Habeas Corpus shall not be suspended, unless when in Cases of Rebellion or Invasion the public Safety may require it.

No bill of Attainder or ex post facto Law shall be passed.

No capitation, or other direct, Tax shall be laid unless in Proportion to the Census or Enumeration herein before directed to be taken.

No Tax or Duty shall be laid on Articles exported from any State.

No Preference shall be given by any Regulation of Commerce or Revenue to the Ports of one State over those of another: nor shall Vessels bound to, or from, one State, be obliged to enter, clear, or pay Duties in another.

No Money shall be drawn from the Treasury, but in Consequence of Appropriations made by Law; and a regular Statement and Account of the Receipts and Expenditures of all public Money shall be published from time to time.

No Title of Nobility shall be granted by the United States: And no Person holding any Office of Profit or Trust under them, shall, without the Consent of the Congress, accept of any present, Emolument, Office, or Title, of any kind whatever, from any King, Prince, or foreign State.

**Section 10.** No State shall enter into any Treaty, Alliance, or Confederation; grant Letters of Marque and Reprisal; coin Money; emit Bills of Credit; make any Thing but gold and silver Coin a Tender in Payment of Debts; pass any Bill Attainder, ex post facto Law, or Law impairing the Obligation of Contracts, or grant any title of Nobility.

No State shall, without the Consent of the Congress, lay any Imposts or Duties on Imports or Exports, except what may be absolutely necessary for executing its inspection Laws; and the net Produce of all Duties and Imposts, laid by any State on Imports or Exports, shall be for the use of the Treasury of the United States; and all such Laws shall be subject to the Revision and Control of the Congress.

No state shall, without the Consent of Congress, lay any duty of Tonnage, keep Troops, or Ships of War in time of Peace, enter into any Agreement or Compact with another State, or with a foreign Power, or engage in War, unless actually invaded, or in such imminent Danger as will not admit of delay.

## *Article II*

**Section 1.** The executive Power shall be vested in a President of the United States of America. He shall hold his Office during the Term of four years, and, together with the Vice president, chosen for the same Term, be elected, as follows:

Each State shall appoint, in such Manner as the legislature thereof may direct, a Number of Electors, equal to the whole Number of Senators and Representatives to which the State may be entitled in the Congress: but no Senator or Representative, or Person holding an Office of Trust or Profit under the United States, shall be appointed an Elector.

The Electors shall meet in their respective States, and vote by Ballot for two persons, of whom one at least shall not be an Inhabitant of the same State with themselves. And they shall make a List of all the Persons voted for, and of the Number of Votes for each; which List they shall sign and certify, and transmit sealed to the Seat of the Government of the United

States, directed to the President of the Senate. The President of the Senate shall, in the Presence of the Senate and House of Representatives, open all the Certificates, and the Votes shall then be counted. The Person having the greatest Number of Votes shall be the President, if such Number be a Majority of the whole Number of Electors appointed; and if there be more than one who have such Majority, and have an equal Number of Votes, then the House of Representatives shall immediately choose by Ballot one of them for President; and if no Person have a majority, then from the five highest on the List the said House shall in like Manner choose the President. But in choosing the President, the Votes shall be taken by States, the Representation from each State having one Vote; a quorum for this Purpose shall consist of a Member or Members from two-thirds of the States, and a Majority of all the states shall be necessary to a Choice. In every Case, after the Choice of the President, the Person having the greatest Number of Votes of the Electors shall be the Vice-President.  But if there should remain two or more who have equal votes, the Senate shall chuse from them by Ballot the Vice-President.

The Congress may determine the Time of choosing the Electors, and the Day on which they shall give their Votes; which Day shall be the same throughout the United States.

No person except a natural-born Citizen, or a Citizen of the United States, at the time of the Adoption of this Constitution, shall be eligible to the Office of President; neither shall any Person be eligible to that Office who shall not have attained to the Age of thirty-five Years, and been fourteen Years a Resident within the United States.

In Case of the Removal of the President from Office, or of his Death, Resignation, or Inability to discharge the Powers and Duties of the said Office, the same shall devolve on the Vice-President, and the Congress may by Law provide for the Case of Removal, Death, Resignation, or Inability, both of the President and Vice-President, declaring what Officer shall then act as President, and such Officer shall act accordingly, until the disability be removed or a President shall be elected.

The President shall, at stated Times, receive for his Services a Compensation, which shall neither be increased nor diminished during the Period for which he shall have been elected, and he shall not receive within that Period any other Emolument from the United States, or any of them.

Before he enter on the execution of his Office, he shall take the following Oath or Affirmation:—"I do solemnly swear (or affirm) that I will faithfully execute the Office of President of the United States, and will, to the best of my Ability, preserve, protect, and defend the Constitution of the United States."

**Section 2.** The President shall be Commander in Chief of the Army and Navy of the United States, and of the Militia of the several States, when called into the actual Service of the United States; he may require the Opinion, in writing, of the principal Officer in each of the executive Departments, upon any subject relating to the Duties of their respective Offices, and he shall have power to Grant Reprieves and Pardons for Offenses against the United States, except in Cases of Impeachment.

He shall have Power, by and with Advice and Consent of the Senate, to make Treaties, provided two thirds of the Senators present concur; and he shall nominate, and by and with the Advice and Consent of the Senate, shall appoint Ambassadors, other public Ministers and Consuls, Judges of the supreme Court, and all other Officers of the United States, whose Appointments are not herein otherwise provided for, and which shall be established by Law: but the Congress may by Law vest the Appointment of such inferior Officers, as they think proper, in the President alone, in the Courts of Law, or in the Heads of Departments.

The President shall have Power to fill up all Vacancies that may happen during the Recess of the Senate, by granting Commissions which shall expire at the End of their next Session.

**Section 3.** He shall from time to time give to the Congress Information of the State of the Union, and recommend to their Consideration such Measures as he shall judge necessary and expedient; he may, on extraordinary occasions, convene both Houses, or either of them, and in Case of Disagreement between them, with respect to the Time of Adjournment, he may adjourn them to such Time as he shall think proper; he shall receive Ambassadors and other public Ministers; he shall take care that the Laws be faithfully executed, and shall Commission all the Officers of the United States.

**Section 4.** The President, Vice President and all civil Officers of the United States, shall be removed from Office on Impeachment for, and Conviction of, Treason, Bribery, or other high Crimes and Misdemeanors.

## *Article III*

**Section 1.** The judicial Power of the United States, shall be vested in one supreme Court, and in such inferior Courts as the Congress may from time to time ordain and establish. The Judges, both of the supreme and inferior Courts, shall hold their Offices during good Behaviour, and shall, at stated Times, receive for their Services, a Compensation, which shall not be diminished during their Continuance in Office.

**Section 2.** The judicial Power shall extend to all Cases, in Law and Equity, arising under this Constitution, the Laws of the United States, and Treaties made, or which shall be made, under their Authority; — to all Cases affecting Ambassadors, other public Ministers and Consuls;—to all cases of admiralty and maritime Jurisdiction;—to Controversies to which the United

States shall be a Party; — to Controversies between two or more States;—between a State and Citizens of another State;—between Citizens of different States:—between Citizens of the same State claiming Lands under Grants of different States, and between a State, or the Citizens thereof, and foreign States, Citizens or Subjects.

In all Cases affecting Ambassadors, other public Ministers and Consuls, and those in which a State shall be Party, the supreme Court shall have original Jurisdiction. In all the other Cases before mentioned, the supreme Court shall have appellate Jurisdiction, both as to Law and Fact, with such Exceptions, and under such Regulations as the Congress shall make.

The trial of all Crimes, except in Cases of Impeachment, shall be by Jury; and such Trial shall be held in the State where the said Crimes shall have been committed; but when not committed within any State, the Trial shall be at such Place or Places as the Congress may by Law have directed.

**Section 3.** Treason against the United States, shall consist only in levying War against them, or in adhering to their Enemies, giving them Aid and Comfort. No Person shall be convicted of Treason unless on the Testimony of two Witnesses to the same overt Act, or on Confession in open Court.

The Congress shall have Power to declare the Punishment of Treason, but no Attainder of Treason shall work Corruption of Blood, or Forfeiture except during the Life of the Person attained.

## *Article IV*

**Section 1.** Full Faith and Credit shall be given in each State to the public Acts, Records, and judicial Proceedings of every other State. And the Congress may by general Laws prescribe the Manner in which such Acts, Records and Proceedings shall be proved, and the Effect thereof.

**Section 2.** The Citizens of each State shall be entitled to all Privileges and Immunities of Citizens in the several States.

A Person charged in any State with Treason, Felony, or other Crime, who shall flee from Justice, and be found in another State, shall on demand of the executive Authority of the State from which he fled, be delivered up, to be removed to the State having Jurisdiction of the Crime.

No Person held to Service or Labour in one State, under the Laws thereof, escaping into another, shall, in Consequence of any Law or Regulation therein, be discharged from such Service or Labour, but shall be delivered up on Claim of the Party to whom such Service or Labour may be due.

**Section 3.** New States may be admitted by the Congress into this Union; but no new State shall be formed or erected within the Jurisdiction of any other State; nor any State be formed by the Junction of two or more States, or parts of States, without the Consent of the Legislatures of the States concerned as well as of the Congress.

The Congress shall have Power to dispose of and make all needful Rules and Regulations respecting the Territory or other Property belonging to the United States; and nothing in this Constitution shall be so construed as to Prejudice any Claims of the United States or of any particular State.

**Section 4.** The United States shall guarantee to every State in this union a Republican Form of Government, and shall protect each of them against Invasion; and on Application of the Legislature, or of the Executive (when the Legislature cannot be convened) against domestic Violence.

## Article V

The Congress, whenever two-thirds of both Houses shall deem it necessary, shall propose Amendments to this Constitution, or, on the Application of the Legislatures of two-thirds of the several States, shall call a Convention for proposing Amendments, which, in either Case, shall be valid to all Intents and Purposes, as part of this Constitution, when ratified by the Legislatures of three-fourths of the several States, or by Conventions in three-fourths thereof, as the one or the other Mode of Ratification may be proposed by the Congress; Provided that no Amendment which may be made prior to the Year One thousand eight hundred and eight shall in any Manner affect the first and fourth Clauses in the Ninth Section of the first Article; and that no State, without its Consent, shall be deprived of its equal Suffrage in the Senate.

## Article VI

All Debts contracted and Engagements entered into, before the Adoption of this Constitution, shall be as valid against the United States under this Constitution, as under the Confederation.

This Constitution, and the Laws of the United States which shall be made in Pursuance thereof; and all Treaties made, or which shall be made, under the Authority of the United States, shall be the supreme Law of the Land; and the Judges in every State shall be bound thereby, any Thing in the Constitution or Laws of any State to the Contrary notwithstanding.

The Senators and Representatives before mentioned, and the Members of the several State Legislatures, and all executive and judicial Officers, both of the United States and of the several States, shall be bound by Oath or Affirmation to support this Constitution; but no religious Test shall ever be required as a qualification to any Office or public Trust under the United States.

## Article VII

The Ratification of the Conventions of nine States shall be sufficient for the Establishment of this Constitution between the States so ratifying the same.

Done in Convention by the Unanimous Consent of the States present the Seventeenth Day of September in the Year of our Lord one thousand seven hundred and Eighty seven, and of the Independence of the United

States of America the Twelfth.   In Witness whereof We have hereunto subscribed our Names.

*[Names omitted]*

Articles in Addition to, and Amendment of, the Constitution of the United States of America, Proposed by Congress, and Ratified by the Legislatures of the Several States, Pursuant to the Fifth Article of the Original Constitution.

*[The first ten amendments went into effect in 1791.]*

### AMENDMENT I

Congress shall make no law respecting an establishment of religion, or prohibiting the free exercise thereof; or abridging the freedom of speech, or of the press; or the right of the people peaceably to assemble, and to petition the Government for a redress of grievances.

### AMENDMENT II

A well regulated Militia, being necessary to the security of a free State, the right of the people to keep and bear Arms shall not be infringed.

### AMENDMENT III

No Soldier shall, in time of peace, be quartered in any house, without the consent of the Owner, nor in time of War, but in a manner to be prescribed by law.

### AMENDMENT IV

The right of the people to be secure in their persons, houses, papers, and effects, against unreasonable searches and seizures, shall not be violated, and no Warrants shall issue, but upon probable cause, supported by Oath or affirmation, and particularly describing the place to be searched, and the persons or things to be seized.

### AMENDMENT V

No person shall be held to answer for a capital or otherwise infamous crime, unless on a presentment or indictment of a Grand Jury, except in cases arising in the land or naval forces, or in the Militia, when in actual service in time of War or public danger; nor shall any person be subject for the same offence to be twice put in jeopardy of life or limb; nor shall be compelled in any criminal case to be a witness against himself, nor be deprived of life, liberty, or property, without due process of law; nor shall private property be taken for public use, without just compensation.

## AMENDMENT VI

In all criminal prosecutions, the accused shall enjoy the right to a speedy and public trial, by an impartial jury of the State and district wherein the crime shall have been committed, which district shall have been previously ascertained by law, and to be informed of the nature and cause of the accusation; to be confronted with the witnesses against him; to have compulsory process for obtaining witnesses in his favour, and to have the Assistance of Counsel for defence.

## AMENDMENT VII

In suits at common law where the value in controversy shall exceed twenty dollars, the right of trial by jury, shall be preserved, and no fact tried by a jury shall be otherwise reexamined in any Court of the United States, than according to the rules of the common law.

## AMENDMENT VIII

Excessive bail shall not be required, nor excessive fines imposed, nor cruel and unusual punishments inflicted.

## AMENDMENT IX

The enumeration in the Constitution, of certain rights, shall not be construed to deny or disparage others retained by the people.

## AMENDMENT X

The powers not delegated to the United States by the Constitution, nor prohibited by it to the States, are reserved to the States respectively, or to the people.

## AMENDMENT XI (1798)

The Judicial power of the United States shall not be construed to extend to any suit in law or equity, commenced or prosecuted against one of the United States by Citizens of another State, or by Citizens or Subjects of any Foreign State.

## AMENDMENT XII (1804)

The Electors shall meet in their respective States and vote by ballot for President and Vice-President, one of whom, at least, shall not be an inhabitant of the same State with themselves; they shall name in their ballots the person voted for as President, and in distinct ballots the person voted for as Vice-President, and they shall make distinct lists of all persons voted for as President, and of all persons voted for as Vice-President, and of the number of votes for each, which lists they shall sign and certify, and transmit sealed to the seat of the government of the United States, directed to the President of the Senate;—The President of the Senate shall, in the presence of the Senate and House of Representatives, open all the certificates and the votes shall then be counted; — The person having the greatest number of votes for President, shall be the President, if such number be a majority of the whole number of Electors appointed; and if no person have such majority, then from the persons having the highest numbers not exceeding three on the list of those voted for as President, the House of Representatives shall choose immediately, by ballot, the President. But in choosing the President, the votes shall be taken by states, the representation from each state having one vote; a quorum for this purpose shall consist of a member or members from two-thirds of the states, and a majority of all the states shall be necessary to a choice. And if the House of Representatives shall not choose a President whenever the right of choice shall devolve upon them, before the fourth day of March next following, then the Vice-President shall act as President, as in the case of the death or other constitutional disability of the President.—The person having the greatest number of votes as Vice-President, shall be the Vice-President, if such number be a majority of the whole number of Electors appointed, and if no person have a majority, then from the two highest numbers on the list, the Senate shall choose the Vice-President; a quorum for the purpose shall consist of two-thirds of the whole number of Senators, and a majority of the whole number shall be necessary to a choice. But no person constitutionally ineligible to the office of President shall be eligible to that of Vice-President of the United States.

## AMENDMENT XIII (1865)

**Section 1.** Neither slavery nor involuntary servitude, except as a punishment for crime whereof the party shall have been duly convicted, shall exist within the United States, or any place subject to their jurisdiction.

**Section 2.** Congress shall have power to enforce this article by appropriate legislation.

## AMENDMENT XIV (1868)

**Section 1.** All persons born or naturalized in the United States, and subject to the jurisdiction thereof, are citizens of the United States and of the State wherein they reside. No State shall make or enforce any law which shall abridge the privileges or immunities of citizens of the United States; nor shall any State deprive any person of life, liberty, or property, without due process of law; nor deny to any person within its jurisdiction the equal protection of the laws.

**Section 2.** Representatives shall be apportioned among the several States according to their respective numbers, counting the whole number of persons in each State, excluding Indians not taxed. But when the right to vote at any election for the choice of electors for President and Vice-President of the United States, Representatives in Congress, the Executive and

Judicial officers of a State, or the members of the Legislature thereof, is denied to any of the male inhabitants of such State, being twenty-one years of age, and citizens of the United States, or in any way abridged, except for participation in rebellion, or other crime, the basis of representation therein shall be reduced in the proportion which the number of such male citizens shall bear to the whole number of male citizens twenty-one years of age in such State.

**Section 3.** No person shall be a Senator or Representative in Congress, or elector of President and Vice-President, or hold any office, civil or military, under the United States, or under any State, who, having previously taken an oath, as a member of Congress, or as an officer of the United States, or as member of any State legislature, or as an executive or judicial officer of any State, to support the Constitution of the United States, shall have engaged in insurrection or rebellion against the same, or given aid or comfort to the enemies thereof. But Congress may by a vote of two-thirds of each House, remove such disability.

**Section 4.** The validity of the public debt of the United States, authorized by law, including debts incurred for payment of pensions and bounties for services in suppressing insurrection or rebellion, shall not be questioned. But neither the United States nor any State shall assume or pay any debt or obligation incurred in aid of insurrection or rebellion against the United States, or any claim for the loss or emancipation of any slave; but all such debts, obligations, and claims shall be held illegal and void.

**Section 5.** The Congress shall have the power to enforce, by appropriate legislation, the provisions of this article.

### AMENDMENT XV (1870)

**Section 1.** The right of citizens of the United States to vote shall not be denied or abridged by the United States or by any State on account of race, color, or previous condition of servitude—

**Section 2.** The Congress shall have power to enforce this article by appropriate legislation.

### AMENDMENT XVI (1913)

The Congress shall have power to lay and collect taxes on incomes, from whatever source derived, without apportionment among the several States, and without regard to any census or enumeration.

### AMENDMENT XVII (1913)

The Senate of the United States shall be composed of two Senators from each State, elected by the people thereof, for six years; and each Senator shall have one vote. The electors in each State shall have the qualifications requisite for electors of the most numerous branch of the State legislatures.

When vacancies happen in the representation of any State in the Senate, the executive authority of such State shall issue writs of election to fill such vacancies: *Provided,* That legislature of any State may empower the executive thereof to make temporary appointments until the people fill the vacancies by election as the legislature may direct.

This amendment shall not be so construed as to affect the election or term of any Senator chosen before it becomes valid as part of the Constitution.

### AMENDMENT XVIII (1919)

**Section 1.** After one year from the ratification of this article the manufacture, sale, or transportation of intoxicating liquors within, the importation thereof into, or the exportation thereof from the United States and all territory subject to the jurisdiction thereof for beverage purposes is hereby prohibited.

**Section 2.** The Congress and the several States shall have concurrent power to enforce this article by appropriate legislation.

**Section 3.** This article shall be inoperative unless it shall have been ratified as an amendment to the Constitution by the legislatures of the several States, as provided in the Constitution, within seven years from the date of the submission hereof to the States by the Congress.

### AMENDMENT XIX (1920)

The right of citizens of the United States to vote shall not be denied or abridged by the United States or by any State on account of sex.

Congress shall have power to enforce this article by appropriate legislation.

### AMENDMENT XX (1933)

**Section 1.** The terms of the President and Vice-President shall end at noon on the 20th day of January, and the terms of Senators and Representatives at noon on the 3d day of January, of the years in which such terms would have ended if this article had not been ratified; and the terms of their successors shall then begin.

**Section 2.** The Congress shall assemble at least once in every year, and such meeting shall begin at noon on the 3d day of January, unless they shall by law appoint a different day.

**Section 3.** If, at the time fixed for the beginning of the term of the President, the President elect shall have died, the Vice-President elect shall become President. If a President shall not have been chosen before the time fixed for the beginning of his term, or if the President elect shall have failed to qualify, then the Vice-President elect shall act as President until a President shall have qualified; and the Congress may by law provide for the case wherein neither a President elect nor a Vice-President elect shall have qualified, declaring who shall then act as President, or the manner in which one who is to act shall be selected, and such person shall act accordingly until a President or Vice-President shall have qualified.

**Section 4.** The Congress may by law provide for the case of the death of any of the persons from whom the House of Representatives may choose a President whenever the right of choice shall have devolved upon them, and for the case of the death of any of the persons from whom the Senate may choose a Vice-President whenever the right of choice shall have devolved upon them.

**Section 5.** Sections 1 and 2 shall take effect on the 15th day of October following the ratification of this article.

**Section 6.** This article shall be inoperative unless it shall have been ratified as an amendment to the Constitution by the legislatures of three-fourths of the several States within seven years from the date of its submission.

## AMENDMENT XXI (1933)

**Section 1.** The eighteenth article of amendment to the Constitution of the United States is hereby repealed.

**Section 2.** The transportation or importation into any State, Territory, or possession of the United States for delivery or use therein of intoxicating liquors, in violation of the laws thereof, is hereby prohibited.

**Section 3.** This article shall be inoperative unless it shall have been ratified as an amendment to the Constitution by conventions in the several States, as provided in the Constitution within seven years from the date of the submission hereof to the States by the Congress.

## AMENDMENT XXII (1951)

**Section 1.** No person shall be elected to the office of the President more than twice, and no person who has held the office of President, or acted as President, for more than two years of a term to which some other person was elected President shall be elected to the office of the President more than once.

But this Article shall not apply to any person holding the office of President when this Article was proposed by the Congress, and shall not prevent any person who may be holding the office of President, or acting as President, during the term within which this article becomes operative from holding the office of President or acting as President during the remainder of such term.

**Section 2.** This article shall be inoperative unless it shall have been ratified as an amendment to the Constitution by the legislatures of three-fourths of the several states within seven years from the date of its submission to the states by the Congress.

### AMENDMENT XXIII (1961)

**Section 1.** The District constituting the seat of Government of the United States shall appoint in such manner as the Congress may direct:

A number of electors of President and Vice-President equal to the whole number of Senators and Representatives in Congress to which the District would be entitled if it were a State, but in no event more than the least populous State; they shall be in addition to those appointed by the States, but they shall be considered, for the purposes of the election of President and Vice-President, to be electors appointed by a State; and they shall meet in the District and perform such duties as provided by the twelfth article of amendment.

**Section 2.** The Congress shall have power to enforce this article by appropriate legislation.

### AMENDMENT XXIV (1964)

**Section 1.** The right of citizens of the United States to vote in any primary or other election for President or Vice President, for electors for President or Vice President, or for Senator or Representative in Congress, shall not be denied or abridged by the United States or any other State by reason of failure to pay any poll tax or other tax.

**Section 2.** The Congress shall have the power to enforce this article by appropriate legislation.

### AMENDMENT XXV (1967)

**Section 1.** In case of the removal of the President from office or of his death or resignation, the Vice President shall become President.

**Section 2.** Whenever there is a vacancy in the office of the Vice President, the President shall nominate a Vice President who shall take office upon confirmation by a majority vote of both Houses of Congress.

**Section 3.** Whenever the President transmits to the President pro tempore of the Senate and the Speaker of the House of Representatives his written declaration that he is unable to discharge the powers and duties of his office, and until he transmits to them a written declaration to the contrary, such powers and duties shall be discharged by the Vice President as Acting President.

**Section 4.** Whenever the Vice President and a majority of either the principal officers of the executive departments or of such other body as Congress may by law provide, transmit to the President pro tempore of the Senate and the Speaker of the House of Representatives their written declaration that the President is unable to discharge the powers and duties of his office, the Vice President shall immediately assume the powers and duties of the office as Acting President.

Thereafter, when the President transmits to the President pro tempore of the Senate and the Speaker of the House of Representatives his written declaration that no inability exists, he shall resume the powers and duties of his office unless the Vice President and a majority of either the principal officers of the executive departments or of such other body as Congress may by law provide, transmit within four days to the President pro tempore of the Senate and the Speaker of the House of Representatives their written declaration that the President is unable to discharge the powers and duties of his office. Thereupon Congress shall decide the issue, assembling within forty-eight hours for that purpose if not in session. If the Congress, within twenty-one days after receipt of the latter written declaration, or, if Congress is not in session, within twenty-one days after Congress is required to assemble, determines by two-thirds vote of both Houses that the President is unable to discharge the powers and duties of his office, the Vice President shall continue to discharge the same as Acting President; otherwise, the President shall resume the powers and duties of his office.

### AMENDMENT XXVI (1971)

**Section 1.** The right of citizens of the United States, who are eighteen years of age or older, to vote shall not be denied or abridged by the United States or by any State on account of age.

**Section 2.** The Congress shall have the power to enforce this article by appropriate legislation.

### AMENDMENT XXVII (1992)

**Section 1.** No law varying the compensation for the services of the Senators and Representatives shall take effect until an election of Representatives shall have intervened.

# Appendix D

---

## THE FEDERALIST NO. 10

*(First published November 22, 1787)*

**TO THE PEOPLE OF THE STATE OF NEW YORK:**

Among the numerous advantages promised by a well-constructed Union, none deserves to be more accurately developed than its tendency to break and control the violence of faction. The friend of popular governments never finds himself so much alarmed for their charter and fate, as when he contemplates their propensity to this dangerous vice. The instability, injustice, and confusion introduced into the public councils, have, in truth, been the mortal diseases under which popular governments have everywhere perished; as they continue to be the favorite and fruitful topics from which the adversaries to liberty derive their most specious declamations. The valuable improvements made by the American constitutions on the popular models, both ancient and modern, cannot certainly be too much admired; but it would be an unwarrantable partiality to contend that they have as effectively obviate the danger on this side as was wished and expected. Complaints are everywhere heard from our most considerate and virtuous citizens, equally the friends of public and private faith, and of public and personal liberty, that our governments are too unstable, that the public good is disregarded in the conflicts of rival parties, and that measures are too often decided, not according to the rules of justice and the rights of the minor party, but by the superior force of an interested and overbearing majority. However anxiously we may wish that these complaints had no foundation, the evidence of known facts will not permit us to deny that they are in some degree true. . . . [The] distresses under which we labor [must] be chiefly, if not wholly, effects of the unsteadiness and injustice with which a factious spirit has tainted our public administrations.

By a faction, I understand a number of citizens, whether amounting to a majority or minority of the whole, who are united and actuated by some common impulse of passion, or of interest, adverse to the rights of other citizens, or to the permanent and aggregate interests of the community.

There are two methods of curing the mischiefs of faction: the one, by removing its causes; the other, by controlling its effects.

There are again two methods of removing the causes of faction: the one by destroying the liberty which is essential to its existence; the other, by giving to every citizen the same opinions, the same passions, and the same interests.

It could never be more truly said than of the first remedy, that it was worse than the disease. Liberty is to faction what air is to fire, an aliment without which it instantly expires. But it could not be less folly to abolish liberty, which is essential to political life, because it nourishes faction, than it would be to wish the annihilation of air, which is essential to animal life, because it imparts to fire its destructive agency.

The second expedient is as impracticable as the first would be unwise. As long as the reason of man continues fallible, and he is at liberty to exercise it, different opinions will be formed. As long as the connection subsists between his reason and his self-love, his opinions and his passions will have a reciprocal influence on each other; and the former will be objects to which the latter will attach themselves. The diversity in the faculties of men, from which the rights of property originate, is not less an insuperable obstacle to a uniformity of interests. The protection of these faculties is the first object of government. From the protection of different and unequal faculties of acquiring property, the possession of different degrees and kinds of property immediately results; and from the influence of these on the sentiments and views of the respective proprietors, ensues a division of the society into different interests and parties.

The latent causes of faction are thus sown in the nature of man; and we see them everywhere brought into different degrees of activity, according to the different circumstances of civil society. A zeal for different opinions, concerning religion, concerning government, and many other points, as well as speculation as of practice; an attachment to different leaders ambitiously contending for preeminence and power; or to persons of other descriptions whose fortunes have been interesting to the human passions, have, in turn, divided mankind into parties, inflamed them with mutual animosity, and rendered them much more disposed to vex and oppress each other than to co-operate for their common good. So strong is this propensity of mankind to fall into mutual animosities, that where no substantial occasion presents itself, the most frivolous and fanciful distinctions have been sufficient to kindle their unfriendly passions and excite their most violent conflicts. But the most common and durable source of factions has been the various and unequal distribution of property. Those who hold and those who are without property have ever formed distinct interests in society. Those who are creditors, and those who are debtors, fall under a like discrimination. A landed interest, a manufacturing interest, a mercantile interest, a moneyed interest, with many lesser interests, grow up of necessity in civilized nations, and divide them into different classes, actuated by different sentiments and views. The regulation of these various and interfering interests forms the principal task of modern legislation, and involves the spirit of party and faction in the necessary and ordinary operations of the government.

No man is allowed to be a judge in his own cause, because his interest would certainly bias his judgment, and, not improbably, corrupt his integrity. With equal, nay with greater reason, a body of men are unfit to be both judges and parties at the same time; yet what are many of the most important acts of legislation, but so many judicial determinations, not indeed concerning the rights of single persons, but concerning the rights of large bodies of citizens? And what are the different classes of legislators but advocates and parties to the cause which they determine? Is a law proposed concerning private debts? It is a question to which the creditors are parties on one side and the debtors on the other. Justice ought to hold the balance between them. Yet the parties are, and must be, themselves the judges; and the most numerous party, or, in other words, the most powerful faction must be expected to prevail. Shall domestic manufacturers be encouraged, and in what degree, by restrictions on foreign manufactures? are questions which would be differently decided by the landed and the manufacturing classes and probably by neither with a sole regard to justice and the public good. . . .

It is in vain to say that enlightened statesmen will be able to adjust these clashing interests, and render them all subservient to the public good. Enlightened statesmen will not always be at the helm. . . .

The inference to which we are brought is, that the *causes* of faction cannot be removed, and that relief is only to be sought in the means of controlling its *effects*.

If a faction consists of less than a majority, relief is supplied by the republican principle, which enables the majority to defeat its sinister views by regular vote. It may clog the administration, it may convulse the society; but it will be unable to execute and mask its violence under the forms of the Constitution. When a majority is included in a faction, the form of popular government, on the other hand, enables it to sacrifice to its ruling passion or interest both the public good and the rights of other citizens. To secure the public good and private rights against the danger of such a faction, and at the same time to preserve the spirit and the form of popular government, is then the great object to which our inquiries are directed. Let me add that it is the great desideratum by which this form of government can be rescued from the opprobrium under which it has so long labored, and be recommended to the esteem and adoption of mankind.

By what means is this object attainable? Evidently by one of two only: Either by the existence of the same passion or interest in a majority at the same time must be prevented, or the majority, having such coexistent passion or interest, must be rendered, by their number and local situation, unable to concert and carry into effect schemes of oppression. If the impulse and the opportunity be suffered to coincide, we well know that neither moral nor religious motives can be relied on as an adequate control. They are not found to be such on the injustice and violence of individuals, and lose their efficacy in proportion to the number combined together, that is, in proportion as their efficacy becomes needful.

From this view of the subject it may be concluded that a pure democracy, by which I mean a society consisting of a small number of citizens, who assemble and administer the government in person, can admit of no cure for the mischiefs of faction. A common passion or interest will, in almost every case, be felt by a majority of the whole; a communication and concert result from the form of government itself; and there is nothing to check the inducements to sacrifice the weaker party or an obnoxious individual. Hence it is that such democracies have ever been spectacles of turbulence and contention; have ever been found incompatible with personal security or the rights of property; and have in general been as short in their lives as they have been violent in their deaths. Theoretic politicians, who have patronized this species of government, have erroneously supposed that by reducing mankind to a perfect equality in their political rights, they would, at the same time, be perfectly equalized and assimilated in their possessions, their opinions, and their passions.

A republic, by which I mean a government in which the scheme of representation takes place, opens a different prospect, and promises the cure for which we are seeking. . . .

The two great points of difference between a democracy and a republic are: first, the delegation of the government, in the latter, to a small number of citizens elected by the rest; secondly, the greater number of citizens, and greater sphere of country, over which the latter may be extended.

The effect of the first difference is, on the one hand, to refine and enlarge the public views, by passing them through the medium of a chosen body of citizens, whose wisdom may best discern the true interest of their country, and whose patriotism and love of justice will be least likely to sacrifice it to temporary or partial considerations. Under such a regulation, it may well happen that the public voice, pronounced by the representatives of the people, will be more consonant to the public good than if pronounced by the people themselves, convened for the purpose. On the other hand, the effect may be inverted. Men of factious tempers, of local prejudices, or of sinister designs, may, by intrigue, by corruption, or by other means, first obtain the suffrages, and then betray the interests of the people. The question resulting is whether small or extensive republics are more favorable to the election of proper guardians of the public weal; and it is clearly decided in favor of the latter by two obvious considerations:

In the first place, it is to be remarked that, however small the republic may be, the representatives must be raised to a certain number, in order to guard against the cabals of a few; and that, however large it may be, they must be limited to a certain number, in order to guard against the confusion of a multitude. Hence the number of representatives in the two cases not being in proportion to that of the two constituents, and being proportionally greater in the small republic, it follows that, if the proportion of fit characters be not less in the large than in the small republic, the former will present a greater option, and consequently a greater probability of a fit choice.

In the next place, as each representative will be chosen by a greater number of citizens in the large than in the small republic, it will be more difficult for unworthy candidates to practice with success the vicious arts by which elections are too often carried; and the suffrages of the people being more free, will be more likely to centre in men who possess the most attractive merit and the most diffusive and established characters.

It must be confessed that in this, as in most other cases, there is a mean, on both sides of which inconveniences will be found to lie. By enlarging too much the numbers of electors, you render the representative too little acquainted with all their local circumstances and lesser interests as by reducing it too much, you render him unduly attached to these, and too little fit to comprehend and pursue great and national objects. The federal Constitution forms a happy combination in this respect; the great and aggregate interests being referred to the national, the local and particular to the State legislatures.

The other point of difference is, the greater number of citizens and extent of territory which may be brought within the compass of republican than of democratic government; and it is this circumstance principally which renders factious combinations less to be dreaded in the former than in the latter. The smaller the society, the fewer probably will be the distinct parties and interests composing it; the fewer the distinct parties and interests, the more frequently will a majority be found of the same party; and the smaller the number of individuals composing a majority, and the smaller the compass within which they are placed, the more easily will they concert and execute their plans of oppression. Extend the sphere, and you take in a greater variety of parties and interests; you make it less probable that a majority of the whole will have a common motive to invade the rights of other citizens; or if such a common motive exists, it will be more difficult for all who feel it to discover their own strength, and to act in unison with each other. Besides other impediments, it may be remarked that where there is a consciousness of unjust or dishonorable purposes, communication is always checked by distrust in proportion to the number whose concurrence is necessary.

Hence, it clearly appears, that the same advantage which a republic has over a democracy, in controlling the effects of faction, is enjoyed by a large over a small republic,—is enjoyed by the Union over the States composing it. Does the advantage consist in the substitution of representatives whose enlightened views and virtuous sentiments render them superior to local prejudices and to schemes of injustice? It will not be denied that the representation of the Union will be most likely to possess these requisite endowments. Does it consist in the greater security afforded by a greater variety of parties, against the event of any one party being able to outnumber and oppress the rest? In an equal degree does the increased variety of parties comprised within the Union, increase this security? Does it, in fine, consist in the greater obstacles opposed to the concert and accomplishment of the secret wishes of an unjust and interested majority? Here, again, the extent of the Union gives it the most palpable advantage.

The influence of factious leaders may kindle a flame within their particular States, but will be unable to spread a general conflagration through the other States. A religious sect may degenerate into a political faction in a part of the Confederacy; but the variety of sects dispersed over the entire face of it must secure the national councils against any danger from that source. A rage for paper money, for an abolition of debts, for an equal division of property, or for any other improper or wicked project, will be less apt to pervade the whole body of the Union than a particular member of it; in the same proportion as such a malady is more likely to taint a particular county or district than an entire State.

In the extent and proper structure of the Union, therefore, we behold a republican remedy for the diseases most incident to republican government. And according to the degree of pleasure and pride we feel in being republicans, ought to be our zeal in cherishing the spirit and supporting the character of Federalists.

Publius [*James Madison*]

# Appendix E

---

## THE FEDERALIST NO. 51
## (HAMILTON OR MADISON)
## (1788)

In order to lay a due foundation for that separate and distinct exercise of the different powers of government, which to a certain extent is admitted on all hands to be essential to the preservation of liberty, it is evident that each department should have a will of its own; and consequently should be so constituted that the members of each should have as little agency as possible in the appointment of the members of the others. Were this principle rigorously adhered to, it would require that all the appointments for the supreme executive, legislative, and judiciary magistracies should be drawn from the same fountain of authority, the people, through channels having no communication whatever with one another. [Some] difficulties, and some additional expense would attend the execution of it. Some deviations, therefore, from the principle must be admitted. In the constitution of the judiciary department in particular, it might be inexpedient to insist rigorously on the principle: first, because peculiar qualifications being essential in the members, the primary consideration ought to be to select that mode of choice which best secures these qualifications; secondly, because the permanent tenure by which the appointments are held in that department, must soon destroy all sense of dependence on the authority conferring them.

It is equally evident, that the members of each department should be as little dependent as possible on those of the others, for the *emoluments* annexed to their offices. Were the executive magistrate, or the judges, not independent of the legislature in this particular, their independence in every other would be merely nominal.

But the great security against a gradual concentration of the several powers in the same department, consists in giving to those who administer each department the necessary constitutional means and personal motives to resist encroachments of the others. The provision for defence must in this, as in all other cases, be made commensurate to the danger of attack. Ambition must be made to counteract ambition. The interest of the man must be connected with the constitutional rights of the place. It may be a reflection on human nature, that such devices should be necessary to control the abuses of government. But what is government itself, but the greatest of all reflections on human nature? If angels were to govern men, neither external nor internal controls on government would be necessary. In framing a government which is to be administered by men over men, the great difficulty lies in this: you must first enable the government to control the governed; and in the next place oblige it to control itself. A dependence on the people is, no doubt, the primary control on the government; but experience has taught mankind the necessity of auxiliary precautions.

This policy of supplying, by opposite and rival interests, the defect of better motives, might be traced through the whole system of human affairs, private as well as public. We see it particularly displayed in all the subordinate distributions of power, where the constant aim is to divide and arrange the several offices in such a manner as that each may be a check on the other—that the private interest of every individual may be a sentinel over the public rights. These inventions of prudence cannot be less requisite in the distribution of the supreme powers of the State.

But it is not possible to give to each department an equal power of self-defence. In republican government, the legislative authority necessarily predominates. The remedy for this inconveniency is to divide the legislature into different branches; and to render them, by different modes of election and different principles of action, as little connected with each other as the nature of their common functions and their common dependence on the society will admit. It may even be necessary to guard against dangerous encroachments by still further precautions. As the weight of the legislative authority requires that it should be thus divided, the weakness of the executive may require, on the other hand, that it should be fortified. An absolute negative on the legislature appears, at first view, to be the natural defence with which the executive magistrate should be armed. But perhaps it would be neither altogether safe nor alone sufficient. On ordinary occasions it might not be exerted with the requisite firmness, and on extraordinary occasions it might be perfidiously abused. May not this defect of an absolute negative be supplied by some qualified connection between this weaker department and the weaker branch of the stronger department, by which the latter may be led to support the constitutional rights of the former, without being too much detached from the rights of its own department?

There are, moreover, two considerations particularly applicable to the federal system of America, which place that system in a very interesting point of view.

*First.* In a single republic, all the power surrendered by the people is submitted to the administration of a single government; and the usurpations are guarded against by a division of the government into distinct and separate departments. In the compound republic of America, the power surrendered by the people is first divided between two distinct governments, and then the portion allotted to each subdivided among distinct and separate departments. Hence a double security arises to the rights of the people. The different governments will control each other, at the same time that each will be controlled by itself.

*Second.* It is of great importance in a republic not only to guard the society against the oppression of its rulers, but to guard one part of the society against the injustice of the other part. Different interests necessarily exist in different classes of citizens. If a majority be united by a common interest, the rights of the minority will be insecure. There are but two methods of providing against this evil: the one by creating a will in the community independent of the majority—that is, of the society itself; the other, by comprehending in the society so many separate descriptions of citizens as will render an unjust combination of a majority of the whole very improbable, if not impracticable. The first method [is] but a precarious security; because a power independent of the society may as well espouse the unjust views of the major, as the rightful interests of the minor party, and may possible be turned against both parties. The second method will be exemplified in the federal republic of the United States. Whilst all authority in it will be derived from and dependent on the society, the society itself will be broken into so many parts,, interests and classes of citizens, that the rights of individuals, or of the minority, will be in little danger from interested combinations of the majority. In a free government the security for civil rights must be the same as that for religious rights. It consists in the one case in the multiplicity of interests, and in the other in the multiplicity of sects. The degree of security in both cases will depend on the number of interests and sects; and this may be presumed to depend on the extent of country and number of people comprehended under the same government. This view of the subject must particularly recommend a proper federal system to all the sincere and considerate friends of republican government, since it shows that in exact proportion as the territory of the Union may be formed into more circumscribed Confederacies, or States, oppressive combinations of a majority will be facilitated; the best security, under the republican forms, for the rights of every class of citizens, will be diminished; and consequently the stability and independence of some member of the government the only other security, must be proportionally increased.

[In] a society under the forms of which the stronger faction can readily unite and oppress the weaker, anarchy may as truly be said to reign as in a state of nature, where the weaker individual is not secured against the violence of the stronger; and as, in the latter state, even the stronger individuals are prompted, by the uncertainty of their condition, to submit to a government which may protect the weak as well as themselves; so, in the former state, will the more powerful factions or parties be gradually induced, by a like motive, to wish for a government which will protect all parties, the weaker as well as the more powerful. It can be little doubted that if the State of Rhode Island was separated from the Confederacy and left to itself, the insecurity of rights under the popular form of government, within such narrow limits would be displayed by such reiterated oppressions of factious majorities that some power altogether independent of the people would soon be called for by the voice of the very factions whose misrule had proved the necessity of it. In the extended republic of the United States, and among the great variety of interests, parties, and sects which it embraces, a coalition of a majority of the whole society could seldom take place on any other principles than those of justice and the general good; whilst there being thus less danger to a minor from the will of a major party, there must be less pretext, also, to provide for the security of the former, by introducing into the government a will not dependent on the latter, or, in other words, a will independent of the society itself. It is no less certain than it is important, notwithstanding the contrary opinions which have been entertained, that the larger the society, provided it lie within a practical sphere, the more duly capable it will be of self-government. And happily for the *republican cause,* the practicable sphere may be carried to a very great extent, by a judicious modification and mixture of the *federal principle.*

*Publius*

# Appendix F

## THE MONROE DOCTRINE

### Message to Congress from President James Monroe (December 2, 1823)

... At the proposal of the Russian Imperial Government, made through the minister of the Emperor [the Russian Tsar] residing here, a full power and instructions have been transmitted to the minister of the United States at St. Petersburg to arrange by amicable negotiations the respective rights and interests of the two nations on the northwest coast of this continent. A similar proposal had been made by His Imperial Majesty to the Government of Great Britain, which has likewise been acceded to. The Government of the United States has been desirous by this friendly proceeding of manifesting the great value which they have invariably attached to the friendship of the Emperor and their solicitude to cultivate the best understanding with his Government. In the discussions to which this interest has given rise and in the arrangements by which they may terminate, the occasion has been judged proper for asserting, as a principle in which the rights and interests of the United States are involved, that the American continents, by the free and independent condition which they have assumed and maintain, are henceforth not to be considered as subjects for future colonization by any European powers. ...

It was stated at the commencement of the last session that a great effort was then making in Spain and Portugal to improve the condition of the people of those countries, and that it appeared to be conducted with extraordinary moderation. It need scarcely be remarked that the result has been so far very different from what was then anticipated. Of events in that quarter of the globe, with which we have so much intercourse and from which we derive our origin, we have always been anxious and interested spectators. The citizens of the United States cherish sentiments the most friendly in favor of the liberty and happiness of their fellow-men on that side of the Atlantic. In the wars of the European powers in matters relating to themselves we have never taken any part, nor does it comport with our policy so to do. It is only when our rights are invaded or seriously menaced that we resent injuries or make preparation for our defense. With the movements in this hemisphere we are of necessity more immediately connected, and by causes which must be obvious to all enlightened and impartial observers. The political system of the allied powers is essentially different in this respect from that of America. This difference proceeds from that which exists in their respective Governments; and to the defense of our own, which has been achieved by the loss of so much blood and treasure, and matured by the wisdom of their most enlightened citizens, and under which we have enjoyed unexampled felicity. . . . We owe it, therefore, to candor and to the amicable relations existing between the United States and those [allied] powers to declare that we should consider any attempt on their part to extend their system to any portion of this hemisphere as dangerous to our peace and safety. With the existing colonies or dependencies of any European power we have not interfered and shall not interfere. But with the [Latin American] Governments who have declared their independence and maintained it, and whose independence we have, on great consideration and on just principles, acknowledged, we could not view any interposition for the purpose of oppressing them, or controlling in any other manner their destiny, by any European power in any other light than as the manifestation of any unfriendly disposition toward the United States. In the war between those new Governments and Spain we declared our neutrality at the time of their recognition, and to this we have adhered, and shall continue to adhere, provided no change shall occur which, in the judgment of the competent authorities of this Government, shall make a corresponding change on the part of the United States indispensable to their security.

The late events in Spain and Portugal show that Europe is still unsettled. Of this important fact no stronger proof can be adduced than that the allied powers should have thought it proper, on any principle satisfactory to themselves, to have interposed by force in the internal concerns of Spain. To what extent such interposition may be carried, on the same principle, is a question in which all independent powers whose governments differ from theirs are interested, even those most remote, and surely none more so than the United States. Our policy in regard to Europe, which was adopted at an early stage of the wars which have so long agitated that quarter of the globe, nevertheless remains the same, which is, not to interfere in the internal concerns of any of its powers; to consider the government *de facto* as the legitimate government for us; to cultivate friendly relations with it, and to preserve those relations by a frank, firm, and manly policy, meeting in all instances the just claims of every power, submitting to injuries from none. But in regard to those continents circumstances are eminently and conspicuously different. It is impossible that the allied powers should extend their political system to any portion of either continent without endangering our peace and happiness; nor can anyone believe that our southern brethren, if left to themselves, would adopt it of their own accord. It is equally impossible, therefore, that we should behold such interposition in any form with indifference. If we look to the comparative strength and resources of Spain and those new [Latin American] Governments, and their distance from each other, it must be obvious that she can never subdue them. It is still the true policy of the United States to leave the parties to themselves, in the hope that other powers will pursue the same course. . . .

# Appendix G

## WOMEN'S RIGHTS

### Declaration of Sentiments and Resolutions
### Woman's Rights Convention
### (Seneca Falls, N.Y., July 19, 1848)

**I. Declaration of Sentiments**

When, in the course of human events, it becomes necessary for one portion of the family of man to assume among the people of the earth a position different from that which they have hitherto occupied, but one to which the laws of nature and of nature's God entitle them, a decent respect to the opinions of mankind requires that they should declare the causes that impel them to such a course.

We hold these truths to be self-evident: that all men and women are created equal; that they are endowed by their Creator with certain inalienable rights; that among these are life, liberty, and the pursuit of happiness; that to secure these rights governments are instituted, deriving their just powers from the consent of the governed. Whenever any form of government becomes destructive of these ends, it is the right of those who suffer from it to refuse allegiance to it, and to insist upon the institution of a new government, laying its foundation on such principles, and organizing its powers in such form, as to them shall seem most likely to effect their safety and happiness. Prudence, indeed, will dictate that governments long established should not be changed for light and transient causes; and accordingly all experience hath shown that mankind are more disposed to suffer while evils are sufferable, than to right themselves by abolishing the forms to which they are accustomed. But when a long train of abuses and usurpations, pursuing invariably the same object, evinces a design to reduce them under absolute despotism, it is their duty to throw off such government, and to provide new guards for their future security. Such has been the patient sufferance of the women under this government, and such is now the necessity which constrains them to demand the equal station to which they are entitled.

The history of mankind is a history of repeated injuries and usurpations on the part of man toward woman, having in direct object the establishment of an absolute tyranny over her. To prove this, let facts be submitted to a candid world.

He has never permitted her to exercise her inalienable right to the elective franchise.

He has compelled her to submit to laws, in the formation of which she has no voice.

He has withheld from her rights which are given to the most ignorant and degraded men—both natives and foreigners.

Having deprived her of this first right of a citizen, the elective franchise, thereby leaving her without representation in the halls of legislation, he has oppressed her on all sides.

He has made her, if married, in the eye of the law, civilly dead.

He has taken from her all right in property, even to the wages she earns.

He has made her, morally, an irresponsible being, as she can commit many crimes with impunity, provided they be done in the presence of her husband. In the covenant of marriage, she is compelled to promise obedience to her husband, he becoming, to all intents and purposes, her master—the law giving him power to deprive her of her liberty, and to administer chastisement.

He has so framed the laws of divorce, as to what shall be the proper causes, and in case of separation, to whom the guardianship of the children shall be given, as to be wholly regardless of the happiness of women— the law, in all cases, going upon a false supposition of the supremacy of man, and giving all power into his hands.

After depriving her of all rights as a married woman, if single, and the owner of property, he has taxed her to support a government which recognizes her only when her property can be made profitable to it.

He has monopolized nearly all the profitable employments, and from those she is permitted to follow, she receives but a scanty remuneration. He closes against her all the avenues to wealth and distinction which he considers most honorable to himself. As a teacher of theology, medicine, or law, she is not known.

He has denied her the facilities for obtaining a thorough education, all colleges being closed against her.

He allows her in Church, as well as State, but a subordinate position, claiming Apostolic authority for her exclusion from the ministry, and, with some exceptions, from any public participation in the affairs of the Church.

He has created a false public sentiment by giving to the world a different code of morals for men and women, by which moral delinquencies which exclude women from society, are not only tolerated, but deemed of little account in man.

He has usurped the prerogative of Jehovah himself, claiming it as his right to assign for her a sphere of action, when that belongs to her conscience and to her God.

He has endeavored, in every way that he could, to destroy her confidence in her own powers, to lessen her self-respect and to make her willing to lead a dependent and abject life.

Now, in view of this entire disfranchisement of one-half the people of this country, their social and religious degradation—in view of the unjust laws above mentioned, and because women do feel themselves aggrieved, oppressed, and fraudulently deprived of their most sacred rights, we insist that they have immediate admission to all the rights and privileges which belong to them as citizens of the United States.

In entering upon the great work before us, we anticipate no small amount of misconception, misrepresentation, and ridicule; but we shall use every instrumentality within our power to effect our object. We shall employ agents, circulate tracts, petition the State and National legislatures, and endeavor to enlist the pulpit and the press in our behalf. We hope this Convention will be followed by a series of Conventions embracing every part of the country.

## II. Resolutions

WHEREAS, The great precept of nature is conceded to be, that "man shall pursue his own true and substantial happiness." [William] Blackstone in his *Commentaries* [on the Laws of England 3(1765-69)] remarks, that this law of Nature being coeval with mankind, and dictated by God himself, is of course superior in obligation to any other. It is binding over all the globe, in all countries and at all times; no human laws are of any validity if contrary to this, and such of them as are valid, derive all their force, and all their validity, and all their authority, mediately and immediately, from this original; therefore,

*Resolved*, That all laws which prevent woman from occupying such a station in society as her conscience shall dictate, or which place her in a position inferior to that of man, are contrary to the great precept of nature, and therefore of no force or authority.

*Resolved*, That woman is man's equal—was intended to be so by the Creator, and the highest good of the race demands that she should be recognized as such.

*Resolved*, That the women of this country ought to be enlightened in regard to the laws under which they live, that they may no longer publish their degradation by declaring themselves satisfied with their present position, nor their ignorance, by asserting that they have all the rights they want.

*Resolved*, That inasmuch as man, while claiming for himself intellectual superiority, does accord to woman moral superiority, it is pre-eminently his duty to encourage her to speak and teach, as she has an opportunity, in all religious assemblies.

*Resolved*, That the same amount of virtue, delicacy, and refinement of behavior that is required of woman in the social state, should also be required of man, and the same transgressions should be visited with equal severity on both man and woman.

*Resolved*, That the objection of indelicacy and impropriety, which is so often brought against woman when she addresses a public audience, comes with a very ill-grace from those who encourage, by their attendance, her appearance on the stage, in the concert, or in feats of the circus.

*Resolved*, That woman has too long rested satisfied in the circumscribed limits which corrupt customs and a perverted application of the Scriptures have marked out for her, and that it is time she should move in the enlarged sphere which her great Creator has assigned her.

*Resolved*, That it is the duty of the women of this country to secure to themselves their sacred right to the elective franchise.

*Resolved*, That the equality of human rights results necessarily from the fact of the identity of the race in capabilities and responsibilities.

*Resolved*, That the speedy success of our cause depends upon the zealous and untiring efforts of both men and women, for the overthrow of the monopoly of the pulpit, and for the securing to women an equal participation with men in the various trades, professions, and commerce.

*Resolved, therefore* That, being invested by the Creator with the same capabilities, and the same consciousness of responsibility for their exercise, it is demonstrably the right and duty of woman, equally with man, to promote every righteous cause by every righteous means; and especially in regard to the great subjects of morals and religion, it is self-evidently her right to participate with her brother in teaching them, both in private and in public, by writing and by speaking, by any instrumentalities proper to be used, and in any assemblies proper to be held; and this being a self-evident truth growing out of the divinely implanted principles of human nature, any custom or authority adverse to it, whether modern or wearing the hoary sanction of antiquity, is to be regarded as a self-evident falsehood, and at war with mankind.

# Appendix H

## THE EMANCIPATION PROCLAMATION

*Proclamation by President Abraham Lincoln*
*(January 1, 1863)*

Whereas, on the twenty-second day of September, in the year of our Lord one thousand eight hundred and sixty-two, a proclamation was issued by the President of the United States, containing, among other things, the following, to wit:

"That on the first day of January, A.D. 1863, all persons held as slaves within any State or designated part of a State, the people whereof shall then be in rebellion against the United States, shall be then, thence forward, and forever free; and the executive government of the United States, including the military and naval authority thereof, will recognize and maintain the freedom of such persons, and will do no act or acts to repress such persons, or any of them, in any efforts they may make for their actual freedom.

"That the executive will on the first day of January aforesaid, by proclamation, designate the states and parts of states, if any, in which the people thereof, respectively, shall then be in rebellion against the United States; and the fact that any state, or the people thereof, shall on that day be in good faith represented in the Congress of the United States, by members chosen thereto at elections wherein a majority of the qualified voters of such states shall have participated, shall, in the absence of strong countervailing testimony, be deemed conclusive evidence that such state, and the people thereof are not then in rebellion against the United States."

Now, therefore, I, Abraham Lincoln, President of the United States, by virtue of the power in me vested as Commander-in-Chief of the Army and Navy of the United States, in time of actual armed rebellion against the authority and government of the United States, and as a fit and necessary war measure for suppressing said rebellion, do, on this first day of January, in the year of our Lord one thousand eight hundred and sixty-three, and in accordance with my purpose so to do, publicly proclaimed for the full period of one hundred days from the day first above mentioned, order and designate as the States and parts of States wherein the people thereof, respectively, are this day in rebellion against the United States, the following, to wit:

Arkansas, Texas, Louisiana (except the parishes of St. Bernard, Plaquemines, Jefferson, St. John, St. Charles, St. James, Ascension, Assumption, Terre Bonne, Lafourche, St. Mary, St. Martin, and Orleans, including the city of New Orleans), Mississippi, Alabama, Florida, Georgia, South Carolina, North Carolina, and Virginia (except the forty-eight counties designated as West Virginia, and also the counties of Berkeley, Accomac, Northampton, Elizabeth City, York, Princess Anne, and Norfolk, including the cities of Norfolk and Portsmouth), and which excepted parts are for the present left precisely as if this proclamation were not issued.

And by virtue of the power and for the purpose aforesaid, I do order and declare that all persons held as slaves within said designated States and parts of States are, and henceforward shall be, free; and that the Executive Government of the United States, including the military and naval authorities thereof, will recognize and maintain the freedom of said persons.

And I hereby enjoin upon the people so declared to be free to abstain from all violence, unless in necessary self-defense; and I recommend to them that, in all cases when allowed, they labor faithfully for reasonable wages.

And I further declare and make known that such persons of suitable condition will be received into the armed service of the United States to garrison forts, positions, stations, and other places, and to man vessels of all sorts in said service.

And upon this act, sincerely believed to be an act of justice, warranted by the Constitution upon military necessity, I invoke the considerate judgment of mankind and the gracious favor of Almighty God.

In witness whereof, I have hereunto set my hand and caused the seal of the United States to be affixed. . . .

# Appendix I

## THE CONSTITUTION OF THE CONFEDERATE STATES OF AMERICA

### (March 11, 1861)

WE, the people of the Confederate States, each State acting in its sovereign and independent character, in order to form a permanent federal government, establish justice, insure domestic tranquility, and secure the blessings of liberty to ourselves and our posterity—invoking the favor and guidance of Almighty God—do ordain and establish this Constitution for the Confederate States of America.

**Article I**

Section 1—All legislative powers herein delegated shall be vested in a Congress of the Confederate States, which shall consist of a Senate and House of Representatives.

Section 2. (1) The House of Representatives shall be chosen every second year by the people of the several States; and the electors in each State shall be citizens of the Confederate States, and have the qualifications requisite for electors of the most numerous branch of the State Legislature; but no person of foreign birth, not a citizen of the Confederate States, shall be allowed to vote for any officer, civil or political, State or Federal.

(2) No person shall be a Representative who shall not have attained the age of twenty-five years, and be a citizen of the Confederate States, and who shall not, when elected, be an inhabitant of that State in which he shall be chosen.

(3) Representatives and direct taxes shall be apportioned among the several States which may be included within this Confederacy, according to their respective numbers, which shall be determined by adding to the whole number of free persons, including those bound to service for a term of years, and excluding Indians not taxed, three-fifths of all slaves. The actual enumeration shall be made within three years after the first meeting of the Congress of the Confederate States, and within every subsequent term of ten years, in such manner as they shall by law direct. The number of Representatives shall not exceed one for every fifth thousand, but each State shall have at least one Representative; and until such enumeration shall be made, the State of South Carolina shall be entitled to choose six; the State of Georgia ten; the State of Alabama nine; the State of Florida two; the State of Mississippi seven; the State of Louisiana six; and the State of Texas six.

(4) When vacancies happen in the representation of any State, the Executive authority thereof shall issue writs of election to fill such vacancies.

(5) The House of Representatives shall choose their Speaker and other officers; and shall have the sole power of impeachment; except that any judicial or other federal officer resident and acting solely within the limits of any State, may be impeached by a vote of two-thirds of both branches of the Legislature thereof.

**Section 3.** (1) The Senate of the Confederate States shall be composed of two Senators from each State, chosen for six years by the Legislature thereof, at the regular session next immediately preceding the commencement of the term of service; and each Senator shall have one vote.

(2) Immediately after they shall be assembled, in consequence of the first election, they shall be divided as equally as may be into three classes. The seats of the Senators of the first class shall be vacated at the expiration of the second year; of the second class at the expiration of the fourth year; and of the third class at the expiration of the sixth year; so that one-third may be chosen every second year; and if vacancies happen by resignation or otherwise during the recess of the Legislature of any State, the Executive thereof may make temporary appointments until the next meeting of the Legislature, which shall then fill such vacancies.

(3) No person shall be a Senator, who shall not have attained the age of thirty years, and be a citizen of the Confederate States; and who shall not, when elected, be an inhabitant of the State for which he shall be chosen.

(4) The Vice-President of the Confederate States shall be President of the Senate, but shall have no vote, unless they be equally divided.

(5) The Senate shall choose their other officers, and also a President *pro tempore*, in the absence of the Vice-President, or when he shall exercise the office of President of the Confederate States.

(6) The Senate shall have sole power to try all impeachments. When sitting for that purpose they shall be on oath or affirmation. When the President of the Confederate States is tried, the Chief-Justice shall preside; and no person shall be convicted without the concurrence of two-thirds of the members present.

(7) Judgment in cases of impeachment shall not extend further than removal from office and disqualification to hold and enjoy any office of honor, trust, or profit, under the Confederate States; but the party convicted shall, nevertheless, be liable to and subject to indictment, trial, judgment, and punishment according to law.

**Section 4.** (1) The times, places, and manner of holding elections for Senators and Representatives, shall be prescribed in each State by the Legislature thereof, subject to the provisions of this Constitution; but the Congress may, at any time, by law, make or alter such regulations, except as to the times and places of choosing Senators.

(2) The Congress shall assemble at least once in every year; and such meeting shall be on the first Monday in December, unless they shall, by law, appoint a different day.

**Section 5.** (1) Each House shall be the judge of the elections, returns, and qualifications of its own members, and a majority of each shall constitute a quorum to do business; but a smaller number may adjourn from day to day, and may be authorized to compel the attendance of absent members, in such manner and under such penalties as each House may provide.

(2) Each House may determine the rules of its proceedings, punish its members for disorderly behavior, and, with the concurrence of two-thirds of the whole number, expel a member.

(3) Each House shall keep a journal of its proceedings, and from time to time publish the same, excepting such part as may in its judgment require secrecy, and the ayes and nays of the members of either House, on any question, shall, at the desire of one-fifth of those present, be entered on the journal.

(4) Neither House, during the session of Congress, shall, without the consent of the other, adjourn for more than three days, nor to any other place than that in which the two Houses shall be sitting.

**Section 6.** (1) The Senators and Representatives shall receive a compensation for their services, to be ascertained by law, and paid out of the Treasury of the Confederate States. They shall, in all cases except treason and breach of the peace, be privileged from arrest during their attendance at the session of their respective Houses, and in going to and returning from the same; and for any speech or debate in either House, they shall not be questioned in any other place.

(2) No Senator or Representative shall, during the time for which he was elected, be appointed to any civil office under the authority of the Confederate States, which shall have been created, or the emoluments whereof shall have been increased during such time; and no person holding any office under the Confederate States shall be a member of either House during his continuance in office. But Congress may, by law, grant to the principal officer in each of the Executive Departments a seat upon the floor of either House, with the privilege of discussing any measure appertaining to his department.

**Section 7.** (1) All bills for raising revenues shall originate in the House of Representatives; but the Senate may propose or concur with amendments as on other bills.

(2) Every bill which shall have passed both Houses shall, before it becomes a law, be presented to the President of the Confederate States; if he approve he shall sign it; but if not, he shall return it with his objections to that House in which it shall have originated, who shall enter the objections at large on their journal, and proceed to reconsider it. If, after such reconsideration, two-thirds of that House shall agree to pass the bill, it shall be sent, together with the objections, to the other House, by which it shall likewise be reconsidered, and if approved by two-thirds vote of that House, it shall become a law. But in all such cases, the votes of both Houses shall be determined by yeas and nays, and the names of the persons voting for and against the bill shall be entered on the journal of each House respectively. If any bill shall not be returned by the President within ten days (Sundays excepted) after it shall have been presented to him, the same shall be a law in like manner as if he had signed it, unless the Congress, by their adjournment, prevent its return; in which case it shall not be a law. The President may approve any appropriation and disapprove any other appropriation in the same bill. In such case he shall, in signing the bill, designate the appropriations disapproved; and shall return a copy of such appropriations, with his objections, to the House in which the bill shall have originated; and the same proceedings shall then be had as in case of other bills disapproved by the President.

(3) Every order, resolution, or vote, to which the concurrence of both Houses may be necessary (except on questions of adjournment) shall be presented to the President of the Confederate States; and before the same shall take effect shall be approved by him; or being disapproved by him, may be repassed by two-thirds of both Houses according to the rules and limitations prescribed in case of a bill.

**Section 8.** The Congress shall have power —

(1) To lay and collect taxes, duties, imposts, and excises, for revenue necessary to pay the debts, provide for the common defence, and carry on the Government of the Confederate States; but no bounties shall be granted

from the treasury; nor shall any duties or taxes on importations from foreign nations be laid to promote or foster any branch of industry; and all duties, imposts, and excises shall be uniform throughout the Confederate States.

(2) To borrow money on the credit of the Confederate States.

(3) To regulate commerce with foreign nations, and among the several States, and with the Indian tribes; but neither this, nor any other clause contained in the Constitution shall be construed to delegate the power to Congress to appropriate money for any internal improvement intended to facilitate commerce; except for the purpose of furnishing lights, beacons, and buoys, and other aids to navigation upon the coasts, and the improvement of harbors, and the removing of obstructions in river navigation, in all which cases, such duties shall be laid on the navigation facilitated thereby, as may be necessary to pay the costs and expenses thereof.

(4) To establish uniform laws of naturalization, and uniform laws on the subject of bankruptcies throughout the Confederate States, but no law of Congress shall discharge any debt contracted before the passage of the same.

(5) To coin money, regulate the value thereof, and of foreign coin, and fix the standard of weights and measures.

(6) To provide for the punishment of counterfeiting the securities and current coin of the Confederate States.

(7) To establish post-offices and post-routes; but the expenses of the Post-office Department, after the first day of March, in the year of our Lord eighteen hundred and sixty-three, shall be paid out of its own revenues.

(8) To promote the progress of science and useful arts, by securing for limited times to authors and inventors the exclusive right to their respective writings and discoveries.

(9) To constitute tribunals inferior to the Supreme Court.

(10) To define and punish piracies and felonies committed on the high seas, and offences against the law of nations.

(11) To declare war, grant letters of marque and reprisal, and make rules concerning captures on land and water.

(12) To raise and support armies; but no appropriation of money to that use shall be for a longer term than two years.

(13) To provide and maintain a navy.

(14) To make rules for government and regulation of the land and naval forces.

(15) To provide for calling forth the militia to execute the laws of the Confederate States; suppress insurrections, and repel invasions.

(16) To provide for organizing, arming, and disciplining the militia, and for governing such part of them as may be employed in the service of the Confederate States; reserving to the States, respectively, the appointment of the officers, and the authority of training the militia according to the discipline prescribed by Congress.

(17) To exercise exclusive legislation, in all cases whatsoever, over such district (not exceeding ten miles square) as may, by cession of one or more States, and the acceptance of Congress, become the seat of the Government of the Confederate States; and to exercise a like authority over all places purchased by the consent of the Legislature of the State in which the same shall be, for the erection of forts, magazines, arsenals, dock-yards, and other needful buildings, and

(18) To make all laws which shall be necessary and proper for carrying into execution the foregoing powers, and all other powers vested by this Constitution in the Government of the Confederate States, or in any department or officer thereof.

**Section 9.** (1) The importation of negroes of the African race, from any foreign country, other than the slaveholding States or Territories of the United States of America, is hereby forbidden; and Congress is required to pass such laws as shall effectually prevent the same.

(2) Congress shall also have power to prohibit the introduction of slaves from any State not a member of, or Territory not belonging to, this Confederacy.

(3) The privilege of the writ of *habeas corpus* shall not be suspended, unless when in cases of rebellion or invasion the public safety may require it.

(4) No bill of attainder, or *ex post facto* law, or law denying or impairing the right of property in negro slaves shall be passed.

(5) No capitation or other direct tax shall be laid unless in proportion to the census or enumeration hereinbefore directed to be taken.

(6) No tax or duty shall be laid on articles exported from any State, except by a vote of two-thirds of both Houses.

(7) No preference shall be given by any regulation of commerce or revenue to the ports of one State over those of another.

(8) No money shall be drawn from the treasury but in consequence of appropriations made by law; and a regular statement and account of the receipts and expenditures of all public money shall be published from time to time.

(9) Congress shall appropriate no money from the treasury except by a vote of two-thirds of both Houses, taken by yeas and nays, unless it be asked and estimated for by some one of the heads of departments, and submitted to Congress by the President; or for the purpose of paying its own expenses and contingencies; or for the payment of claims against the Confederate States, the justice of which shall have been judicially declared by a tribunal for the investigation of claims against the Government, which it is hereby made the duty of Congress to establish.

(10) All bills appropriating money shall specify in federal currency the exact amount of each appropriation and the purposes for which it is made; and Congress shall grant no extra compensation to any public contractor,

officer, agent, or servant, after such contract shall have been made or such service rendered.

(11) No title of nobility shall be granted by the Confederate States; and no person holding any office of profit or trust under them shall, without the consent of the Congress, accept of any present, emoluments, office, or title of any kind whatever, from any king, prince, or foreign state.

(12) Congress shall make no law respecting an establishment of religion, or prohibiting the free exercise thereof; or abridging the freedom of speech or of the press; or the right of the people peaceably to assemble and petition the Government for a redress of grievances.

(13) A well-regulated militia being necessary to the security of a free State, the right of the people to keep and bear arms shall not be infringed.

(14) No soldier shall, in time of peace, be quartered in any house without the consent of the owner; nor in time of war, but in a manner prescribed by law.

(15) The right of the people to be secure in their persons, houses, papers, and against unreasonable searches and seizures, shall not be violated; and no warrant shall issue but upon probable cause, supported by oath or affirmation, and particularly describing the place to be searched, and the person or things to be seized.

(16) No person shall be held to answer for a capital or otherwise infamous crime, unless on a presentment or indictment of a grand jury, except in cases arising in the land or naval forces, or in the militia, when in actual service, in time of war, or public danger; nor shall any person be subject for the same offence to be twice put in jeopardy of life or limb; nor be compelled in any criminal case to be a witness against himself; nor be deprived of life, liberty, or property, without due process of law; nor shall any private property be taken for public use without just compensation.

(17) In all criminal prosecutions the accused shall enjoy the right to a speedy and public trial, by an impartial jury of the State and district wherein the crime shall have been committed, which district shall have been previously ascertained by law, and to be informed of the nature and cause of the accusation; to be confronted with the witnesses against him, to have compulsory process for obtaining witnesses in his favor; and to have the assistance of counsel for his defence.

(18) In suits at common law, where the value in controversy shall exceed twenty dollars, the right of trial by jury shall be preserved; and no fact so tried by a jury shall be otherwise reexamined in any court of the Confederacy, than according to the rules of the common law.

(19) Excessive bail shall not be required, nor excessive fines imposed, nor cruel or unusual punishment inflicted.

(20) Every law or resolution having the force of law, shall relate to but one subject, and that shall be expressed in the title.

**Section 10.** (1) No State shall enter into any treaty, alliance or confederation; grant letters of marque and reprisals; coin money; make any thing but gold and silver coin a tender in payment of debts; pass any bill of attainder, or *ex post facto* law, or law impairing the obligation of contracts; or grant any title of nobility.

(2) No State shall, without the consent of Congress, lay any imposts or duties on imports or exports except what may be absolutely necessary for executing its inspection laws; and the net produce of all duties and imposts, laid by any State on imports or exports, shall be for the use of the Treasury of the Confederate States; and all such laws shall be subject to the revision and control of Congress.

(3) No State shall, without the consent of Congress, lay any duty of tonnage, except on sea-going vessels for the improvement of its rivers and harbors navigated by the said vessels; but such duties shall not conflict with any treaties of the Confederate States with foreign nations; and any surplus of revenue, thus derived, shall after making such improvement, be paid into the common treasury; nor shall any State keep troops or ships of war in time of peace, enter into any agreement or compact with another State, or with a foreign power, or engage in war, unless actually invaded or in such imminent danger as will not admit of delay. But when any river divides or flows through two or more States, they may enter into compacts with each other to improve the navigation thereof.

## Article II

**Section 1.** (1) The Executive power shall be vested in a President of the Confederate States of America. He and the Vice-President shall hold their offices for the term of six years; but the President shall not be reeligible. The President and Vice-President shall be elected as follows:

(2) Each State shall appoint in such manner as the Legislature thereof may direct, a number of electors equal to the whole number of Senators and Representatives to which the State may be entitled in Congress; but no Senator or Representative, or person holding an office of trust or profit under the Confederate States shall be appointed an elector.

(3) The electors shall meet in their respective States, and vote by ballot for President and Vice-President, one of whom at least, shall not be an inhabitant of the same State with themselves; they shall name in their ballots the person voted for as President, and in distinct ballots the person voted for as Vice-President and they shall make distinct lists of all persons voted for as President, and of all persons voted for as Vice-President, and of the number of votes for each; which list they shall sign and certify, and transmit, sealed, to the Government of the Confederate States, directed to the President of the Senate. The President of the Senate shall, in the presence of the Senate and House of Representatives, open all the certificates, and the votes shall then be counted; the person having the greatest number of votes for

President shall be the President, if such number be a majority of the whole number of electors appointed; and if no person shall have such a majority, then, from the persons having the highest numbers not exceeding three, on the list of those voted for as President, the House of Representatives shall choose immediately, by ballot the President. But, in choosing the President the votes shall be taken by States, the Representative from each State having one vote; a quorum for this purpose shall consist of a member or members from two-thirds of the States, and a majority of all the States shall be necessary to a choice. And if the House of Representatives shall not choose a President, whenever the right of choice shall devolve upon them, before the fourth day of March next following, then the Vice-President shall act as President, as in case of the death, or other constitutional disability of the President.

(4) The person having the greatest number of votes as Vice-President shall be the Vice-President, if such number be a majority of the whole number of electors appointed; and if no person have a majority, then from the two highest numbers on the list, the Senate shall choose the Vice-President; a quorum for the purpose shall consist of two-thirds of the whole number of Senators, and a majority of the whole number shall be necessary for a choice.

(5) But no person constitutionally ineligible to the office of President shall be eligible to that of Vice-President of the Confederate States.

(6) The Congress may determine the time of choosing the electors, and the day on which they shall give their votes; which day shall be the same throughout the Confederate States.

(7) No person except a natural born citizen of the Confederate States, or a citizen thereof, at the time of the adoption of this Constitution, or a citizen thereof born in the United States prior to the 20th December, 1860, shall be eligible to the office of President; neither shall any person be eligible to that office who shall not have attained the age of thirty-five years, and been fourteen years a resident within the limits of the Confederate States, as they may exist at the time of his election.

(8) In case of the removal of the President from office or of his death, resignation, or inability to discharge the powers and duties of the said office, the same shall devolve on the Vice-President; and the Congress may, by law, provide for the case of the removal, death, resignation or inability both of the President and the Vice-President, declaring what officer shall then act as President, and such officer shall then act accordingly until the disability be removed or a President shall be elected.

(9) The President shall, at stated times, receive for his services a compensation, which shall neither be increased nor diminished during the period for which he shall have been elected; and he shall not receive within that period any other emolument from the Confederate States, or any of them.

(10) Before he enters on the execution of the duties of his office he shall take the following oath or affirmation:

> "I do solemnly swear (or affirm) that I will faithfully execute the office of President of the Confederate States, and will, to the best of my ability, preserve, protect, and defend the Constitution thereof."

**Section 2.** (1) The President shall be commander-in-chief of the army and navy of the Confederate States, and of the militia of the several States, when called into the actual service of the Confederate States; he may require the opinion, in writing, of the principal officer in each of the Executive Departments, upon any subject relating to the duties of their respective offices; and he shall have power to grant reprieves and pardons for offences against the Confederate States, except in cases of impeachment.

(2) He shall have power, by and with the advice and consent of the Senate, to make treaties, provided two-thirds of the Senators present concur; and he shall nominate, and by and with the advice and consent of the Senate, shall appoint ambassadors, other public ministers, and consuls, Judges of the Supreme Court, and all other officers of the Confederate States, whose appointments are not herein otherwise provided for, and which shall be established by law; but the Congress may by law vest the appointment of such inferior officers, as they think proper, in the President alone, in the courts of law, or in the heads of departments.

(3) The principal officer in each of the Executive Departments, and all persons connected with the diplomatic service, may be removed from office at the pleasure of the President. All other civil officers of the Executive Department may be removed at any time by the President, or other appointing power, when their services are unnecessary, or for dishonesty, incapacity, inefficiency, misconduct, or neglect of duty; and when so removed, the removal shall be reported to the Senate, together with the reasons therefor.

(4) The President shall have power to fill all vacancies that may happen during the recess of the Senate, by granting commissions which shall expire at the end of the next session, but no person rejected by the Senate shall be reappointed to the same office during their ensuing recess.

**Section 3.** (1) The President shall, from time to time, give the Congress information of the state of the Confederacy, and recommend to their consideration such measures as he shall judge necessary and expedient; he may, on extraordinary occasions, convene both Houses, or either of them; and, in case of disagreement between them, with respect to the time of adjournment he may adjourn them to such time as he shall think proper; he shall receive ambassadors and other public ministers; he shall take care that the laws be faithfully executed, and shall commission all the officers of the Confederate States.

**Section 4.** (1) The President and Vice-President, and all civil officers of the Confederate States, shall be removed from office on impeachment for, or conviction of, treason, bribery, or other high crimes and misdemeanors.

## Article III

**Section 1.** (1) The judicial power of the Confederate States shall be vested in one Superior Court, and in such inferior courts as the Congress may from time to time ordain and establish. The judges, both of the Supreme and inferior courts, shall hold their offices during good behavior, and shall, at stated times, receive for their services a compensation, which shall not be diminished during their continuance in office.

**Section 2.** (1) The judicial power shall extend to all cases arising under the Constitution, the laws of the Confederate States, or treaties made or which shall be made under their authority; to all cases affecting ambassadors, other public ministers, and consuls; to all cases of admiralty or maritime jurisdiction; to controversies to which the Confederate States shall be a party; to controversies between two or more States; between a State and citizens of another State, where the State is plaintiff; between citizens claiming lands under grants of different States, and between a State or the citizens thereof, and foreign States, citizens, or subjects; but no State shall be sued by a citizen or subject of any foreign State.

(2) In all cases affecting ambassadors, other public ministers, and consuls, and those in which a State shall be a party, the Supreme Court shall have original jurisdiction. In all the other cases before mentioned, the Supreme Court shall have appellate jurisdiction, both as to law and fact, with such exceptions, and under such regulations as the Congress shall make.

(3) The trial of all crimes, except in cases of impeachment, shall be by jury, and such trial shall be held in the State where the said crimes shall have been committed; but when not committed within any State, the trial shall be at such place or places as the Congress may by law have directed.

**Section 3.** (1) Treason against the Confederate States shall consist only in levying war against them, or in adhering to their enemies, giving them aid and comfort. No person shall be convicted of treason unless on the testimony of two witnesses to the same overt act, or on confession in open court.

(2) The Congress shall have power to declare the punishment of treason but no attainder of treason shall work corruption of blood, or forfeiture, except during the life of the person attainted.

*Article IV*

**Section 1.** (1) Full faith and credit shall be given in each State to the public acts, records, and judicial proceedings of every other State. And the Congress may, by general laws, prescribe the manner in which such acts, records, and proceedings shall be proved, and the effect thereof.

**Section 2** (1) The citizens of each State shall be entitled to all the privileges and immunities of citizens of the several States, and shall have the right of transit and sojourn in any State of this Confederacy, with their slaves and other property; and the right of property in said slaves shall not be thereby impaired.

(2) A person charged in any State with treason, felony, or other crime against the laws of such State, who shall flee from justice, and be found in another State, shall, on demand of the executive authority of the State from which he fled, be delivered up to be removed to the State having jurisdiction of the crime.

(3) No slave or other person held to service or labor in any State or Territory of the Confederate States, under the laws thereof, escaping or unlawfully carried into another, shall, in consequence of any law or regulation therein, be discharged from such service or labor; but shall be delivered up on claim of the party to whom such slave belongs, or to whom such service or labor may be due.

**Section 3.** (1) Other States may be admitted into this Confederacy by a vote of two-thirds of the whole House of Representatives, and two-thirds of the Senate, the Senate voting by States; but no new State shall be formed or erected within the jurisdiction of any other State; nor any State be formed by the junction of two or more States, or parts of States, without the consent of the Legislatures of the States concerned as well as of the Congress.

(2) The Congress shall have power to dispose of and make all needful rules and regulations concerning the property of the Confederate States, including the lands thereof.

(3) The Confederate States may acquire new territory; and Congress shall have power to legislate and provide governments for the inhabitants of all territory belonging to the Confederate States, lying without the limits of the several States, and may permit them, at such times, and in such manner as it may by law provide, to form States to be admitted into the Confederacy. In all such territory, the institution of negro slavery, as it now exists in the Confederate States, shall be recognized and protected by Congress and by the territorial government; and the inhabitants of the several Confederate States and Territories shall have the right to take to such territory any slaves lawfully held by them in any of the States or Territories of the Confederate States.

(4) The Confederate States shall guarantee to every State that now is or hereafter may become a member of this Confederacy, a Republican form of Government, and shall protect each of them against invasion; and on

application of the Legislature, (or of the Executive when the Legislature is not in session) against domestic violence.

## Article V

**Section 1.** (1) Upon the demand of any three States, legally assembled in their several Conventions, the Congress shall summon a Convention of all the States, to take into consideration such amendments to the Constitution as the said States shall concur in suggesting at the time when the said demand is made; and should any of the proposed amendments to the Constitution be agreed on by the said Convention—voting by States—and the same be ratified by the Legislatures of two-thirds of the several States, or by conventions in two-thirds thereof—as the one or the other mode of ratification may be proposed by the general convention—they shall thenceforward form a part of this Constitution. But no State shall, without its consent, be deprived of its equal representation in the Senate.

## Article VI

1. The Government established by this Constitution is the successor of the Provisional Government of the Confederate States of America, and all the laws passed by the latter shall continue in force until the same shall be repealed or modified; and all the officers appointed by the same shall remain in office until their successors are appointed and qualified, or the offices abolished.

2. All debts contracted and engagements entered into before the adoption of this Constitution shall be as valid against the Confederate States under this Constitution as under the Provisional Government.

3. This Constitution, and the laws of the Confederate States, made in pursuance thereof, and all treaties made, or which shall be made, under the authority of the Confederate States, shall be the supreme law of the land; and the judges in every State shall be bound thereby, any thing in the Constitution or laws of any State to the contrary notwithstanding.

4. The Senators and Representatives before mentioned, and the members of the several State Legislatures, and all executive and judicial offices, both of the Confederate States and of the several States, shall be bound, by oath or affirmation, to support this Constitution; but no religious test shall ever be required as a qualification to any office or public trust under the Confederate States.

5. The enumeration in the Constitution of certain rights, shall not be construed to deny or disparage others retained by the people of the several States.

6. The powers not delegated to the Confederate States by the Constitution, nor prohibited by it to the States, are reserved to the States, respectively, or to the people thereof.

## Article VII

1. The ratification of the conventions of five States shall be sufficient for the establishment of this Constitution between the States so ratifying the same.

2. When five States shall have ratified this Constitution in the manner before specified, the Congress, under the provisional Constitution, shall prescribe the time for holding the election of President and Vice-President, and for the meeting of the electoral college, and for counting the votes and inaugurating the President. They shall also prescribe the time for holding the first election of members of Congress under this Constitution, and the time for assembling the same. Until the assembling of such Congress, the Congress under the provisional Constitution shall continue to exercise the legislative powers granted them; not extending beyond the time limited by the Constitution of the Provisional Government.

Adopted unanimously by the Congress of the Confederate States of South Carolina, Georgia, Florida, Alabama, Mississippi, Louisiana, and Texas, sitting in convention at the capitol, in the city of Montgomery, Ala. on the eleventh day of March, in the year eighteen hundred and sixty-one.

[*Signatures omitted*]

# Index

Johnson, Lyndon
  and civil rights, 17
  in election of 1964, 69, 74
  and Great Society programs, 20, 21
  use of media by, 37
  as vice-president, 81
Johnson, William, 6
Joint Chiefs of Staff (JCS), 179
Joint resolutions, 96
Journalists, personal backgrounds of, 38–39
Judges, 133
  backgrounds of, 133
  selection of federal, 134
Judicial activism versus judicial restraint, 141
Judicial constraint on presidential power, 110
Judicial power, constraints on, 140
Judicial restraint versus judicial activism, 141
Judicial system. *See also* Courts; Supreme Court, U.S.; Supreme Court, U.S., cases
  and affirmative rights, 158–159
  and civil liberties, 144–151
  and civil rights, 151–162
  organization of federal system, 133–136
  participants in, 132–133
  and sex discrimination, 156–159
  types of law, 130–132
  and women's equality, 156
Judiciary Committee, Senate, 137
Jurisdiction, 133
  appellate, 134, 135, 136
  concurrent, 134
  exclusive, 133
  original, 134, 136
Justice, U.S. Department of, 123

**K**

Kassebaum, Nancy, 91
Kemp, Jack, 78
Kennedy, Anthony M., 140
Kennedy, John F.
  and bureaucracy, 125
  communicative skills of, 109
  in election of 1960, 73, 81, 84
  as political parties, 45
  as president, 104, 112, 125
  in televised debate, 33, 73
  use of media by, 33
Kerry, Bob, 78
Keynes, John Maynard, 169
Keynesian economics, 169
Keynote address, 190

King, Martin Luther, Jr., 17, 154
Kissinger, Henry, 113, 125, 178
"Kitchen cabinet," 114
Know-Nothing party, 46
Korean conflict, removal of MacArthur from, 106
Kuwait, Iraqi invasion of, 175

**L**

Labor, U.S. Department of, 125
Laissez-faire economic policy, 190
"Lame duck" chief executives, 111
Landon, Alfred, 29
Lasswell, Harold, 2
Law, types of, 130–132
Lawyers, 132
League of United Latin American Citizens, 159
League of Women Voters, 59
Lee, Richard Henry, 5
Legislation, role of president in, 107–108
Legislative courts, 136
Legislative veto, 111, 190
Legislator-constituent relationships, 92–93
Legislators, ratings of, 54
Legislature. *See* Congress, U.S.
Libel, 145–146, 190
Lincoln, Abraham, 46, 113
Line agency, 190
*Literary Digest*, 190
  mistake of 1936, 29, 31
Litigants, 132
Lobbying Act (1946), 61
Lobbyist, 54, 190
Locke, John, 8–9

**M**

MacArthur, Douglas, 106
"MacNeil-Lehrer Newshour," 41
Madison, James, 5, 7, 9, 10, 18, 45
Majority rule, 9
Mandates, 21
*Mapp* v. *Ohio*, 148
*Marbury* v. *Madison*, 136
Marines, killing of, in Lebanon, 107
Marshall, John, 18, 138
Marshall, Thomas R., 115
Marshall, Thurgood, 140
Matching funds, 78
Material benefits, 190
*McClure's*, 32
*McCulloch* v. *Maryland*, 18, 89
McGovern, George, 50

Media
  as agents of political socialization, 27
  concentration of, 35–36
  constraint on presidential power, 111–112
  coverage of Congress, 40
  coverage of courts, 41
  coverage of presidency, 40
  coverage of presidential elections, 40
  and democracy, 41
  and foreign and defense policy, 180
  history of, 32–34
  political roles of, 36–38
  and public opinion polls, 31–32
  role of, in news presentation, 38–40
  scope of, 35
  structure of, 35
Media "circles," 190
Media "concentration," 190
Medicaid, 20, 21, 26, 173
Medicare, 26, 174
Merit Systems Protection Board (MSPB), 121
Mexican American/Puerto Rican Legal Defense and Education Fund, 159
Migratory Bird Conservation Commission, 123
Mikulski, Barbara, 91
Military, women in, 158
Minority rights, 9
Minor parties, 190
  categories of, 50–51
  importance of third parties, 51
Mint, Bureau of the, 122
*Missouri ex rel. Gaines* v. *Canada*, 152
Model cities programs, 21
Mondale, Walter
  in election of 1984, 31, 70, 73, 81, 110
  in TV debate, 73
  as vice-president, 115
"Monetarist" school of economics, 168
Monetary policy, 168–169, 190
Monroe, James, 46
Monroe Doctrine, 176, 232–234
Montesquieu, Baron de, 10
Montgomery, Alabama, boycott, 154
Moral Majority, 59
Mothers Against Drunk Driving (MADD), 53
Muckrakers, 32

# OTHER BOOKS IN THE HARPERCOLLINS COLLEGE OUTLINE SERIES

## ART
History of Art  0-06-467131-3
Introduction to Art  0-06-467122-4

## BUSINESS
Business Calculus  0-06-467136-4
Business Communications  0-06-467155-0
Introduction to Business  0-06-467104-6
Introduction to Management  0-06-467127-5
Introduction to Marketing  0-06-467130-5

## CHEMISTRY
College Chemistry  0-06-467120-8
Organic Chemistry  0-06-467126-7

## COMPUTERS
Computers and Information Processing  0-06-467176-3
Introduction to Computer Science and Programming
   0-06-467145-3
Understanding Computers  0-06-467163-1

## ECONOMICS
Introduction to Economics  0-06-467113-5
Managerial Economics  0-06-467172-0

## ENGLISH LANGUAGE AND LITERATURE
English Grammar  0-06-467109-7
English Literature From 1785  0-06-467150-X
English Literature To 1785  0-06-467114-3
Persuasive Writing  0-06-467175-5

## FOREIGN LANGUAGE
French Grammar  0-06-467128-3
German Grammar  0-06-467159-3
Spanish Grammar  0-06-467129-1
Wheelock's Latin Grammar  0-06-467177-1
Workbook for Wheelock's Latin Grammar
   0-06-467171-2

## HISTORY
Ancient History  0-06-467119-4
British History  0-06-467110-0
Modern European History  0-06-467112-7
Russian History  0-06-467117-8
20th Century United States History  0-06-467132-1
United States History From 1865  0-06-467100-3
United States History to 1877  0-06-467111-9
Western Civilization From 1500  0-06-467102-X

Western Civilization To 1500  0-06-467101-1
World History From 1500  0-06-467138-0
World History to 1648  0-06-467123-2

## MATHEMATICS
Advanced Calculus  0-06-467139-9
Advanced Math for Engineers and Scientists
   0-06-467151-8
Applied Complex Variables  0-06-467152-6
Basic Mathematics  0-06-467143-7
Calculus with Analytic Geometry  0-06-467161-5
College Algebra  0-06-467140-2
Elementary Algebra  0-06-467118-6
Finite Mathematics with Calculus  0-06-467164-X
Intermediate Algebra  0-06-467137-2
Introduction to Calculus  0-06-467125-9
Introduction to Statistics  0-06-467134-8
Ordinary Differential Equations  0-06-467133-X
Precalculus Mathematics: Functions & Graphs
   0-06-467165-8
Survey of Mathematics  0-06-467135-6

## MUSIC
Harmony and Voice Leading  0-06-467148-8
History of Western Music  0-06-467107-7
Introduction to Music  0-06-467108-9
Music Theory  0-06-467168-2

## PHILOSOPHY
Ethics  0-06-467166-6
History of Philosophy  0-06-467142-9
Introduction to Philosophy  0-06-467124-0

## POLITICAL SCIENCE
The Constitution of the United States  0-06-467105-4
Introduction to Government  0-06-467156-9

## PSYCHOLOGY
Abnormal Psychology  0-06-467121-6
Child Development  0-06-467149-6
Introduction to Psychology  0-06-467103-8
Personality: Theories and Processes  0-06-467115-1
Social Psychology  0-06-467157-7

## SOCIOLOGY
Introduction to Sociology  0-06-467106-2
Marriage and the Family  0-06-467147-X

Available at your local bookstore or directly from HarperCollins at 1-800-331-3761.